The Other Side of the Family

The Other Side of the Family

A Book for Recovery
from Abuse, Incest and Neglect

Ellen F. Ratner

Health Communications, Inc.
Deerfield Beach, Florida
1990

The following publishers have generously given permission to use material from copyrighted works:

From *American Psychiatric Glossary*, compiled and edited by Evelyn M. Stone. Copyright 1988 by American Psychiatric Press, Inc. Permission granted by the publisher, American Psychiatric Press, Inc.

From *Ego Development: Conceptions and Theories*, by Jane Loevinger. Copyright 1976 by Jossey-Bass. Permission granted by the publisher, Jossey-Bass Publishers.

From *Family Adaptability and Cohesion Evaluation Scale III (F.A.C.E.S. III)*, by David Olson, Joyce Portner, and Yoav Lavee. Copyright 1988 by Department of Social Science, University of Minnesota. Permission granted by the publisher, Department of Social Science, University of Minnesota.

From *knots*, by R. D. Laing. Copyright 1970 by The R. D. Laing Trust. Permission granted by the publisher, Random House, Inc.

From *Manwatching: A Field Guide to Human Behavior*, by Desmond Morris. Copyright 1977 by Desmond Morris. Permission granted by the publisher, Harry N. Abrams, Inc., New York.

From *Messages: The Communication Skills Book*, by Matthew McKay, Martha Davis, and Patrick Fanning. Copyright 1983 by New Harbinger Publications. Permission granted by the publisher, New Harbinger Publications.

From *Treatment of Adult Survivors of Abuse*, by Eliana Gil. Copyright 1988 by Eliana Gil. Permission granted by the publisher, Launch Press.

From *Unmasking the Face: A Guide to Recognizing Emotions from Facial Clues*, by Paul Ekman and Wallace V. Friesen. Copyright 1984 by Consulting Psychologists Press, Inc. Permission granted by the publisher, Consulting Psychologists Press, Inc.

The author may be contacted at The ARC Research Foundation, 12300 Twinbrook Parkway, Suite 150, Rockville, Maryland 20852, or call 301–816–9700.

for

the Ratners, who have a great sense of family
the Spotts, who are discovering it

and

Terry Ciulla
Joanne Cutter
Pam Dugas
Jack D. Green
Mona Jewell
and
Ceena Wallack

Contents

Acknowledgments

This book began 19 years ago in a class taught by Robert Ziegler, M.D. Throughout the next 15 years, much of my learning was the result of Bob's mentoring. I also appreciate the help of my colleagues Peter Musliner, M.D., and Patricia Ziegler, M.S.W., both great friends and critics.

Many lively discussions took place at Boundaries Therapy Center, and I am especially grateful to Bonnie Broe, M.S.W., Jeremiah Donohue, C.A.C., and Rysia Lombroso, Ed.D., for their insights.

Fred Duhl, M.D., and Bunny Duhl, Ed.D., were two of my teachers, and many of the ideas and exercises in this book are the direct result of Fred Duhl's input.

The lion's share of editorial and technical work for this book was completed by John Burns and Steven Pederson of Delta Publications; Ellen Hermanson provided valuable editing as well.

In the early phases of the book, Margot Fromer and Louise Taylor offered valuable advice. Clair Handalian, Kathleen McAleer, Gary Midora, and Danna Vranes were indispensable for typing. Help in researching the book was given by Margaret S. Boone, Ph.D., and Anna Donovan.

I am grateful to many friends who provided collegial as well as personal support: Louis and Brenda Brewer, Dana Finnegan, Ph.D., Betsy Fontes, Professor Regina Herzlinger, Richard Horman, Ph.D., Barbara Karanian, Deniston Kay, Ph.D., Mim Landry, Emily McNally, Ph.D., Laura Noble, Mel Pohl, M.D., William Scott, M.S.W., Winfield Scott, Ph.D., David Smith, M.D., Susan Taney, Greg Thomas, P.A., Gail Walsh, Michael Weeks, Michael Shernoff, M.S.W., Dennis Wilson, and Pierre Zimmerman.

My theological and spiritual discussions with Rev. Anne Gehman, Joan Biando, Rev. Sherre Boothman, and Rabbi Harold White helped focus my views and understanding.

I could not have competed this project without the support and understanding of many friends. I thank Diane Waldo and Janice Worswick for hanging in there, and Chris Waldron and Debra Murray for their sense of humor. Conchita Balinong, Linda Chase, Joe Donovan, Mary Krayer, Theone and Robert Mark, Brenda Notini, Linda Randall, JoAnn Webb, and Suzanne Leone have helped me maintain a sense of well being.

Michael Avery has been the attorney I can always count on.

My family and family-like network of MaryAnn Krayer, Lisa Myers, Larry and Sheila Bienemann, Robert Berkowitz, Lynn Dubal, Lorri Webb, Pam Nates, and Roz and Harlow Hermanson, have been great support through this project. My brothers Michael and Bruce, my sisters-in-law Julie and Karen, and my nieces Rebbie and Lizzie have only been a phone call away.

Caitlin C. Ryan has provided loving support and encouragement as well as editorial input from the beginning.

Introduction

On a bleak November morning, a six-year-old child was found beaten to death. Her brother, age 16 months, was discovered chained to his high chair in a room littered with filth. For ten years, the children's adoptive mother had been physically and emotionally abused—repeatedly—by their adoptive father. This case—one case—among the thousands of children who are battered, neglected, sexually assaulted, verbally and emotionally abused each year electrified the nation and made the horror and shame of child abuse a household word: Lisa Steinberg.

For untold others, however, living in households dominated by shame and guilt, living in alcoholic and dysfunctional family systems, those who are ignored, neglected, and less publicly abused, there is no public forum for their pain. Fact is, no one knows exactly how many children are abused and neglected each year. Incidents are underreported but statistics appear to be rising as more attention is paid to all forms of abuse and domestic violence. (One national study of child abuse by a noted expert finds that the rate of abuse was 26 times higher than that reported by the National Center on Child Abuse and Neglect. For definitions and frequency of child abuse, see Appendix I.)

Public vs Private Pain

Focusing on the drama and horror of the Lisa Steinberg case, the public often overlooks and ignores the personal and private suffering of more than one out of seven children who are physically abused each year, one out of seven female children who experience incest, or the uncounted numbers of children who are emotionally and verbally abused or neglected, as well as ignored.

The scars of abuse and neglect are just as deep for them, although at times, adults abused as children may try to deny their experience or repress it by saying, "It wasn't so bad." You may try to compare what little you remember

1

of your early childhood experience with that of others—such as the widely reported case of Lisa Steinberg. And next to that stark, highly publicized tragedy of her life and early death, you may minimize your suffering, fear, depression, lack of joy, or inability to experience a full range of emotions and feelings.

Recovery is Possible

However, regardless of how much is denied or what assaults are repressed, all kinds of abuse have repercussions. All kinds of abuse are harmful. But recovery is possible. Support, helpful therapy, 12-Step programs, and simply learning more about the process and results of abuse will help you develop the skills and identify the strengths that can bring you to full recovery from abuse, incest, and neglect.

Recovery takes determination and support. Do not try to do it alone. Just as abuse did not occur in a vacuum—it happened in relation to your parents or other early caretakers—so recovery cannot occur without the experience of support and empathy from others that will allow you to feel compassion for yourself and give you the freedom to express who you really are.

Using This Book

As Fred Duhl has said, "The first task of every child is to survive his or her own family." This book is an opportunity for growth and change, a chance to give up—at last—painful ways you have needed to survive. *The Other Side of the Family* has been written for adults who want to begin the process of recovery. It can be used alone, as part of a 12-Step or self-help recovery group, or together with your therapist. By opening this book, you have embarked on a journey of self-discovery and healing. I encourage you to try as many exercises as you can: to take time, to think, to feel, to remember, to observe, to listen, to write, to draw, to share, and ultimately, to heal.

There is no "correct" time period for reading this book or completing the exercises, nor are there any "correct" answers to the questions. While the book was designed to encourage a flow from one phase of recovery to another, you may choose to complete some sections out of sequence. Take as much time as you need. Use this book to give you the tools you need to change and to grow. If you need to take a break, save some exercises for later when you will feel more ready to work them through or when you will have developed more support.

You may find it useful to have a special notebook or journal to explore the written exercises and to record your thoughts and feelings. You can keep this notebook in a private place or with this book. You might also like to supply yourself with a set of paints, colored pencils, or markers to create the drawings recommended in many of these exercises.

In using this book, you will explore a painful chapter in your life. Although initially, abuse and neglect may have occurred during a relatively short time period, they have long-term repercussions, affecting how you behave, how you feel about yourself and others, how you express yourself, and your creativity. Be gentle with yourself. As you explore the past and its impact on the present, take time to build up the support you need. If at any time you feel overwhelmed, stop at once and get help. Call one of the friends you have identified as part of your support system, your therapist, or a crisis hotline, but do not try to work out crises on your own.

Part of recovery is joining the human family. In your family of origin, because you might have been neglected or abused, you learned to enact and expect the same negative or unproductive behavior from others. As you work through this book, you will learn to understand and embrace as part of your daily life the very positive, life-sustaining, and supportive experiences that were denied you as a child.

The quality of your life, relationships, and work will change as you begin to identify and change the hold the past has over you. At times, your journey may seem almost too much to bear, but that is part of the legacy of child abuse: its rootedness is found in the center of your being.

Working through—all the way through—is what recovery is about. I hope this book will assist you in your recovery process, and I welcome your comments and suggestions as to how it was or might be useful.

Ellen F. Ratner
Washington, D.C.

1
The First Steps Toward Recovery

Acknowledging a history of abuse is step one on the road of emotional recovery. Taking action is the necessary second step. Understanding what has happened, accepting one's emotions, and working through the abuse are the major tasks for persons using this book. It is even possible that ritual, cult, or satanic abuse may have occurred in your family—these kinds of abuse are much more prevalent than has previously been acknowledged. This book can be helpful if such is the case for you. Recognizing and adopting behaviors that allow people to grow and develop into mature, happy adults are the goals of this work.

People once abused can learn as adults to act in ways they choose. The exercises in *The Other Side of the Family* were planned with such learning in mind. Each section presents a lesson from which something can be learned. Every so often, you may want to review what you have learned and how you judge it to have been helpful. Occasionally, you may want to share your learning and observations with someone else.

When you are ready to work through the abuse, to take action by acknowledging what has happened, you are taking that first important step toward recovery. You are now ready to begin to understand the effects of the abuse.

Through Others' Eyes

Although the idea may sound strange when first heard, it is worth thinking about: abused people tend to see themselves only as others have seen them. Their self-perception has never been self-generated. At one time, the abuser may have said that they were this or that kind of person. For whatever reason, they accepted that judgment. Ever after, they have been what someone else told them they were. Their behavior has always been judged to be what someone else told them it was.

5

How Does This Affect Me?

What does this mean to you in practical terms? It may mean that you feel worthless, fearful, guilty. It may mean that a seemingly easy and uncomplicated decision for another person—starting a conversation or deciding what to wear, for example—may be an extremely difficult task for you.

Why do abused people have such negative attitudes? Why are simple tasks so difficult for victims of abuse? Because an abused person has received little—if any—accurate, positive reinforcement (or feedback) about the kind of human being he or she is. A child brought up in a "well-functioning" home is sure to hear how pretty or handsome he or she is, how nice a new outfit looks, how well he or she has shoveled the driveway or raked the leaves. An abused child may receive few or no compliments or be punished as a result of efforts to please.

The best efforts of an abused child are likely to be met with silence, a comment about failure at another time, or just more abuse. Almost inevitably the child grows into an adult with distorted self-perception: "I'm no good; I can't do anything right," are haunting refrains in their awareness.

The very ability of abused children to be themselves, to develop normally, ask questions, and receive honest answers—simply to feel safe and secure—may not have happened. A book like this one can suggest ways for some readers to make up for those losses, not by giving them substitute experiences—what has been lost in childhood has been lost forever—but by giving them methods for developing realistic and positive images of themselves today. To develop a positive self-image is to turn oneself into a healthy, "normal" person.

The Other Side of the Family will help you tell your own story—or construct it—in your own unique style, a way that is personal because it has been chosen out of your own growth. In writing your own history and thereby becoming a strong, creative, independent man or woman no longer controlled by past abuse, you can give up living only by reaction as an adult.

Abuse is a strong force that establishes patterns of behavior to which every thought, feeling, and action becomes connected. Sadly, it is the abuser who sets the patterns more often than not. However, as old patterns and habits are broken and healthy new ones established, the abuser's power can be reduced. After you become comfortable with the process of this book, you can encourage trusted persons to reflect to you the positive images you are trying to develop. By sharing thoughts, goals, and actions with trusted friends, a reader can begin building a new—and positive—collection of memories, feelings, and events.

Human relationships, whether therapeutic, casual, intimate, or abusive, are mirrors in which people see themselves. Abuse, particularly if it was perpetrated by a parent or other close authority figure, created a distorted image. Looking into that mirror is like seeing the curved image of oneself at a carnival fun house. Fortunately, talking about old images of self with trusted others actually does change the way persons see themselves. The image that comes back to the speaker by way of the conversation is reflected in an accurate and polished mirror (the friend), and that friend only reflects the image that is presented.

Addictions

Addictions, whether to alcohol or drugs, someone or something else (sex, a person, work, spending), will prevent you from working through the abuse. Every addiction is really an addiction to the process of mood change, and this kind of mood change diverts your attention from your feelings: "I'm depressed—I think I'll go shopping," or "I had a bad day—I better take a pill or have a drink" are common ways of changing feelings.

It is necessary to get help for any addiction before beginning to work through abuse. Twelve-Step programs such as Alcoholics Anonymous, Debtors Anonymous, and similar organizations can help you recover from addictions. Do not attempt to work on past abuse issues without first dealing with addictive problems.

Getting Help

Only you can decide if you need to work through the material of abuse with a professional. When you are making your choice, remember that it does not have to be an all-or-nothing decision. You may want to work through some portions of your recovery from abuse alone, some with friends, some with a professional. What is important is that you receive validation for your feelings and feed-back on how your behavior affects others as you go through the process of working on past abuse.

If you are in a relationship, be cautious about entering therapy that does not include your partner on a regular basis. Seeing two or more therapists (i.e., you seeing one, your partner seeing another, and you both seeing a third) will probably be confusing at best, and may even be destructive. If possible, it is best that one therapist see you and your partner.

Good medical care is essential, and the body-mind connection will be evident to you as you work through the abuse. As certain medical problems may be stress induced, it is important to choose a sensitive physician, make regular appointments, and talk about your past abuse history.

Medication may be necessary if symptoms get in the way of your day-to-day ability to function and relate to others. Often, medication can be used on a short-term basis. In any event, do not prescribe for yourself. See a physician.

Getting Started—Avoid Procrastination

At times, abused people have thought about settling some old family issues, feelings, or memories. Many, however, have felt or said: "I'm too busy with 'other' things in my life. I can't deal with that stuff now." Time passes by but the feelings never change. Fear, anxiety, and depression continue, but the feelings are not faced. Invariably, the bad feelings remain.

The development of a cycle of procrastination can be recognized in passing thoughts such as:

- "I've got to start looking at this soon."
- "It's been so long—how bad could it get if I never start?"
- "I should have started sooner (self-blame)."
- "I'm doing lots of important things in my life—is this more important? Since I've survived till now, I'll get by."
- "There's plenty of time. I can get to these issues later."
- "I hope no one finds out that there's something wrong with me," or, "If I do this now, someone will be hurt."
- "There has to be a better time. But later."*

People give yet other reasons for procrastinating:

- "It's safer to do nothing than to risk failure."
- "They may remember everything." Or, "They may not remember anything."
- "If I start and succeed, someone else may get hurt."
- "If I expose who I am, I will find out I'm really bad."
- "Somehow I will magically be relieved of my pain."
- "I can't do this perfectly, so I won't do it at all."
- "I'm not allowed to feel better or to get well."

Procrastination is an indirect way to continue feeling bad and suffering pain or anxiety. For many reasons, people cannot easily let go of their pain. You yourself may look at this book, do a section, then put it away for a few weeks, perhaps even longer.

That is all right. No one needs to hold on to shame or blame because of the way feelings and memories are faced. Each of us will have our own way of approaching abuse. Probably the best way to avoid procrastination is to make a deal or contract with someone in your life whom you trust, even though any contract is really a promise you make to yourself. There is a side-benefit in talking to another person in that someone else is now contracted to act as your cheerleader and anti-procrastination squad.

*Adopted from *Procrastination: Why You Do It, What to Do About It,* by Jane Burka and Lenora Yuen.

Making a Recovery Contract

Your contract should be fulfillable.
Example:
- I will go to my support group weekly.
- I will read a chapter of the book every two or three weeks.
- I will call _____ when I am unable to do either of the above.

Your chosen champion or cheerleader should be someone outside your family of origin. You can select a friend, self-help group member, spouse, or professional. Write up your contract or promise, make a copy for both you and your cheerleader, then put your copy in a place you will frequently see it—desk, night stand, refrigerator, appointment book, or wallet. Be sure to write an affirming, positive phrase on both the top and bottom of the paper—a phrase such as "I can do this work" or "I want to feel better." Sign it—make it official!

Stages of Recovery

The process of recovery is marked by specific and predictable stages. They are:
- Denial
- Pre-Awareness (glimpsing)
- Awareness
- Exploration
- Bottoming Out
- Working Through
- Resolution and Integration

The Process of Recovery

Deciding to begin the journey of recovery from abuse is difficult. It requires great courage to re-experience feelings and memories you may believe would be better left buried. Some persons who confront old feelings may temporarily become depressed, anxious, or—in extreme cases—even suicidal. Re-examining the past may ultimately require a person to give up some family relationships and sense of belonging, sometimes for long periods of time.

Why should a person who has experienced abuse need to be ready to risk all these things because someone else caused pain? In fairness, the abuser should have to do the work or somehow make up for the pain. But the cliche holds true: life is not fair, and you cannot change what has been done.

Why wait to begin healing until the one who hurt you makes apologies? An abuser is not likely to apologize, and what reparations can be made?

Better simply to take control of your life and make a commitment to become a fully functional person. Now.

The process of recovering from abuse is not like surgery in which some malfunction can be cut out. Working through abuse may take years, but the results can be gratifying and long-lasting. At the end you will own your heart and soul. You will be able to live with ordinary fear and anxiety, and, best of all, you will be able to cope with life's problems without the pall of past abuse.

Stage I—Denial

Denial is a common, significant way in which the mind protects a person from psychological pain. When active, denial allows a person to accomplish life tasks without being conscious of certain bad feelings or memories. For some persons, denial may last only a short time or it may not occur at all. Those persons find a way of dealing directly with the abuse. For others, however, denial may run the course of an entire lifetime. They are persons who fail to deal with past abuse, and it is not uncommon for them to look for refuge from pain in alcohol, drugs, food, or compulsive spending. Because denial blocks the pain of conscious memories, it precludes the opportunity to deal directly with past abuse. Unconsciously, a person may reason that "If I don't remember it, it didn't happen. If I don't feel it, it didn't happen." Another person could deny how abuse felt or acknowledge the fact of abuse while only remembering certain aspects.

Denial may allow you to carry out some rash agreements you made with others. One simple example: as a small child, you promised your mother you would always love her; later, she abused you, and as a loving child, you interpreted the abuse as something other than it was ("only ordinary discipline," you said) in order to keep your word to always love her.

Denial can be the force maintaining family relationships in the face of the anger you feel toward some relatives. Many people remember being abused by their families; few admit that it affected them. They say such things as, "Every kid got whipped. So what?" or "It's OK that Mom left; she was very upset." Such thinking is a form of denial called minimizing, because its effect is minimized.

Almost all persons who have experienced abuse deny its painful parts until they are ready to cope with that difficult segment of their memories.

What have you denied in the past? _____

_____

How did denial help you at the time? _____

_____

When did the denial end? _____

_____

What else might you be denying? (It's OK to take a wild guess.) _____

_____

Stage II—Pre-Awareness or Glimpsing

The stage that follows denial—Pre-awareness or Glimpsing—is closely tied to the denial stage. You may find yourself moving from the denial ("It never happened," or "So what if it did happen?" or "It wasn't abnormal") to glimmers or glimpses of memories and feelings. These glimpses may come to you in dream form or as quick flashes during wakefulness. Sometimes the glimpse may come to you only as a vague feeling. Whether the memory comes as a dream, vague feeling, or a flash, you may not remember it a few hours or even minutes later. What is happening is that your unconscious mind is testing your ability to handle painful information or feelings.

An example. You may feel fear upon meeting someone. There seems to be no reason for the feeling. However, if you analyze your feeling of fear, you may find that something about that person (tone of voice, body language, clothing) may have reminded you of someone you feared in the past. Your felt-fear has to do with a past memory, not the present meeting.

At times in the pre-awareness/glimpsing stage, you may try to do what Elizabeth Kübler-Ross calls bargaining if you do not like the feelings you get with the glimpses. The bargain—like the contract referred to on page 8— is a promise you make to yourself. You may say, "If I stay busy, go to school, and join community activities, then the glimpses will go away and I'll just carry on as always," or "If I don't see my family, I won't have any more of those feelings and I'll be all right." Bargains may limit glimpses. They may keep memories and feelings suppressed and repressed. Bargainers try to stay where they are.

What glimpses have you had of:

Feelings _____

Memories _____

Sensations in your body _____

Smells or odors _____

Have you made any bargains with yourself to shut these glimpses off? What are they? _____

Stage III—Awareness

This is the phase during which you begin to reconcile what happened. You acknowledge the fact that you were indeed the victim of abuse, and you face the reality of how it felt. You are likely to minimize ("It wasn't that bad." "It probably didn't happen the way I thought it did.") or negate the effects of the abuse on your present life.

Many people possess a vague sense of having been abused as a child, but either they lack specific memories of the abuse or they have pushed the memories far back. Denial may take over, and they may even go to professional helpers to reinforce/deny that abuse ever took place. These reactions are the mind's way of coping with stress, and they often create symptoms that will begin to abate when specific incidences of abuse are recalled. It is important to know that what is remembered in fact does not have to be remembered in symptoms.

Sometimes memories of abuse can be overwhelming, and simply to survive, the body transforms emotional feelings into physical reactions or worries about other matters. While transformation and the resulting physical reaction may be troublesome and even frightening, it is a natural defense against the pain of memory.

One or two of the following symptoms do not necessarily indicate a history of abuse, but the presence of a cluster of them suggest another story. As you read the list that follows, think of symptoms you have experienced: the time in your life they appeared, what made them disappear—and then reappear. You might also think about the symptoms of others in your family to give yourself a view into their styles of coping with the stress of having witnessed or participated in your abuse.

Behavioral symptoms	When these feelings occurred
Worry about or being obsessed with harming someone else	_____
Self-destructive or self-endangering behavior	_____
Compulsions such as overeating or gambling	_____
Abusing children or animals	_____
Overly active sexual behavior	_____
Alcohol and/or drug abuse	_____
Running away during childhood and adolescence	_____

Behavioral symptoms	When these feelings occurred
Learning and concentration difficulties not related to a specific learning disability	_____
Allowing yourself to be physically or sexually abused	_____
Extreme irritability	_____
Impulsively irresponsible behavior	_____
Suicidal attempts, constant suicidal feelings, or planning suicide attempts	_____

Feeling/emotional symptoms	When these feelings occurred
Feelings that there is a frightening, evil entity in your home	_____
Fear of being alone or being vulnerable	_____
Persistent sense of overwhelming helplessness	_____
Ability to cut off sensations in certain body parts	_____
Episodes of weeping for no apparent reason	_____
Frequent feelings of confusion	_____
Feelings of intense embarrassment, guilt or shame	_____
Chronic sense of anxiety and panic	_____
Feelings of worthlessness or extremely low self-esteem	_____
Recurrent feelings of disassociation: feeling removed from family members or past experiences	_____
Persistent phobias—e.g., dislike of bedrooms or bathrooms	_____
Choosing relationships in which you are used or taken advantage	_____

Feeling/emotional symptoms	When these feelings occurred
Fear of intimacy or close relationships	_____
Lack of trust or too much trust	_____
Difficulty in relating sexually	_____
Sexual phobias; anxiety or panic during sexual encounters	_____
Inability to put down roots: moving often, changing jobs or friends frequently	_____
Abusive anger with others	_____
Inability to say no to others	_____
Generally poor relationships with others	_____

Bodily symptoms	When these feelings occurred
Feeling of choking	_____
Auditory hallucinations (hearing things): hearing sounds of intruders, such as footsteps, tampering at doors or windows	_____
Visual hallucinations, such as objects moving in your peripheral vision, shadowy figures or dark, featureless figures	_____
Tactile hallucinations: the sense of being pushed, touched, grasped, or thrown	_____
Seizures without biological origin	_____
Recurring violent nightmares and flashbacks with themes of catastrophes	_____
Aches, pains, or unexplained illnesses	_____
Migraine headaches	_____

Stage IV—Exploration Stage

In the stage of exploration, many things happen. In this stage, most persons have a strong interest in finding out more about their pasts, but some feel leery about initiating a serious investigation. Many abused adults find that exploration is a time of great ambivalence, a kind of betwixt and between time filled with indecision about willingness to explore past experiences.

Take a look at your own situation. You know that the past was painful. So painful, you may be reluctant to look at it. The future might seem equally frightening if you sense that during the exploration phase your relationships with your family, friends, and even co-workers may change drastically. Exploring past abuse is a trying process during which you may take out the most negative aspects of your feelings on other people. Anger is apt to emerge at some point: appropriate anger at the people who abused you and displaced anger aimed at people who never had to go through what you did. You may even become abusive to others. This period may come to feel so overwhelming, you may be tempted to run back to the comfort of the denial stage.

So why should you explore your memory? Because eventually you will come to trust in your ability to pass safely through this period, especially as you begin identifying with others who have also been abused. You will feel empathy with people you see on television talk shows about abuse, with those you read about in newspapers and magazines. Suddenly, you will discover that you have concrete information about the subject of abuse, and you will find a willingness in yourself both to talk about and learn more about your experiences.

Now—at this time—the most important task is to keep the good relationships you have and to reach out to others in order to continue your growth process.

Ways I want to explore my past are _____

_____

_____

_____

My fears of exploration are _____

_____

_____

_____

Stage V—Bottoming Out

The exploration period leaves many people emotionally and physically exhausted. As you near the end of exploration, you may feel as though there is no place to go, nowhere to hide, because you now recognize the feelings, problems, and memories. As you sift through the recalled events, feelings and memories of pain may emerge—as strongly and painfully as if they were occurring for the first time.

Now you are immersed in the re-experience of having been abused. Do not be surprised if you become preoccupied by it. Daily work may suffer; you may begin evaluating all current relationships in light of your past. Sometimes it may seem that everything mirrors the past—as if you were going through it all again.

This part of recovery is what many people refer to as the "it-has-to-get-worse-before-it-gets-better" phase, and in a sense it is true. In order to get to the point of being able to work through abuse, you need to re-experience the feelings in order to look at them through a fresh, adult perspective. It is important to understand that the feelings did not kill you then and will not make things worse now. Working on self-esteem, stress reduction, and transference issues in relationships will help you minimize the effects of this stage.

Stage VI—Working Through

As you re-experience events that happened to you as a child, learn to make sense of them in a different way. Understand that, as a child, you had no control over what happened to you; perhaps the people who abused you had little control over themselves because they in turn had been abused as children.

You will feel stable and alive as you discover new ways of solving problems. You may begin to contact members of your family—perhaps even those who abused you—establishing new relationships with them. Though you may not feel relaxed and buoyant, you are recovering now. You are discovering your own feelings and are beginning to have a sense of yourself as a person in control of your life. You are turning into a full-fledged responsible adult.

You clearly recognize that your perception of abuse is genuine, that you were not responsible for it, and that you can pattern your life differently now because you are an adult and have much control over what happens to you. Positive support networks are essential at this stage of recovery.

Stage VII—Resolution and Integration

You have now reached the time to begin exchanging the old you for the new you, of deciding who you want to be and how you want to live your life. You are letting go of denial as you form a healthy, new picture from the jumbled puzzle pieces of your past life. You probably will start to sense yourself as a whole person who matters and who does have a place in the world.

The goal during resolution and integration is not to forget your past but rather to wrap it into your past life exactly for what it is, to know that you have moved beyond it, and to know that you can have healthy, positive relationships with others—and to help others who have been abused.

As you proceed through this book and experience the different stages of recovery, you will get a clearer idea of how each recovery stage builds on previous work. This realization will give you much encouragement to continue and the knowledge that there will come a time when abuse no longer controls your life.

Types of Abuse

The following list of common acts of child abuse is by no means exhaustive. Unfortunately, no one can list every atrocity that humans are capable of perpetrating on other humans. One man sold his daughter to pay off gambling debts. His action reinforced for the author a lesson that this book is trying to teach: never deny abuse because you think it is too bad to have happened.

There is no scale by which to measure child abuse, and it is very difficult to say that some types of abuse are always worse than others. It is also unhelpful to make such comparisons. Physical abuse, for example, is not necessarily worse than emotional abuse, and incest is not always worse or more damaging than neglect. All abuse is long-lasting, damaging, painful, and prevents healthy growth. All abuse needs to be talked about and worked through.

At first you may remember only one or two examples of abuse, but as you proceed through the stages of recovery and open up painful memories, you will probably recall more. For now, at the outset of your road to recovery, try not to force yourself to remember. Read the following list, checking the items that apply to you and/or your family members. Then go over this list periodically; it may help you to remember other deeply suppressed occasions of abuse.

	Happened to me	Happened to others in family
Emotional Abuse		
Calling you names, constantly embarrassing you/others or putting you down	❏	❏
Belittling or rejecting you, blocking your attempts at self-acceptance	❏	❏
Harassing you or making you the object of malicious or sadistic jokes	❏	❏
Making you steal or do other illegal things	❏	❏
Blackmail	❏	❏
Punishing you unfairly	❏	❏
Making you perform cruel or degrading tasks	❏	❏
Criticizing your independent thoughts and feelings	❏	❏
Telling you that you have no right to be alive or that you are unworthy	❏	❏
Telling you that you are always or usually wrong; dictating religious thoughts	❏	❏
Making you feel hopeless	❏	❏
Punishing you in public or in front of other family members	❏	❏
Always comparing you to others	❏	❏
Making you eat something you spilled on the floor	❏	❏
Deliberately raising you as a member of the opposite sex	❏	❏
Preventing you from going to school	❏	❏
Terrorizing or bullying you	❏	❏
Isolating you from others	❏	❏
Rejecting you by openly preferring your siblings	❏	❏
_____	❏	❏
_____	❏	❏
_____	❏	❏

	Happened to me	Happened to others in family
Neglect		
Leaving you alone for days or weeks in the care of others	❏	❏
Ignoring you or not responding to your needs	❏	❏
Not feeding you or providing you needed clothing, or making you feed yourself before you were able	❏	❏
Not washing your clothes	❏	❏
Ignoring your physical needs and/or not getting you required medical attention	❏	❏
Providing little physical nurturing, such as holding you or talking to you	❏	❏
Leaving you with an irresponsible caretaker	❏	❏
Not providing proper nutrition or not giving you enough to eat	❏	❏
Providing an uninhabitable place to live: drafty, unclean, or unsafe	❏	❏
Your parents were drug or alcohol abusers and neglected you as a result	❏	❏
Your parents didn't get out of bed to care for you	❏	❏
Not allowing you to leave your room or your home for long hours, days, or weeks	❏	❏
_____	❏	❏
_____	❏	❏
Physical Abuse		
Shoving	❏	❏
Throwing	❏	❏
Slapping, hitting, spanking that caused marks or bruises	❏	❏
Scratching or biting	❏	❏
Burning	❏	❏
Cutting	❏	❏

	Happened to me	Happened to others in family
Breaking your bones or making you bleed	❑	❑
Not allowing you to defecate or urinate	❑	❑
Tying or locking you up or restraining you in other ways	❑	❑
Using heat or cold (usually water) to cause pain	❑	❑
Using rubber bands or other materials in your hair to cause pain	❑	❑
Holding your head under water or otherwise trying to suffocate you	❑	❑
Making you sit or stand for unreasonable periods of time	❑	❑
Using hunger as a consistent punishment	❑	❑
Confining you to a small space for long periods of time	❑	❑
Forcing you to eat unhealthy or unsanitary food or food designed for animals	❑	❑
Forcing you into toilet training too early	❑	❑
Medicating or drugging you when you were not ill	❑	❑
Locking you out of the house as punishment	❑	❑
Forcing you into child labor	❑	❑
Hurting or killing your pets	❑	❑
Serving your pets to you as food	❑	❑
_____	❑	❑
_____	❑	❑

Sexual

	Happened to me	Happened to others in family
Lying nude or being provocative	❑	❑
Showing you pornographic pictures or movies	❑	❑
Flirting with you or engaging in provocative behavior	❑	❑

	Happened to me	Happened to others in family
Kissing, holding, or touching you inappropriately	❏	❏
Raping you	❏	❏
Touching, biting, or fondling your sexual parts	❏	❏
Giving you enemas or douches for no medical reason	❏	❏
Forcing you to observe or participate in adult bathing, undressing, toilet, or sexual activities	❏	❏
Making you engage in forced or mutual masturbation	❏	❏
Forcing you to be nude with others	❏	❏
Making you share your parents' bed when other beds were available	❏	❏
Making you look at or touch adults' sexual parts	❏	❏
Allowing you to be sexually molested	❏	❏
Telling you about their explicit sexual behavior	❏	❏
_____	❏	❏
_____	❏	❏

As you work your way through this book, you may begin to be fearful, even feel unsafe or frightened. Rest assured that these are the feelings you had as a child. It is not unusual to re-experience these feelings when you sense yourself back in a vulnerable position. Although these feelings will be discussed later in *The Other Side of the Family,* it is important to identify such feelings as you go along.

What are some of the feelings you are re-experiencing now as you begin your journey into recovery? List them:

_____

_____

_____

_____

Family Maps, Myths, and Organizing Principles

As you work through the book, you will see how important it is to understand your family's patterns and systems. Generational patterns such as alliances and feuds, as well as patterns of illness and health, will be evident if you draw your family map. Two excellent books, *Genograms* by Emily Marlin and *Genograms in Family Assessment* by Monica McGoldrick and Randy Gerson, will help you map family traits, relationships, talents, and personality types. The information you gain will deepen your understanding of your family's dynamics and help you with the important work of healing.

A family is a system in which actions produce reactions. Events do not happen without something to precede them. Expressed emotions and feelings lead to other expressed emotions and feelings. Nothing occurs in a vacuum, and each person is affected by the actions of others, even if the effect is denied. No clue is too small to be useful; you might not understand its significance, but as you continue your work, the clue may acquire meaning.

You may find it helpful in your work to think about your family's organizing principles. An organizing principle is a system or thought process by which an entity arranges itself to work as a unit. All families have them; some are organized around obedience to a patriarchal (father) figure; others may be organized around feelings of shame or guilt.

As you think about some possible organizing principles of your own family, try to identify those on the surface, then speculate on the underlying principles. This is an exercise you can return to many times during your recovery: your insights will change and deepen.

You may also find that you remember stories about your family that seem like myths or fairy tales. Whether these stories are true or were made up, they reflect what the storyteller has heard and understands about the family. A family myth may tell of heroic actions during wartime, or it may describe generous and charitable ancestors. Myths can also be negative: a father may tell a story about the mother's family to make his own relatives seem normal and healthy (or vice versa). These family myths and stories can reveal your family's organizing principles and help illuminate puzzling or disturbing experiences.

Keeping a Journal

Writing down your thoughts and feelings as you embark on this journey toward recovery from abuse might seem like an odd thing to do. After all, aren't memories of the abuse permanent enough?

The rationale for keeping a journal comes from the experience of many women and men who have worked their way through abuse. Keeping a journal is an excellent way of telling your story to yourself. You can refer to your journal from time to time, and as you remember your feelings and reactions from childhood, you can re-evaluate them as an adult.

Children are often told that they really are not feeling what they know they feel; are not remembering what they do remember; not experiencing what they are experiencing. Conditioned as they are by the adults who tell them these things, children eventually begin to deny their past. They become quite good at convincing themselves that reality is not what they experienced. Your journal today can be a clear, adult record of your reality. It will be there for you when you are tempted to say, "It wasn't that bad," or "I don't think I ever really felt that way."

A journal is also a record of progress. In your journal you will be able to keep track of insights, feelings, and behaviors, and you will learn to define yourself by the thoughts and feelings you have recorded. You will not be able to deny experience because your own name will be stamped on those thoughts and experiences.

Some people find it difficult to write, but even that need not be a hindrance. You are not being graded on the correctness or cleverness of your grammar and language; the only truly important thing to write is your most accurate expression of your feelings. You can do that simply by writing a series of words that represent what is going on in your heart or mind. You may write words or phrases such as scared, angry, bad dreams last night. Little by little, though, you will find yourself becoming more fluent, and you will spend more time recording what you are feeling.

You might want to scribble a picture sometime, using colored pens or pencils to represent emotions. Many people use their journals to record dreams and fantasies, or how they feel about a certain event in their present lives if it brings up memories of the past. If you cannot write words, then cut out magazine pictures, newspaper articles, or headlines that represent the way you feel.

Since the experience of having been abused can bring feelings of uncertainty and fear about life and the future, you may want to include representations of life in your journal: pressed flowers, dried leaves from a walk in the woods, a card or letter that meant something to you, a term paper you wrote, a piece of artwork, the program from a concert or play.

The content of your journal does not really matter as a long as it is truly a representation of your thoughts and reflects your feelings at that moment.

Long-term Effects

People who have been abused, neglected, or experienced incest carry several effects with them until the experience has been worked through. In this book, we will address each of them, and you will gain new skills and learn new ways for overcoming old behaviors.

Although this list is far from complete, many of the long-term effects of abuse, neglect, and incest fall into the following areas:
- Decreased ability to enjoy life
- Lack of peer relationships
- Impaired relationships
- Impulsive, inappropriate, or unsavory relationships
- Low self-esteem
- Loss of the ability to empathize
- Withdrawal and isolation
- Dissociation
- Fear or distrust of others
- Vigilance/almost suspiciousness
- Self-injurious behavior

Using the above-mentioned list, write down the effects you feel that abuse, neglect, or incest has had on you:

_____

_____

_____

_____

_____

_____

_____

As research is still not complete on what kinds of abuse cause what kinds of long-term effects, it is difficult to say how abuse may have affected any one person. You will be the best judge of its long-term effects on you.

Post-trauma Stress (PTSD)

Post-traumatic stress, also known as PTSD, has been identified since the time of World War I. In that era, the disorder was called "shell shock," "being shell shocked," or "war neurosis." After the Vietnam war, the disorder was studied more carefully, and several different health care specialists called for its assignment under a recognized classification in the *Diagnostic and Statistical Manual III* (DSM-III). The disorder consists of characteristic symptoms following a remarkable psychologically distressing event outside the usual range of human experience. Post-traumatic stress reaction can occur anytime following the abuse, even decades after the traumatic occurrence. The three major symptoms are: (1) avoidance of anything that reminds the person of the event, (2) numbing of emotional responsiveness, and (3) increased arousal and responsiveness.

Some characteristics of PTSD include the following:

- Physical reaction to small stresses as if they were the original trauma.
- Sleep and dream disturbances. People may sleep as if poised for flight or sleep with their eyes open. Symptoms may increase with changes in routine, such as beginning to sleep next to another person. Dreams may be either vivid and symbolic or they may be exact re-creations of the abuse.
- Irritability—extreme irritation and reaction to noise or minor stimulants.
- Increase in the startle response.
- Fixation on the trauma.
- Explosive behavior and/or trouble modulating and controlling anger. Rage must go somewhere, either to the self or others. It sometimes manifests itself in physical illness.
- Reduced ability to function. Some persons with PTSD can function quite well; however, it has been shown that after the resolution of PTSD, functioning increases.
- Fantasy is used as a means to cope with stress.
- Development into a career patient, either physical or psychiatric.
- Helplessness and passivity—an inability to look for and find problem-solving solutions.
- Inability to differentiate emotions.
- Sensory (body) experiences.
- Having defensive over- or undercontrol.
- Trouble in forming attachments or increased idealization and/or hate of people recently met.
- Attachment to trauma. Relationships that resemble the original trauma are sought. TV programs or movies in which people are victimized are selected. Involvement with helping figures may end in an attempt to become one with the helper or in total rejection of the helper. A person with PTSD may vacillate between the two reactions.
- Self-blame and a sense of being tainted or evil. They may be prevalent even in individuals who have experienced trauma at a later age and understand the context. Abnormal EEG (Brain Wave Abnormality) may occur as a result of PTSD. Some research shows EEG abnormalities as well as hysterical seizures, learning disabilities, and attentional disorders can be results of early abuse.

Most of the research has also identified a learned helplessness* to be a result of PTSD. Learned helplessness in animals has been shown to manifest itself in the following ways:
- Inability to learn new behavior
- Decreased immune response
- Lower social dominance in a troop or tribe. In some studies, monkeys have difficulty fitting in, develop huddling behavior, socially withdraw, and either develop self-aggression or unpredictable aggression toward others. (They often became confused and had difficulty developing positive sex partners.)

People with PTSD find it hard to think their way through an emotional situation. Negotiation may be perceived as a power game, since that is how the trauma taught them to communicate. PTSD people often organize their world through action, by rage reaction, control of family, mental action manifested in fear or panic, compulsive work, and being ill or getting help. Anger is used as a way of maintaining bonds with others. Rigidity may be used to defend against recurrence of the trauma.

Recovery from PTSD — Some Steps

The trauma must be placed in an historical context.

1. The seeming inability of the PTSD person to feel or respond indicates that all energy is devoted to blocking remembrance of the trauma. PTSD people need to understand what happened before, during, and after the trauma, and the trauma needs to be put into a context that makes sense.

2. The trauma must be put into words. Often, people with PTSD are left only with visual images or sensual feelings in their bodies. Words express the trauma.

3. PTSD people need to understand that they do have power to control their lives, and that they have power to effect change now in their lives.

4. It is important to create a sense of safety for the PTSD person. Visualizations of boundaries and "no-entry" zones inside the mind are helpful.

5. PSTD people need to develop a future orientation. It is necessary for them to understand that they have a future and a tomorrow.

---

*Learned helplessness may prevent people who have been abused from fighting for themselves, standing up for themselves, or becoming assertive. Dissociation may take the form of feeling detached from your body, feeling as if someone else is performing your body's actions, or (a more total dissociation) the development of multiple personality, in which different "selves" take over, often without awareness or memory from the other selves. Memory recall may trigger PTSD, just as the loss of someone close may trigger a trauma response. The sense of helplessness is very painful and makes it hard to participate in a normal give and take.

6. PTSD people need to learn to differentiate their feelings.

7. PSTD people need to develop a slow working-through of memory that allows both body and mind to adjust to remembered events.

8. Others must understand what the PTSD person is verbalizing. Good communication is needed.

9. Elimination of felt-trauma. Any stimulus that makes traumatic feelings recur—e.g., surprises, a scary movie or book, or contact with the abuser—should be avoided.

10. Development of confidence and self-esteem. Resolution of the trauma will be noticeable when the person can recall the trauma, then attend to other matters at will. Some current research has investigated biological changes in brain chemistry that have resulted from the trauma. Medical intervention may be needed to achieve that ability. Medication may be very useful.

Other factors that influence the ability to recover from PTSD include:
- severity of abuse
- genetics: some people are more or less stress-resistant
- mental development at the time of the abuse and the person's ability to understand the abuse and its context
- current social support

Do you have symptoms of PTSD? What are they? _____

_____

_____

Of the ten recovery areas listed above, what do you think you need to do to complete recovery?

_____

_____

What kind of internal time frame do you have for beginning and ending the work of resolving the trauma?

_____

_____

Whom do you want on your team? Whom do you want to help you resolve the trauma?

_____

_____

2
Support Networks

Children experience abuse, incest, or neglect alone, even if others in their family system were also abused, or if they were around while the abuse was happening. Abuse of any kind is like illness: people encounter it alone. Part of the problem of abuse is its uniqueness. No two people experience the same thing. Your experience of abuse is solely your experience, your feelings. And the effects of abuse are different for each person.

What does this mean for an abused person? Sisters or brothers who lived in the same household will not have the same memories or experience of being abused that you have. Blocking negative memories, they may only recall positive family experiences. If you attempt to share your experience of fear, isolation, and pain, they may say you are wrong—or crazy—that your childhood was never like that, or that your parents were hardworking, caring individuals who did the best they could under difficult circumstances.

But do not deny your feelings or experiences. The impact of abuse—as well as the way each of us reacts and responds—can be quite different in the different periods of childhood and adulthood. In one of those periods, you might have been shy and withdrawn, frightened of groups or of too much attention. In another period, you might have been the life of the party, talking animatedly—almost babbling—in a frantic attempt to fill up the silences. Other people have their memories and experiences; you have your own.

Personal styles of abused people vary. Some persons collect acquaintances but avoid having close friends. Others have a rich fantasy life they do not share with anyone. Most abused people, however, have difficulty sharing and opening up to others. That may be another reason why brothers and sisters cannot support your known experiences. As a child, you may have learned that you could neither trust nor rely on your parents or other adults—or your brothers and sisters. You may have learned that it was not safe to trust. Your bothers and sisters may have had the same experience. Thus, it is possible that all the children in your family grew up feeling

29

vulnerable and frightened, especially when they were faced with exploring or thinking about intimacy and closeness.

People tend to keep their experiences of abuse or incest to themselves. Now, you have a chance to challenge your negative feelings of being different, spoiled, or inadequate. Resolving the trauma of abuse, incest, and neglect requires reaching out, opening up, and sharing with others. It means taking a risk for growth, making friends, and building a support system. Even though the recovery process can feel frightening at times — and may leave you feeling vulnerable and exposed — do not hold back from reaching out to others. No one can heal the scars of abuse alone.

Network Building

Developing a network takes time and effort, and finding trustworthy and supportive friends only happens slowly. Building a support network means honing many different skills, such as selecting friends or learning to be a friend. Trust is relying on another person. It does not mean overlooking shortcomings or limitations. Blanket trust of another person is rare and may occur in only one or two relationships in a lifetime.

A reliable personal network that includes friends and family members is an important support to have. A personal network coupled with a professional network that includes a therapist, counselor, spiritual director or physician is the best base from which to begin confronting the abuse in your life. All these relationships must be based on trust.

Personal Network

An example of a personal network might be:

Sally   An old friend from high school with whom you can reminisce; she helps you maintain contact with acquaintances. You may see Sally five to ten times a year.

John   A friend from work you socialize with in the cafeteria or after work. He cheers you up with his jokes.

Lilly   Another friend from work, she is a bit depressed, but is someone who has told you her life story and is sympathetic to you. She has become involved in Adult Children of Alcoholics. You can open up and talk to her.

Mary   Your artistic and talkative next door neighbor. You frequently share late night talks and watch movies together. She takes care of your cat when you are out of town, and occasionally you babysit for her.

What friends might you wish to include in your personal network?

Person	Type of friend and characteristics	How often you see that person
_____	_____	_____
	_____	_____
	_____	_____
_____	_____	_____
	_____	_____
	_____	_____
_____	_____	_____
	_____	_____
	_____	_____

A network is a series of connections linking a person to other people and the community. To function as a network, the separate relationships must be connected to one another in some way. Some friends know each other, and, even if they are not best friends, they realize that they are part of a support system. These individuals can be brought together in small groups to share a concert or film or at an annual large party. A solid personal network is fundamental to learning about a nurturing, positive sense of family that should have been part of a supportive childhood, but was not.

Support allows abused people to risk, to open up, to be vulnerable. It enables them to grow and heal.

Abused people need to select friends carefully to avoid further betrayal and hurt, but before they choose, they need to identify and re-experience past vulnerability. This time—unlike the past when they felt powerless and had no choices—is different. Consider what the concept *vulnerability* means: to risk, hazard, or venture; to lean on and lay oneself open.

There is no one more vulnerable than a child. Children must lean on adults to survive and to grow into adulthood themselves. Open to all, they have no choice as to whom to show their vulnerability. Adults, however, have a choice, and they can choose the people to whom they show it.

Thinking about vulnerability may make you feel like a child and may inhibit you from opening up, from sharing negative feelings, from revealing pain, confusion, loss, or sadness. If you choose the wrong people—those who are not willing to share, to be there for you when you are in need, to show their vulnerability in return—you risk recreating your childhood experience of abuse.

Who are your friends? _____

_____

Who is in your network now? _____

_____

What category would you place them in? _____

_____

How long have you known them? _____

_____

How do they contribute to meeting your needs for growth and support?

_____

_____

Can you count on them to continue meeting those needs? _____

Are you able to be there for them when they are in need of nurturing and support? _____

Identifying Your Personal Network

Needs	My network
To be included:	People who like me, like to have me around, care about my being there: _____ _____
Value sharing:	People who share my values and have similar life styles: _____ _____
To have talents recognized:	People who support and respect me for the things I do well: _____ _____

Needs	**My network**
To have fun, relax:	People with whom I can have fun:
	_____
	_____
To have continuity in a relationship:	People who have known me for a long time, like me, and provide a sense of my past:
	_____
	_____
Crisis support:	People whom I can count on to be there when I'm in trouble; people who can support me when I need it:
	_____
	_____
Closeness, intimacy:	People I can share things with, can give me a hug, and who I know love me and care about me:
	_____
	_____
Intellectual stimulation:	People I can talk with about ideas, world affairs, new interests:
	_____
	_____

As you review your network, do you see areas where you need some additional support? _____

_____

Are any of your needs not being met? _____

Are you counting on just a few people to fill all your needs? _____

Are you spreading out your support network so that no one has a chance to know you too well? _____

   Although it may not always be the case, the people with whom you choose to share closeness and intimacy, along with those you select for crisis support, will probably be the people to whom you will choose to show your vulnerability. Setting limits on physical touch and understanding when and where you feel safe being touched is important as you allow yourself to become vulnerable.

Be careful in choosing. In the past, you may have relied on a certain family member for support in a crisis—someone whom you could count on if you needed to be bailed out. You may still be able to rely on that person for financial help or some other kind of aid. However, negative, unsupportive, or even abusive interactions with that person over the years, may make openness and vulnerability with them now both difficult and unwise.

As a child, you had to rely on and be vulnerable to adults who hurt or abused you. As you choose a support network, be clear with yourself about how much autonomy and dependence you want. In making these decisions you may seesaw over relationships. Clarity about your needs will help you develop a strong network. Think about the idea of feeling vulnerable with a person you may be choosing as a friend. How does being vulnerable to that person make you feel? _____

Words like *unsafe, scared, small,* and *embarrassed* may pop into your mind. If you feel vulnerable, you need to be around people you can trust. That means selecting individuals with care and thought now, not later. Explore and examine their characteristics, behaviors, attitudes, and values to learn if it is safe to risk being vulnerable with them. Before choosing to be vulnerable with another person, ask yourself the following questions.

Alcohol/Drugs
- How frequently does he/she use alcohol or drugs?
- Does he/she have an alcohol or drug problem now?
- Does he/she get drunk, stoned, or high on a regular basis or at inappropriate times?

Directness and Risk-taking without Hostility
- Will your friend tell you and others only what you want to hear (people pleasing), or take risks and tell you unpleasant truths as well? Will your friend give you feedback in a way that you can listen to it?

Jealousy
- Is your friend envious or resentful of your life?
- Can your friend discuss envy if it is an issue to work through?

Life and Friendship Patterns
- What is your friend's previous pattern in friendships? Long-term or rapid turnover?
- Are your friend's personal stories consistent? Does your friend's life match up with what you have been told about the past and what others have said?

Negativity
- Is your friend negative, fault-finding, or critical?
- Does your friend have a biting, hostile sense of humor? Can your friend make jokes that are not mean?
- Are there times when you feel your friend's comments are hostile or biting, but you overlook them anyway?
- Does your friend make a big point of talking about a belief in honesty? (People who make a point of discussing honesty or ethics may be covering up their own dishonest feelings.)
- How important is being truthful to you?

Openness
- Does your friend seem open to what you say? Can this person hear your problems and difficulties, or does your friend minimize what you have to say?
- Does your friend have the ability to listen?

Treatment of Others
- Does your friend make fun of others' problems or is your friend compassionate?
- Does your friend have a reputation for talking about confidences and intimacies of others?

If you excuse or overlook negative or unsupportive behaviors in your friends in the hope that they will change, remember that people do not change without much hard work.

Most important, is your friend loyal, caring, and respectful of who you are? If so, it is probably safe to share some of your childhood feelings and experiences as you work through them.

Have you clarified your dependency/autonomy issues with your friend? Does your friend understand how difficult an issue this may be for you?

Maintaining your network (e.g., letting your friends know when you are feeling stressed, when you would like to call, or even when you might want to stay over for a weekend) is important for your sense of well-being and safety. Even though you may be married or living in an intimate relationship, it is important to maintain a solid network. The dynamics of a couple's relationship may make developing a network outside the relationship very important to continued recovery.

Professional Networks and Support Groups

Choosing a therapist, spiritual counselor, or support group is just as important as choosing a member of your personal network, and it requires just as much forethought and care. Many therapists have had little overt experience with abuse. As a result, they misdiagnose symptoms or do not know which questions to ask. Not all spiritual counselors will be sensitive to a person who has experienced abuse, nor will they understand the deep spiritual violation central to that experience. Some support groups become mired in re-experiencing negative feelings, and they fail to move on after exploring and expressing these feelings.

The following criteria will be helpful in selecting your professional network.

Building a Professional Network

Criteria	Questions to Ask Professionals
Training	1. What kind and level of training have they had? Master's degree, doctorate, para-professional with special nonde-gree training? Is the person a clinical social worker, psychologist, or counselor? If you do not understand the differences, ask about their training.
Experience	2. What experience with incest and abuse does the pro-fessional have? How many clients have been seen from beginning to end of therapy, and over what period of time?
Orientation	3. Does the professional have a systems or family orien-tation? It is often important to become involved in treat-ment with your significant other. Exclusion can strain or even end a relationship. Likewise, seeing two separate counselors or therapists may increase relationship diffi-culties unless there is good communication between the therapists.

It is important to interview providers on the first or second visit to ascertain their skills and capacity to help. You are a consumer and they are providing a service. In most cases you will be required to pay for the service. Lack of assertiveness in selecting a professional network will only delay your recovery.

Support Groups

The work of exploring past abuse and neglect will be easier and more successful if you have an adequate support system. If you cannot afford a spiritual counselor, therapist, or specially trained guide, join a support group. There are many public service agencies that offer support groups to both men and women. Or you might begin to develop a new support group from people you know through a church or a self-help 12-Step group. Some enterprising people have started successful support groups by running ads in a local alternative newspaper, but there are obvious risks in such a course.

The purposes of a support group are to:
- Provide encouragement to all group members
- Share useful information and resources
- Provide a safe place to express feelings
- Offer mutual assistance and encouragement
- Prevent isolation
- Reduce shame and guilt
- Provide feedback and self-understanding.

12-Step Groups

Al-Anon, Adult Children of Alcoholics, or any related 12-Step program can be used as a support group. Attendance at an appropriate 12-Step program can be helpful for anyone who has experienced incest, abuse, a compulsion, or an addiction.

The 12-Step approach as pioneered by Alcoholics Anonymous will be helpful to you because it:
- Helps you get outside yourself
- Curbs negative behaviors and thoughts
- Helps you share with others
- Helps express and relieve guilt and shame.

Groups for incest survivors are available in many communities. Many of these weekly groups are leaderless, and they allow participants to share experience, process feelings, and receive support. At this time, there are few support groups for those persons who have experienced physical or emotional abuse or neglect.

If you decide to begin a leaderless support group, consider the following guidelines:

1. Choose a format that is easy to use. For example, the format could be: (a) topic-related, (b) open discussion, or (c) a combination. You might want to choose a 12-Step format. Or choose a section from this book as a weekly discussion topic, with a leader-of-the-week acting as discussion guide.

2. Choose a gatekeeper/leader for each individual session. Rotate leadership so that everyone has both the chance and responsibility to lead discussion. Power sharing avoids re-creation of abusive or uneven power dynamics.

3. Make sure the meeting starts and ends on time. If meetings begin and end promptly, they serve as models for dealing with others and ensure the existence of checks and balances on intimacy, distance, and closeness.

4. If participants wish, they can make a phone contact list for support outside of the groups. It is usually wise to omit publication of last names.

5. Set ground-rules for name-calling, expression of anger, and similar emotional situations. Follow the suggestions on pages 42–43 for getting and giving feedback. Write a group contract to identify goals, objectives, group process, and individual vulnerabilities.

6. Consider inviting local therapists and spiritual leaders to talk on specific topics. Variety draws out the participation and involvement of most group members.

7. Decide how many sessions you want the group to run, if you want it to be open-ended, as well as rules for entry and exit from the support group.

My Professional Network

Person or group	How you choose them/ characteristics	How often you see them
Therapist/ Counselor	_____	_____
	_____	_____
	_____	_____
Spiritual Counselor	_____	_____
	_____	_____
	_____	_____
Support Group	_____	_____
	_____	_____
	_____	_____

How Can a Group Experience Help Me?

As children adapt and change in response to the stresses of abuse and neglect, it becomes increasingly difficult for them to have an accurate and complete picture of themselves. Treatment they have received from many of the adults in their lives leaves them with a distorted and partial self-portrait. What they see is what other people tell them they are, and all too often, the message is negative. Abusers, having few boundaries, often project what they feel about themselves onto the abused person. Parents who say, "You are a failure; you will never amount to anything in your life," are first making that affirmation of failure about themselves.

In a group experience, the process of receiving accurate feedback from other group members can paint pictures of participants that differ dramatically from the images they have long held about themselves. All group members can use the strength and objectivity of the support group to develop a true, comprehensive picture of self.

The Johari Window

The Johari Window shows what can happen in a positive group. The so-called called Johari Window is named after Johari, two psychologists who developed a teaching device to help people understand what they see and do not see about themselves.*

The four panes of the window represent the whole self.

1 OPEN	2 SECRET
4 BLIND	3 UNKNOWN

The first pane (#1) is visible to all. It is what people know about you, the things you share with the world.

Pane #2 is secret, and it covers what you know about yourself, but do not allow others to see. The secrets are about what has happened to you and how you feel about yourself and others.

Pane #3 is the part of you that is unknown, both by yourself and others.

Pane #4 is the blind spot in your life, the part of you that others see, but which remains hidden from you. It is how others perceive you and describe you.

To open your window (self), you will need to reveal your secret parts and let people give you feedback on the window pane that is blind. The process of gaining self-awareness occurs as you take risks, identify your feelings, let others share your experiences, and then allow them to give you feedback. Through this give-and-take process, you will be able to open your windows and yourself, letting in more of the world.

Sponsors

Alcoholics Anonymous, the world's largest self-help program, recommends that everyone in recovery have a sponsor or mentor. This is a person already in recovery for some time, someone who has looked seriously at issues in life, someone who has had to face the illness of alcoholism or another severe and personally limiting problem.

---

*Luft, Joseph. (1970). *Group process: An introduction to group dynamics*, 11. Palo Alto, Calif.: National Press Books.

Someone who has suffered abuse or neglect is not suffering from a disease. However, because abuse causes pain and suffering and prevents normal growth and development, it does require a recovery process. Like addiction, abuse thrives on denial and secrecy. However, for the abused person, opening up, sharing, and gaining support from others' struggles to recover is most healing and inspiring. Those actions provide both the giver and the receiver the needed courage to face pain and grief.

To recover means to regain, retrieve, recuperate, get back, redeem, reclaim, and take back. In order for the recovery process to happen, most individuals need guidance. Few people, if any, can successfully guide themselves because they have been so hurt and isolated by the abuse.

Everyone in recovery profits from having a sponsor or mentor. Someone who has experienced abuse, incest, or neglect and then worked through the problem into the later stages of recovery can offer insight on the process and be a valuable commentator on your progress toward recovery.

Sponsors should be chosen carefully, be trustworthy, and have no need to elevate, put down, or control the person sponsored. The sponsor/mentor should be there for the sponsored—to call, visit, and share with. A sponsor's main gifts are the role model and the experiences of recovery that can be shared with the person sponsored. A sponsor is not a therapist. A sponsor is a peer role model, someone who chooses to share his or her experience, strength, and hope.

If you are new to recovery, summon your courage, ask someone to sponsor you, and set a time—at least once a week—to meet and share your experiences. A sponsor can help if you become overwhelmed by attacks of isolation, loneliness, despair, and loss of self-worth. A sponsor can be like an ideal older sister or brother, one who cares and helps you learn the ropes of healthy living. Sponsorship can provide a close and growing relationship for both parties, if it is a clear sponsor or mentor relationship. The one factor that will absolutely destroy a sponsorship relation is sexual interaction. Turning sponsorship into a sexual relation may repeat or mimic early family situations and will almost certainly re-create the anxiety and fear of early abuse and neglect.

Some people I might want as a sponsor are: _____

_____

Listening Techniques

Listening is an important part of the support we offer to others. Like talking, writing, or playing a musical instrument, listening is a skill that develops with practice.

Too often a listener begins forming a response before the other person has finished speaking. Most of us are more involved in our need to respond than in hearing what the other person is trying to say.

The listener has a responsibility to help the talker be fully expressive. This responsibility can be satisfied simply by hearing—being able to repeat—what is said, and then giving the other person feedback. The following guidelines are helpful in developing listening and feedback skills.

Focused Listening

- Do not interrupt or disagree while the sender is speaking. Wait until the sender has finished. Otherwise, you will cut off what is being said, and the likely result will be misinterpretation.
- Make sure that the speaker knows you are trying to understand what is being said.
- Use open-ended questions such as:
  —How do you feel?
  —When did that happen? Where did it happen?
  —Why did that happen?
  —Who was involved? What was your mother doing there?
  —What did you do? Did you...?
- Ask for more information. Draw out the speaker by asking questions about topics such as:
  —background
  —descriptions
  —feelings
  —reactions
  —responses and actions
- Show your attention to the speaker by body language. Lean forward, make eye contact, look interested, nod your head, and make supportive comments, such as "Yes, I see," if and when appropriate.
- When you feel your mind wandering, refocus your attention. If you are unsure that you heard what the person said, ask "Would you repeat that so I can be sure I'm hearing what you said?"
- Repeat what you think you heard before you give an answer. By doing so, you confirm that what you heard is what was said.
- Give the speaker enough time to talk, but do not let the conversation wander.
- Direct your response to what was said.

Listening Exercises

With a group member or a friend, time the following exercise. One person talks for three minutes, the other listens. When the speaker stops, the listener should repeat the conversation as accurately as possible. At a minimum, all main ideas should be reflected. The speaker should then judge whether the repeated conversation was accurate. Then reverse roles. If it is comfortable, try the exercise for five minutes, pause, then repeat it for seven minutes. Did your listening skills improve?

Giving Feedback

- Feedback is given to help another person. It is not a stage for your performance.
- Make sure you are ready to hear what the speaker is saying. Pay attention. Do not occupy yourself with some task while someone is speaking.
- Make your feedback as positive as you can.
- Be caring and gentle in your feedback message.
- Be generous with compliments. Be especially concerned to comment favorably on others' accomplishment of difficult tasks.
- Do not be judgmental. Listeners become defensive to judgments.
- Do not give feedback that is ambiguous, vague, or hurtful. Do not let your feedback be divisive of the group.
- Be sure that the time is right for what you have to say.
- Be objective, direct, and specific in what you say. Do not attribute attitudes or emotions to the speaker.
- Be prepared to acknowledge your own discomfort with what you hear or understand.
- Be willing to ask other group members for their opinions about the accuracy and usefulness of your feedback.

Feedback Exercise

Choose a friend with whom to do this exercise. Share something about yourself that you would like to change. Be sure to discuss why you want to change and how you think the behavior or characteristic developed. At the end of the exercise, ask for feedback. Reverse roles and repeat the exercise.

Example:

Speaker: "I would like to change the way I react to my boss. I'm afraid of my boss and I am not sure why. I don't want to be frightened of him for no reason. He reminds me of my uncle who was abusive to me. Does anyone have any ideas?"

Receiver: "I hear you saying you're having a hard time and your boss scares you. Can you tell me more about him? Has this always been the case? Sometimes I notice you seem a little scared here, too. Are you?"

When your support group begins to meet, it is important that everyone understand the rules for giving and receiving feedback. A signed contract concerning the rules for giving feedback will make all feedback more acceptable to participants.

Rules for Receiving Feedback

1. Express appreciation that someone cared enough to give you feedback.

2. Receive feedback openly. It is how the other person views you. Restate what was said to acknowledge what you have heard.

3. Be open and nondefensive. This may be difficult, especially if what is said reminds you of the abuser or reinforces bad feelings about some aspect of yourself.

4. When you do not understand something, ask for clarification.

5. Respond. Talk about how you are going to use or think about the feedback.

6. Make sure your body language and facial expressions say that you are open to receiving feedback.

7. Watch your defenses and your anger. Listen to the message and do not kill the messenger. If you have negative reactions about what is being said, let the other person finish and keep what was said in the present. Example: "Hearing this is making me feel angry. I feel like ignoring both it and you, but I'll try to stay open."

8. If you have spoken and no one gives you feedback, ask for it.

9. Do not second-guess the speaker. Take feedback at face value.

10. Write down the feedback you have gotten. Look at it later when you have more distance. When a person feels defensive or afraid, the feedback might be blocked and forgotten.

Exercise: Giving Feedback Safely

1. Share with a friend or group member a time when someone gave you feedback and it was easy to listen to it. Then, reverse roles.

2. Share with your friend a time when someone gave you feedback and it was difficult to listen to it, or you became defensive. Then, reverse roles.

What makes it safe for you to get feedback? _____

_____

What makes it unsafe for you to get feedback? _____

_____

What makes it safe to give feedback? _____

_____

What makes it unsafe to give feedback? _____
_____

    As you practiced the listening and feedback exercises, what new information did you learn about yourself? What feelings did the exercises bring up? Did you wish that someone would have listened to you as thoughtfully when you were a child? Were you angry or sad that communication patterns in your household were defensive, misinterpreted, or negative? Jot down some of those memories and feelings here so that you can refer to them again as you move through the book.

Thoughts _____
_____

Memories _____
_____

Feelings _____
_____

    Always place great value on words. What you say is important; what you hear is a major link to the outside world. Words constantly influence our thoughts and feelings. Be especially careful to understand what your support people say to you. A good support network supplies both friendship and objectivity. Almost everyone who has ever had a home-base support group knows how unexplainably strengthening it is to participate.

Your Contract with Yourself

12 Success Steps to Participating in a Support Group

Success Step	"What I'll do to make this happen is…"
1. Show up.	_____
2. Be hopeful that this process will work.	_____
3. Be willing to take risks.	_____
4. Ask for what I need.	_____
5. Stay positive.	_____

Success Step	"What I'll do to make this happen is..."
6. Get to know other group members.	_____
7. Be helpful when others seem lost or confused.	_____
8. Make what I say count.	_____
9. Keep the group rules and contract.	_____
10. Trust the group conscience and learn from it.	_____
11. Support others by saying positive things when they are doing well.	_____
12. Understand that being open to others will help me learn more.	_____

Once you have learned more about building a support network and are actively working on creating the positive support you need to recover and grow, you will begin to feel the positive effects of positive support on your self-esteem—how you feel about yourself.

3
Boundaries

A boundary is a limit, a demarcation, an end or a beginning. Personal boundaries define the territory of your personal space. Personal space is usually thought of as the area surrounding your physical self; in some sense, a boundary protects you from anyone or anything outside that space. Personal space might include a bedroom, apartment or house, a car, and objects you might leave outside those spaces like a purse or wallet, mail, and personal papers; to a lesser extent, personal space includes an office and a desk at work. When someone invades our space or even comes too close, we may feel personally violated.

A boundary may also be defined as an understood line marking an individual's inner space, the border a person sets between personal life and the outside world to regulate interactions with that world. Boundaries tell us what is ours and what is outside ourselves, our families, our social circles. Boundaries tell us where we belong, and to some degree, who we are.

Where and when do we learn about our boundaries? Each culture has its own definition of personal limits or boundaries, and they are passed on from generation to generation. As examples of boundary differences, consider the following: people from Hispanic cultures tend to stand closer together when having a conversation than do people from Germanic ones. And the Japanese, because of limited space, greatly respect privacy: they can pretend not to hear conversations that take place on the other side of a paper screen wall. Early in life, our families and experiences teach us about boundaries. When we are very young, we learn to define who and what belongs in and who and what does not—what to keep to ourselves and what to share with others.

This is one of the first tasks of childhood. As infants develop and grow, they begin to define themselves as separate from their mothers and all others, they learn where their own bodies begin and end, and they understand that their bodies are distinct from everything around them.

Recognition of separateness is the beginning of boundary establishment, and by learning it, we learn to interact with others, especially by responding to and respecting others' boundaries.

47

People generally feel insecure if their personal space is invaded. Have you ever felt that someone was standing too close? The difficulty in discussing boundaries is that different people have different ideas of how much personal space they need, and although the phenomenon of boundary definition is usually a cultural determination, there are wide variances within cultures and even among individuals themselves from time to time, depending on the circumstances of their lives.

Problems of communication about boundaries and the need for personal space sometimes arise when people from different cultures do not understand others' needs for and definition of secure personal space. Some people inadvertently stand too close or too far apart during conversations. Others think nothing of making late night phone calls. This simple lack of understanding about boundaries and personal space can create major communication breakdowns.

Abused people may be highly sensitive to their own need for personal space, and if you have experienced abuse, you may need more personal space and privacy than do others of your peer group simply because your personal space was violated when you were a child. By its very nature, abuse infringes on personal space. If someone once entered your space without your permission, it is now understandable that you need to guard your space to prevent this kind of invasion from happening again.

People who have never experienced abuse or incest may also have had their boundaries violated. Think about the following actions as they possibly relate to invasion of personal space or to violation of personal boundaries:

- Having a car or home broken into;
- Being stared at by a stranger for a long period of time;
- Receiving an unsolicited touch in an elevator or other crowded place;
- Having the light turned on suddenly as you are on the verge of falling asleep; or
- Having to listen to a compulsive talker.

What examples of boundary violations do you witness in day-to-day life?

_____

_____

Circle those boundary violations you experienced when you were growing up. Do you violate others' boundaries? In what ways?

_____

Teaching children to maintain their boundaries is an essential for parents. They have the responsibility of teaching boundaries so children can develop a sense of safety. Parents can be very helpful to children by allowing them time and space to play, to move, to think, and to dream. Doing so allows children to learn first hand about their own and others' boundaries.

Children require privacy if they are to develop the freedom to choose. At first, their choices will be over small things, such as what they would like to wear or what they would like to eat for lunch. The time will come for more important choices, such as how they feel about their parents' values, what they think about people and events, and how they will shape their lives. Allowing children to develop their own boundaries means providing room for negative as well as positive experiences, along with the means to understand them.

Sexual and physical abuse either preclude the development of individual boundaries or manifest their severe violation. Neglected children, with little normal human interaction to guide them, are hampered as they practice boundary setting. They lack appropriate role models or mentors, and their life experiences provide little feedback. As a result, they do not know where they belong, what is theirs, and what is outside themselves. They have not been given the opportunity to learn how to separate their own feelings from those of others.

Because people with poor boundary development have difficulty knowing how to differentiate feelings, they sometimes identify the feelings of others as their own. If a bossy girl with poor boundary development is angry at a boy because he will not give up a toy, she may end up feeling guilty for being bossy, although he first felt angry at being bossed around. People with poor boundary awareness avoid or deny what they are feeling, or they experience the feeling without any sense of ownership or identification. People without a sense of their own boundaries sometimes inadvertently intrude on the boundaries of others.

In abusive, neglectful, and incestuous families, boundaries surround secrets, that, if revealed, would make the family look abnormal. Thus, although the boundaries were real because they existed, they were unhealthy because they kept locked up secrets that concealed sick behavior. Where unhealthy boundaries are the only models, children are not likely to learn how to set appropriate boundaries.

Types and Examples of Boundary Violations

Intergenerational

The most common category of boundary violation within families is intergenerational violation in which, as its name indicates, it crosses generations. In intergenerational violation, a member of one generation interferes with the growth, development, or business of a member of another generation.

For example:
- A parent who, when angry at someone else, beats or otherwise hurts a child;
- A parent who puts a child in the center of conflict between two parents, or uses the child as an excuse for refusing to be intimate with or for spending time alone with the partner;
- A parent who, unable to maintain an intimate relationship with a spouse, forces an incestuous relationship upon a child;
- An aging mother who demands that an adult child take care of her (in effect, acting as the child's child), to the detriment of the adult child's primary responsibility such as a spouse or children; or
- A father who insists that a son do exactly what the father did. (Some parents force a particular career choice on a child by threatening a financial and emotional break as the alternative.)

Intergenerational boundary violations are most likely to occur when adult relationships are in trouble, when adults are afraid of closeness and intimacy, or if they themselves have experienced abuse and have not yet learned more appropriate ways of behaving. Children generally trust adults and want to please and accommodate them. They are, therefore, easily pulled into situations of trying to meet parents' needs before meeting their own. If such a situation occurs, the parent or older adult is the one who has inappropriately crossed into another generation to meet his or her needs.

If you have experienced intergenerational boundary violation, you may need to work on freeing yourself of any guilt you feel from it, to grieve for the lack of normal boundary development, and to learn how to establish intimate peer relationships of your own. In short, you need to learn how to set your own boundaries.

Family Boundaries

Try the following: draw a picture of your family, including yourself, and your caretakers when you were young. Then draw a boundary circle around each person. Write each person's name at the top of the circle. Within the circle draw smaller circles and name what is in each small circle (e.g., bedroom, toys, certain clothes, house, car). In your notebook, answer these questions:
- Did the boundaries enclose you or were you left outside?
- At what times and as a result of what events did you feel that your abusers most violated your boundaries?
- List any intergenerational boundary violations that may have occurred when you were a child.
- Did anyone leave the family?
- Why do you think that person left?

- Did you make an effort to protect members of an older generation who violated boundaries?
- Why did you feel you had to do that? Were you protected as a result of your action?
- What made healthy and unhealthy boundaries in your family?
- Who set the most distant boundaries, and who encouraged closeness and intimacy?
- In what circumstances did the boundary relationships change?

Architectural Boundaries

Families, communities, and political entities such as countries set physical boundaries, or what David Kantor calls "architectural boundaries." Architectural boundaries can be set by latitude and longitude and are represented by lines drawn on a map; others are tangible, like the Great Wall of China and the wall that once separated East and West Berlin. Any time there is a boundary, there are rules about who may cross into or out of a particular territory, and breaking the rules may provoke serious consequences. More common are boundaries set by economic, national, racial, and religious heritage. Consequences for violating accepted boundaries in these areas can also be severe.

- Think about the community where you grew up. What were its rules for maintaining boundaries?
- Were there ethnic boundaries (also called neighborhoods) in which only certain types of people lived?
- Who was allowed to live in your community?
- Were there zoning laws about the type of building that could be erected on a piece of property and how large that piece of land must be?
- Did families have to have a certain income or work for a certain employer?
- How did your family fit within both the real (i.e., physical) and unspoken boundaries established by your community?
- Did you feel welcomed by your neighbors?
- Did your family's economic means fit in with your community or neighborhood?
- Was the educational and cultural level of your family similar to those of the people living near you, or were you outsiders?

Approaching Home

Think about the home in which you lived. Was the area immediately outside of your house friendly and welcoming, or did you feel some anxiety each time you stepped outside? Describe how people approached it: did they walk up a sidewalk, or was it part of a larger apartment building with no direct access to the outside? Did you and your neighbors leave doors unlocked, or were you careful to lock them each time you went out? Was lack of physical security an important part of your childhood? Write your answers in your notebook.

Inside the Home

Answer the following questions about the boundaries of your childhood home:

- Did someone come in to take care of the house? Was it well maintained? How?
- Who let visitors in?
- What happened to visitors as soon as they entered the house?
- Were any rooms off limits to visitors? Were any rooms for visitors only?
- Who was allowed to have contact with visitors?
- Were there any rules concerning outsiders? What topics were off limits?
- Did anyone in the family break any of those rules? What happened if the rules were broken?
- How were visitors let out of the house? How did they know it was time to leave?
- Was there ever a time when unwelcome persons were in the house? How did they get there? How did they leave?

Family boundary systems can go from distant/separate to enmeshed, and change over the course of family life depending on events that influence growth and development. Such events may include: illnesses, births, deaths, loss or gain of jobs, family members moving in or out, and many other factors.

Where did your family fit in then and where does it fit now?

	Interpersonal	Personal–Internal
Highly enmeshed	• family loyalty and to-getherness • lots of dependency • shared reality • emotional • physical	• little personal separateness • weak personal or intergenerational boundaries • group decisions • space not respected • most needs met inside family

	Interpersonal	Personal–Internal
Connected but some-what separated	• closeness • family interactions a priority • family involvement and closeness encouraged • some individuality encouraged • physical closeness encouraged	• need for separation recognized but not encouraged • personal boundaries unclear at times • lots of shared family space • decision often made by group
Separated but some connections	• emotional separateness with some connections • sporadic family loyalty • separate activity • occasional physical closeness	• clear intergenerational boundaries • personal distance preferred • private space encouraged • decisions made by individuals, occasionally by group

Adapted from *F.A.C.E.S. III* [*Family Adaptability and Cohesion Evaluation Scale*, 3rd ed.], developed by David H. Olson, Joyce Portner, and Yoav Lavee, University of Minnesota Department of Family Social Science.

Review the exercises you have just completed. Has your understanding of your own boundaries changed? What changes in your own boundaries would you like to make?

Your Perfect Place

Now that you are beginning recovery, it is important to establish your own boundaries and make your own rules about who is invited into your home or other personal space. Take time with this decision. Close your eyes and let your mind wander to a safe and comfortable place. Think about your choice of a perfect place to be and live.

Where are you? Think about the space you have devised for yourself, and when you open your eyes, answer the following questions.

How do you get to your perfect place? _____

_____

_____

How do people know you are there? Is there a doorbell or knocker? Who lets people in?

_____

Who decides when people are welcome to enter? Do you have rules about who is allowed in and who is not? What are those rules?

_____

What areas of your dwelling may visitors enter? Are there areas they are not allowed to enter? Is there any place or thing they are not allowed to see?

_____

Is there a space that is for you alone? What does it look like?

_____

How does your own special dwelling compare to the home where you grew up? What are the boundary differences?

_____

_____

What changes would you like to make in the home you live in now?

_____

Is there anyone who could help you make those changes? From whom would you accept help?

_____

Finding the Best Boundaries for You

Of all the people you know, who has the clearest boundaries?

_____

Who seems self-assured and does not take advantage of others?

_____

Talk to the people you know who seem self-assured. Ask them what they did to achieve harmony in their lives. How do they guard their boundaries and personal space?

_____

_____

Now think about establishing your own boundaries. To whom would you tell:

Secrets and confidences? _____

Your past history? _____

Information about your family? _____

Your problems? _____

Financial issues? _____

Future plans? _____

List the people with whom you share the different aspects of your life.

_____

_____

Do you talk too much? Do you confide in too many people or talk to the wrong people? _____

How can you keep from acting on an impulse to tell someone too much?

_____

Do you trust too many people? _____

The wrong people? _____

Are you so secretive (i.e., careful never to put yourself in a vulnerable position) that you have a hard time telling anyone anything, thus cutting yourself off from the possibility of close personal relationships? _____

What effect does secretiveness have on you? _____

_____

Personal Boundaries

Personal boundaries are harder to identify than are architectural boundaries, especially for people who were abused. For example, emotionally abused children learn negative things from abusive adults or adults around them who ignore the abuse. If an impressionable child is told that he is "just like" a drunken father, that child's self-view will thereafter include the image of a drunken father. If a young child hears, "You'll never amount to anything and will end up on the street just like those bag ladies," then that child's self-view will include the image of an abandoned woman unable to take care of herself.

Although all forms of abuse violate the spirit, people who have been spiritually abused (as when religious values are used to force a child into a mold designed by someone else) have had their boundaries violated by a person wielding a club called "a higher power." Ironically, persons who have been spiritually abused may end up in a 12-Step Group (such as Alcoholics Anonymous) that may teach them how to use a more legitimate, comforting, and healing concept of a higher power.

How do you know when your personal boundaries are being violated, and how can you tell if someone else has poorly defined boundaries? If you experience the following, you may be showing signs of being unclear about proper boundaries:

- Feeling like you always have to be talking;
- Revealing personal data to casual acquaintances;
- Inappropriately revealing personal data to anyone;
- Saying yes to everyone's requests;
- Expecting to be taken care of by friends, employer, or others ;
- Falling apart so others must take care of you;
- Pleasing others even when your principles are violated;
- Letting yourself be consumed by another person;
- Falling in love with anyone who is nice to you;
- Letting people touch you after you have said no;
- Touching another after you have been told no;
- Being sexual only because you fear losing someone's approval;
- Trying to be only what others want you to be;
- Letting others dictate your choices;
- Allowing another to control your life;
- Abusing your body: too much food, dangerous sex, drugs, or alcohol;
- Being recklessly impulsive;
- Giving away what you truly need for your own well being;
- Taking advantage of others by violating their boundaries;
- Taking from others without knowing when to stop;
- Spending your whole life working.

What Were Your Family's Boundaries?

Type of Boundary   **Examples from My Family**

community/political   _____

_____

intergenerational   _____

_____

Type of Boundary	Examples from My Family
architectural	_____
	_____
personal	_____
	_____
emotional	_____
	_____
spiritual/intellectual	_____
	_____

4
Identity and Self-esteem

Women and men who have been abused generally do not feel good about themselves. Why? Because no one is born with a sense of being an individual nor with a sense of self-esteem. Here, self-esteem and identity are virtually interchangeable as terms and they signify an attitude that each person needs. Self-esteem is a process of learning to like oneself through feedback and positive life experiences.

Most often, problems begin during childhood in relationships in which abused children do not receive the respect they need. Instead of growing, they begin to doubt their abilities. They hear few positive messages from the adults in their lives and many loud, negative messages. Often the messages suggest that they are not worthy of being alive. Look at the following four examples of hateful, "nonliving" messages.

Emotional Abuse

"Why can't you be like your brother?" Hidden meaning: "You would be better off as a different person." Message received: "I'd be better off dead or at least not here, since I'm not as good as he is."

Neglect

"I'm going away for a month—I need a rest." Hidden meaning: "You are causing me to go away. If you weren't who you are, I wouldn't go away." Message received: "Everyone would be better off if I weren't here or if I were dead."

Physical Abuse

"I'm going to punish you now. I'm going to spank you so hard you won't be able to sit down." Hidden meaning: "You are a bad person, unworthy of any consideration." Message received: "I am so bad, I deserve to be severely beaten. Maybe I would be better off dead."

Sexual Abuse

(Unspoken but signified through action) "I am touching you now wherever I want to touch you. You belong to me." Hidden meaning: "You have

59

no rights. You will do as I say." Message received: "I am just an object here, not a person; I might as well be dead."

What are some of the negative messages you grew up with? (To complete this exercise, imagine the voice of the abuser. Write down what was said and then translate it.)

Message	Hidden Meaning	From Whom?
_____	_____	_____
_____	_____	_____
_____	_____	_____
_____	_____	_____

The abuser was one of your family members. You may have received positive, "living" messages from that person along with negative ones. Abused people often have trouble making sense of mixed messages and integrating conflict into their lives. Nonetheless, both can be accomplished. Even after severe abuse, you can gain a sense of self and learn to like yourself despite the destructive messages you received.

Begin by writing down the positive living messages you received:

Message	Translation	From Whom?
_____	_____	_____
_____	_____	_____
_____	_____	_____
_____	_____	_____

Before leaving behind the negative messages and moving to a positive attitude, you first must develop a sense of yourself as an independent, separate person who can make choices, have opinions, and develop a life of your own. Prior to getting a sense of who you are and beginning to like yourself, you must fill emotional needs that are fundamental to healthy, full personality development. Until you meet these needs, it will be difficult for you to have the physical or emotional energy necessary to discovering who you are. Study the following basic human needs as developed by Abraham Maslow.

Maslow's "Hierarchy of Needs" includes (1) physiological: food, warmth, shelter, and sleep, as well as bodily needs and even sexual fulfillment; (2) safety and security: physical safety, security from emotional injury, and emotional security; (3) belonging and love: a sense of belonging, of connecting, of giving and receiving both love and affection; (4) self-esteem:

every person needs self-respect along with the love or esteem of others. Self-actualization cannot be achieved until all basic needs are filled. Self-actualization is the process by which a person brings the potential self into operation and works toward becoming all that person is capable of being. Self-actualization is becoming who you are for your own self. For each of the rungs on the hierarchy, answer the following questions.

Looking back at your childhood, list the needs that were met and the needs that were unmet. Which ones are still unmet?

Need	Was it met during childhood?	Is it met now?
Physiological	_____	_____
	_____	_____
Safety	_____	_____
	_____	_____
Belonging	_____	_____
	_____	_____
Esteem	_____	_____
	_____	_____
Self-actualization	_____	_____
	_____	_____

When people are fearful or in danger, they will focus on lower needs first. If your mode as a child was one of basic survival, you may not have been able to develop a sense of self. Development of a sense of self—i.e., of self-esteem leads naturally to developing the ability to like yourself, to hold yourself in regard. But putting first things first, to have a sense of self-esteem you must discover your identity. Eric Erikson defined identity as: "both a persistent sameness within oneself and a persistent need to share some kind of essential character (self) with others…it means that there is some kind of continuity, sameness and congruity of the self. Not having an identity means that you have not made all of your parts and pieces into a whole that is 'yours.'"

Barriers to Self-esteem

1. A negative thought process, especially a "poor me" designation, will keep you in a "victim" position. Self-pity will keep you from discovering the person you are.

2. If you act in an irresponsible manner (e.g., if you do not keep

appointments, if you do not care for yourself, if you do not pay your bills), you will never develop a positive sense of identity.

3. A sense of identity begins with taking care of yourself, i.e., by taking care of the lower three rungs of Maslow's Hierarchy of Needs. You need to provide for your bodily needs (food, warmth, and shelter), keep your house clean, take care of your body, and eat correctly. Your needs for physical safety can be met by living in a place where people do not abuse you. You can develop emotional security to prevent your life from being only a series of changes.

4. Self-identity begins to appear as personal interactions occur. Coming to know what is going on inside yourself and how you relate to the rest of the world can occur at the same time. Personal enlightenment may involve complex interaction with others. It is hard to have self-esteem and a positive sense of who you are if your behaviors consistently are met with negative feedback about how you have been in the past.

The exercises in this chapter will focus on (1) making "I" statements, i.e., finding out what you like and who you are, and (2) self-esteem exercises.

Being Present

Make two signs and place them where you will frequently see them. The first message might say, "What am I doing to keep my focus on today?" Another message: "What am I doing to acknowledge others today?" Focusing on today will help you turn your mindframe away from the abuse; acknowledging others will help you develop the third rung of the hierarchy—the need for belonging.

Working on abuse is not a career. When you find that too much of your mental or physical energy is consumed by past abuse, it is time to focus on positive, daily living tasks so that dealing with past abuse is but one part of your total routine. If you allow abuse to live on in the forefront of your memory, you run the danger of refocusing your thought processes on the abuse.

A major difference underlies attitudes of self-like and self-love on the one hand and narcissism, selfishness, and extreme notions of self-importance on the other. Imagine a see-saw with one side weighted by feelings of unworthiness, dislike of self, an uneasy feeling that you do not deserve to be living; the other side weighted by self-preoccupation, self-importance, and an inflated ego. Neither end of the see-saw reflects a healthy, adult sense of self. Although some may believe that self-centered narcissists have great senses of self, narcissists are far from it, as are persons who feel they have no right to live. Women and men with true self-esteem possess balance and a sense of humility. Both are connected to the center; both are integral to a sense of well-being and a sense of self.

Ice Cream Party

How often have you kept silent about what you wanted to eat, or stuck to familiar foods out of habit or fear? Do you do this often, all the time, or only in certain situations? Describe the situations.

_____

_____

_____

_____

Take two or three friends to a local ice cream parlor. Order three or four kinds of ice cream. Be sure to order at least one flavor you have never tried.

Flavor	Feel/Taste/Color	Memories (if any)
Vanilla	Cold, familiar, rich, satisfying	Going to get hand-packed with father
_____	_____	_____
_____	_____	_____
_____	_____	_____
_____	_____	_____

Which flavor do you like best? _____

Next best? _____

Least liked? _____

What did you learn from this exercise? _____

_____

_____

The Clothing Store

Accompanied by a friend who agrees not to comment on your likes and dislikes, visit a clothing store. Select some clothes to try on.

What style did you choose? _____

What colors did you choose? _____

What features of this particular garment attracted you? _____

Try different garments, and then answer these questions:

What shape do I like best? _____ Least? _____

What color do I like best? _____ Least? _____

What fabric do I like best? _____ Least? _____

What do I like that doesn't look good on me? _____

What looks good on me, but I don't feel comfortable wearing? _____

   If you are having difficulty deciding what you like, simply write "like most" on one side of a piece of paper; on the other side, write "like least." Then, write the answers near "most like" or closer to "least like." This exercise will help you get a sense of order and priority in your likes and dislikes.

Identifying Who You Are

Go to a friend's house and sit quietly in the living room. As you relax, begin to look around the room.

What do you like about the room? _____

In answering the following questions, you may not know what makes you feel welcome and comfortable. If so, you might say, "I feel a little more warmth from the flowers in the vase than from the leather chair."

What objects make you feel most at home? _____

What room colors do you like? _____

Write down three colors in the room. What do the colors make you feel and think? Example: "The red is too strong; I feel suffocated or small in the room."

_____

_____

_____

What in the room makes you feel uncomfortable? _____

_____

Does the room have a style? Can you describe it? _____

_____

Describe your decorating style. (Example: modern, old, bright colors, muted tones, lots of furniture, cluttered)_____

How is your style similar to or different from the style you grew up in?

_____

Has this exercise brought back any memories? What are they?

_____

_____

Making Choices: What You Like And Want

How did you choose your bank? _____

How did you choose your grocery store? _____

How did you choose your dry cleaner? _____

How did you choose your hair stylist? _____

How did you choose the place where you live? _____

What made you choose the car you drive? _____

How did you choose your career or place of work? _____

Do you see a pattern in the way you make choices? What is it?

_____

_____

Your Beliefs

If you were in a march, what placard or sign would you carry? _____

_____

Do you let others know what you believe? _____

What You Represent

Design a cover for a book or record album. Make it as accurate—and as positive—as you can. Show it to friends. Do they think it is accurate? _____

Do you like the cover? _____

Symbols and Images from Different Worlds
(This is a great exercise to do with friends.)

If you were an animal, what animal would you be? _____

Why? _____

If you were a flower, what flower would you be? _____

Why? _____

If you were a house, what kind of house would you be? _____

Why? _____

If you were a song, what kind of song would you be? _____

Why? _____ _____

If you were a star or constellation, what star or constellation would you be?

_____ Why? _____

If you were a food, what kind of food would you be? _____

Why? _____

If you were a country or state, what country or state would you be? _____

_____ Why? _____

If you were a car, what kind of car would you be? _____

Why? _____

On a separate sheet of paper, draw or paint a picture containing as many of the above-mentioned images as you can fit. You will be painting a picture symbolic of yourself. What does your picture look like? What would you like to change in it? What do you feel?

_____

_____

If there are any images you want to change, draw or paint another picture with the changes.

_____

_____

Eight Basic Characteristics for Developing Self-Esteem

To develop a sense of self-esteem or self-like, you need eight things.

1. *Acknowledgment of existence.* This means affirming and acknowledging who you are, what you are, and what you think. Affirmations do not need to have a larger-than-life quality. They can be simple affirmations of reality: for example, "I am 50 years old" or "I am a woman." Acknowledgment of existence means that you begin to own yourself. "Owning yourself" may go against everything the abuser taught or told you. Owning yourself means

recognizing yourself as separate from all others. It means acknowledging your uniqueness, your characteristics, the experiences that have influenced you, the thoughts, desires, and hopes that define who you are.

2. *Belonging.* People identify with a group to be connected with someone or something else. Finding out where they belong and whom they belong with contributes to self-esteem. For some people, belonging may result from the search for personal and family history; for others, it may start from affiliation with a religion or community, a group of friends, a place you identify as "home."

3. *Differentiation between you and others.* Finding out who you are implies finding out how you are the same as or different from others. Having experienced abuse, you may have trouble making this distinction because abused children are taught to see themselves as possessions of the abuser. Feedback from a friend can help you make the differentiation. Since boundaries are poor in families of abuse, asking help from a family member in this matter is not advisable. In your work of developing self-esteem, it is crucial to find the best help as you discover yourself.

4. *Caring curiosity.* Knowing that someone has a "caring curiosity" about you aids in building self-esteem. Realizing that someone is interested, wants to know how you are doing, what you are learning, and what interests or excites you is great motivation to work. The caring curiosity of another person will help you come to like yourself.

5. *Fun.* Laughing and enjoying yourself and others, along with being able to appreciate the lighter sides of life, build self-esteem.

6. *Having a sense of process and sequence.* Getting a sense of "what happened next," and, then, "what happened after that" helps makes sense of past experience. Abused children often feel as if things happened without any cause. It is hard for them to tell the story of growing up in their family because events never seemed to follow a logical sequence or make sense. Beginning to understand process is a component in developing self-esteem.

7. *Sense of context.* Children who have lived in abusive families do not always understand the relationship between "what happens" and "where it happens." They must learn that most events are attached to a proper time, place, and environment. Abused children have been treated in such a way that they seldom understand the context in which things happen. Abuse is always experienced as being unique. No child can develop a sense of context alone. They need another person, a positive "good parent," an adult to help them discover and understand context.

8. *Doing something of value.* There are endless ways in which to do something of value. Examples: helping others, performing work you value, pursuing hobbies, performing tasks that show a sense of mastery and competence, talking with people in a way that makes them feel better.

The following exercises will help you develop some basic self-esteem:

What's You / What's Them

List your patterns, likes, and dislikes in each of the categories below. If you are not sure what suits you, draw a line with something you dislike or do not want on one end, and something you think you might like or know would really please you on the other. The continuum will allow you to mark a range of possibilities.

(example)	You	Them (Family)	Possible Change or Do I Want to Keep It this Way?
Entertaining Guests	Need for perfection	Always had to be perfect	I like treating guests as special, but would like to be more relaxed.
Entertaining Guests	_____	_____	_____
	_____	_____	_____
Financial: Savings, Spending, Bill Paying	_____	_____	_____
	_____	_____	_____
Household Decor	_____	_____	_____
Work Style	_____	_____	_____
Health: Self-care	_____	_____	_____
Children in Family	_____	_____	_____
	_____	_____	_____
Treatment of "Other" Children	_____	_____	_____
Treatment of Service People: Restaurants and Stores	_____	_____	_____

	You	Them (Family)	Possible Change or Do I Want to Keep It this Way?
Personal Habits: Messy, Knuckle Cracking	_____	_____	_____
Politics	_____	_____	_____
Charity and Giving to Others	_____	_____	_____
Interests and Hobbies	_____	_____	_____
Having Fun	_____	_____	_____
Vacations	_____	_____	_____
Sexuality: Sexual Behavior	_____	_____	_____
Friendship Patterns	_____	_____	_____
Phobias, Fears and Anxieties	_____	_____	_____
Secrets	_____	_____	_____

Caring and Curiosity

The following exercise can help you develop curiosity and caring. Begin by asking someone about his or her life. Expand on questions. Be a reporter; ask without criticizing. Try this exercise with a few people. How do they respond? How do people feel when they are asked about themselves without judgment or criticism? After you have played the role of reporter, ask a friend to switch roles. Choose someone who can ask questions about you without being judgmental or critical. How does it feel to be questioned like that? Is it a comfortable way of telling your story?

Humor and Fun

Acquiring a sense of humor is very difficult, if you have never learned to laugh. Rent or go to a funny movie. Can you laugh there? Get some joke books from the library and write down a few that you think are terrific. Tell them to friends. Did they laugh?

List several times when you have done or said something funny. Poll your friends. Do they say you have a sense of humor? Ask them what you do that they find funny or amusing, and why they have fun with you. If depression has robbed you of fun, ask friends or people whom you trust how they enjoy themselves. Can you follow their example? An expression in Alcoholics Anonymous says, "Fake it till you make it." Sometimes the only way to have fun is to fake it until it actually starts to be fun.

Developing a Sense of Process

Think back to a time when things were going well. Write down what happened in one situation involving at least one other person. Be specific; be detailed. Ask yourself what happened at each step. Be sure to include both what you and the other person said and did. When you review your abusive experiences, this method will be helpful in understanding abuse. Although abuse may seem to have happened without a reason, you will discover that you had a sense of the process in which it happened.

Develop a Sense of Context

Ask yourself the following questions (*who, what, where, when,* and *how* will help you answer):

Where am I safe? _____

In what context am I safe? _____

Where am I unsafe? _____

Where do I feel most vulnerable? _____

In what contexts do I do well and function well? _____

At what places do I do work well? Is it the lighting, the people, the workload, the ambiance? _____

What drives me up the wall at work? In what context do I become most anxious or angry? _____

The Sense of Doing Something Valuable

List some things you have done that others feel are valuable:

What I do that others think is valuable:	What I think is valuable:
_____	_____
_____	_____
_____	_____

Confirmation of Who and What You Are

The beginning exercises in the chapter have addressed who and what you are. Review them at this point, understanding that they are builders of self-esteem. Then, answer the following questions.

1. *Belonging.* In his book, *Teachings of Don Juan: A Yaqui Way of Knowledge,* Carlos Castaneda speaks of finding his spot—meaning a place—where he could feel naturally happy and strong. His teacher had given him the task of "finding his spot" and distinguishing that place from all other places. He spent an evening on a porch standing or sitting in many different spaces, including his teacher's spot, but none worked. He continued to try other spots on the porch, finally finding a place that felt right. His inner turmoil stopped, and he went to sleep. He had found a spot. His spot. You, too, can find your spot. Begin by looking around your house.

Where do you go when you most want to feel comfortable? _____

Think about your place at work or in your car. In what position or what place do you feel you have a spot? Where do you belong? What is yours? _____

_____

Now, extend your thoughts to your social network. With whom do you feel you belong?_____

Where do you feel you most belong? In what social group or setting? _____

_____

Negative Mantras as Barriers to Self-esteem

A mantra is a word or group of words used in meditation. Overall relaxation and repetition of the mantra induce a kind of self-hypnosis. Although mantras help produce positive states of mind, it is also true that poor self-image can be reinforced by an unconscious or semi-conscious repetitive or self-disparaging idea. We might call these ideas or comments "negative mantras." Examples of negative mantras are:

I'm helpless. There's something wrong with me. I hate myself. I can't continue. I'm a failure. I'll never have a good relationship. I always cause myself problems. If only I were a better person. I'd be better off dead

Write down some of your negative mantras.

_____

_____

_____

Write positive mantras for yourself below. Positive mantras are sometimes called affirmations, because they affirm a positive characteristic.

Write down positive mantras.

_____ _____

_____

_____

Select several positive mantras and say them out loud five times each, getting louder each time you say them. After that, recite the mantras into a tape recorder. What does the playback sound like? Taping your mantras puts you in a position of being your own "good parent." Replaying the tape provides you the outside affirmation and feedback you missed as a child. You are now both a listener ("good parent") and the experiencer (the speaker). As both, you can match your outside with your inside—always affirming your experience.

Positive affirmations repeated regularly and often can be powerful tools. Besides changing a negative thought process, they can modify the way you look at and approach the world. Try repeating the mantras several times a day, literally a hundred times if you can. Make a tape of them, play it, have friends record you reciting them. After 30–45 days of regular and frequent playing and recitation, you will begin to notice a difference in attitude.

Trust Your Intuition

If you have been abused, it is probable that your instincts and intuition were never affirmed or respected. List times when your "gut" (i.e., feelings) or "intuition" told you something.

Event	Intuition	Did I or Could I Follow My Intuition?
_____	_____	_____
_____	_____	_____
_____	_____	_____
_____	_____	_____
_____	_____	_____

How can I follow my feelings more often? _____

What makes me not listen to myself? _____

All-of-Me Stew

In a way, you are images and pieces of other people. In part, who you are is a reflection of people you have encountered and experiences you have had in your life.

Think of the people you most respect. Write their names below.

_____   _____

_____   _____

_____   _____

Think of the people you least respect. Write their names here.

_____   _____

_____   _____

_____   _____

What experiences have been important in a most positive sense?

_____

_____

Least positive sense?

_____

_____

Who has had most influence on you? (in positive/negative ways?)

_____

Think of some experiences that have contributed to making you who you are. What are they?

_____

_____

Now, think about yourself as a kind of "stew," made up of parts and influences from all these people and experiences.

What is the recipe for you?

_____

_____

What do you have a dash of? _____

List the major ingredients.

_____

_____

What is the flavor? _____

Write your recipe here:

_____

_____

_____

_____

Natural Law and Self-esteem

Some basic natural laws:
  • You have worth as a person.
  • No one is perfect.
  • Every human being has potential.
  • You always have the capacity to change.
  • There is no one else on earth exactly like you.
  • You are capable of giving and receiving love.

Do you agree with these laws about self-esteem? _____

How does each of the laws apply to you? _____

_____

_____

Lemons to Lemonade

Learning to master new skills can only be accomplished if you are willing to make mistakes. List five mistakes you have made in the last two years. What have you learned from them?

  1. _____

  2. _____

  3. _____

  4. _____

  5. _____

Now, list five mistakes you made when you were a child. What did you learn from them?

1. _____

2. _____

3. _____

4. _____

5. _____

How can making mistakes help you feel better about yourself?

_____

_____

_____

If you recognize a time in the past when you liked yourself, what can you do to make the experiences of that time happen again, perhaps in a different context?

_____

_____

I liked myself when: _____

_____

I give myself credit for: _____

_____

Develop Self-esteem

Near the end of the day, review situations you handled well and recount your achievements of the day. Accomplishing even small things can increase your self-esteem. Compliment yourself. Give yourself credit for what you have done well.

What I Like about Me

Keep a running list in front of you (e.g., by your bed or at work) of things you like about yourself. Review the list and save a copy on a daily basis. Your file will help produce self-validation as well as allow you to become your own "good parent" since you will be both the reader (the good parent) and the experiencer (yourself).

5
Stress Reduction and Body Awareness

Self-image is partly the product of our thoughts, feelings, and day-to-day actions. It is also the result of how our bodies respond, move, and sense others and the world around us. All the theory, counseling, and discussion will not help you feel alive without the partnership of your body. Awareness of your body, your movements, and your sensations is central to your feelings of being, of being a part of the world, and of having the world environment respond to you.

There are many parts of your body about which you have little if any awareness. Though these body parts function without your awareness, they play a part in making up the whole person that is you. If you have been physically or sexually abused, it is quite likely that you have blocked awareness of parts of your body simply to survive. Attention to the parts of your body that were the focus of abuse might only cause more pain. You may have even handled the abuse by psychologically detaching whole parts of your body—perhaps by developing a feeling that arms or legs were not attached—or you may have had to deaden your senses to the extent that only extreme physical activity or self-mutilation would help you feel alive.

Or, to the contrary, you may have developed hypersensitivity in parts of your body as reactions to physical or sexual abuse. If you were emotionally abused, you may have been made to feel that a part of your body was ugly or bad or sinful. You may have stopped feeling sensations in your body because your active mind was busy responding to the emotional abuse—so busy you could not attend to the signals and sensations your body was giving.

If neglect was part of your abuse, your body may have responded by developing chronic unmet needs such as hunger, or by deadening your sensations so that you could cope without being cared for.

Many abused people have problems with chronic illness or pain. It is as if the body says, "I can't be cheated — what happened to me will make itself

77

known." If you see a cat or dog that has been abused, notice their body movements—often fear responses or inability to make eye contact. Your body may hold the answers to many questions about your life, questions that your mind may have repressed. It is often by paying attention to your body that memories will come back.

Children learn to restrict their movements as they grow up. "Be still" is a frequent admonishment heard from caretakers. Children tend to diminish their sensing ability if they are not affirmed or valued. Children and adults can learn to prevent their muscles from moving the body in ways that express fear, sadness, or laughter. Blocking emotions from exhibiting themselves is often done on the unconscious level. We miss a valuable part of life and knowledge by taking our body, one of our greatest information sources, and using it only as housing for our mind or perhaps just as a tool of sexuality. Getting in touch with your body makes it possible for you to discover more memories or feelings than you ever knew were there.

Recovering from abuse means reclaiming your body or taking ownership of that which is uniquely yours. If you have "worked things out in your mind" but treat your body as if it were not there, exercise it compulsively, or abuse it with food, alcohol, or drugs, you have not fully recovered.

Think of people you know; let yourself get in touch with their "essence" by closing your eyes and visualizing them and their bodies. You will find that you know more about them than you previously realized simply by attending and focusing on their bodies. By attending to your body, you will learn more about others persons, and you will intuitively and instinctively better understand people in your life.

Evolving Awareness: Your Body

Thoughts, feelings, and day-to-day actions combine with the ways your body responds, moves, and senses the surrounding world to create self-image. Awareness of your body—its movements and sensations—is central to developing an image of self. Your body may hold the answers to many repressed questions about your life, and as you start to pay attention to your body, memories may return.

Most likely, you have some awareness of areas of your body in which you feel cold, heat, pain, pleasure, fear, and anxiety. Symptoms such as aches and pains, which focus attention on specific physical processes, are keys to knowing your body. Dreams, memories, and vague or unrecognized feelings often can be set off by physical position or some other sensation. You can have an awareness of something "not right" within your body even before it can be detected medically. These are all mind/body connections.

The goal of this chapter is to help you begin to be aware of your body and its connection to your mind, and to underline the importance of understanding the mind/body relationship in recovering from abuse.

Body Awareness Exercises

The following exercises will focus on increasing awareness, helping you feel alive and attuned to yourself and others, and helping you find answers in your body. You may say, "I don't like my body; it's ugly", or "I'm too fat, not athletic." Do not decide what you think about your body until you get to know it better. As you are working with yourself, identify negative mantras you have about your body. Before you begin body exploration, repeat positive mantras or "affirmations" about your body. They will open you to accept what is happening within your body. Write your negative body mantras here.

_____

_____

Illness

Write down the times that your body has used illness to cope with your feelings or with reality. To do this, list the following: times in the last year that you have had minor illnesses (colds, backaches, headaches, for example.):

_____

Times in the last two years that your body has had major illnesses (surgery or something that needed a physician's care):

_____

Times as an adolescent or child when you had an illness.

_____

What were you feeling? _____

How did your body express its feelings during these illnesses?

_____

Did you enjoy any "secondary gains" from these illnesses? A secondary gain occurs when a painful or unpleasant event, such as illness, produces benefits such as gifts, visits from friends, and rest and relaxation.

_____

_____

Breathing

Stand or sit comfortably. Then, begin to turn your attention to your breathing, focusing on breathing in and out. As you breathe, stop inhaling and hold your breath. What do you feel? Begin to breathe again. How did it feel to restrain your breathing? If you found calm while holding your breath, it may be a sign that you are able to repress your emotions. However, if you felt some anxiety or unpleasantness, it may be a sign that withholding strong emotional feelings and impulses is more difficult for you.

Your Body

Place a large sheet of paper on the floor and lie down on it, hands at your sides. Have a friend draw your outline. When you are finished, cut out the outline and tack it to the back of a door. As you go through the body exercises and the chapter on relationships and sexuality, color in the parts of your body that feel alive to you and that you are comfortable letting others touch.

Getting in Touch with Breathing

Begin breathing, a light, shallow breathing. Next, begin to breathe more deeply so that you feel as if you are breathing primarily in the chest area. Continue breathing and allow yourself to breathe more deeply, moving your stomach and diaphragm.

How do the different levels of breathing feel? _____

Which level makes you feel more safe? _____

Which level makes you feel more vulnerable? _____

When you are frightened, how do you breathe? _____

When you are sad, where does your breathing come from? _____

When you are relaxed, how do you breathe? _____

When you are tense, where does your breathing come from? _____

Voice Tone

As you are getting in touch with your breathing, try to talk. Modulate your voice as you speak, allowing your breathing to help you regulate your voice. Try to make your voice deep and gruff. Then try to make your voice squeaky. Finally, make your voice soft, then warm, cold, happy, sad, surprised, and scared. Tape yourself as you change your voice. Do you ever listen to your voice to discover how you feel? Practice changing your voice once a week.

Try to become comfortable with the notion that you can modify your voice anyway you want.

Feelings and Your Body

Make a list of five feelings: for example, sad, happy, scared, anxious, and lonely. Begin to feel each feeling in your head, then your shoulders; move on to your neck, chest, arms, stomach, pelvis, hips, knees, legs, ankles, toes, fingers, and eyes. Repeat this exercise. Note the feelings, then try to block them, withholding them from your consciousness. From which parts of your body are feelings easiest to block? The least?

Feeling	What the feeling feels like	What happens when I withhold the feeling
_____	_____	_____
_____	_____	_____
_____	_____	_____

Experiencing Sensations

This exercise is designed to be done in all seasons. Go outside on a particularly windy day, sit and then stand for five minutes each. Feel the wind. What does it feel like? How do you feel? How does the wind feel on your body? Repeat this exercise for snow, falling leaves, sun, and rain.

Reprogramming Your Body and Mind

This exercise is designed to reprogram your mind and body so it can begin to feel good about itself in the way that small children can be taught to feel positive about their bodies.

Go to a playground or visit some very young children. Watch them test how their bodies move. Observe how they give meaning to and delight in finding how their body works.

Record your reactions._____

_____

_____

_____

Next, go to the library or a music store that sells children's music. Select two or three records, tapes, or CDs with songs about children's bodies, such as *Heads, Shoulders, Knees, and Toes*. If your library or record store does not have any, ask friends with young children to look through their collections. Raffi, Sesame Street, and Mr. Rogers are good sources for such songs. As you play these songs, close your eyes and allow your unconscious mind and body to soak in the lyrics. Pretending to be young again, relisten to the music. How does it make you feel?

You've Got Rhythm

All of us respond to natural rhythms, both inside and outside our bodies. Natural rhythm, inside us, includes menstrual cycles, day/evening sleep cycles, and hunger cycles. Outside rhythms may be the change of seasons or the tidal effects of the moon. To help you get in touch with some of your rhythms, try this two-part exercise.

Feel the Rhythm

Without music, begin to do something rhythmically—tap your hand to your chest, stamp your feet in a rhythm, clap your hands, move your head from side to side. Then move your body slowly and upwardly in a circular motion, rhythmically and evenly.

Then, take some music and repeat the same motions in time to it.

What did these exercises put you in touch with? _____

What did you feel? _____

"No One's Looking" Dance

After you feel comfortable with the exercise you have just done, put on some music, and start to dance. If you put on happy music, change the music to sad music and slowly begin to dance. Move your body in any way you choose. Try four different kinds of music, dancing to each one. Let your body follow the music without any thought, any memory, and feeling. After a few hours or a few days, do this again, and after each different mood of music, in your notebook write memories or feelings that come up.

Pantomime

Actors practice getting in touch with their feelings. Do the following in pantomime (pantomime is movement of body without words).
1. Push — make pushing movements with your body.
2. Pull — make pulling movements with your body.
3. Move your body in a way that expresses expectation.
4. Move your body in a way that expresses receiving, getting from someone.

5. Now move your body in a way that expresses giving.
6. Move your body in a way that expresses serenity, calmness.
7. Move the body in a way that expresses joy.
8. Move your body in a way that expresses constriction, pulling in.

What are your feelings? _____

_____

Who are you as you do these exercises? _____

_____

Reaching

Unresolved abuse indicates that your efforts for help were not heard, seen, or acknowledged. Your reaching out never received a response. This exercise involves sitting in a chair, standing up, and lying down. In all three positions, make your body reach out—use your hands, chest, neck, feet—in all three positions.

What does that feel like? _____

Did you prevent your body from reaching out? _____

In what ways? _____

Daily Living

Take any regular task—washing dishes, cleaning up, emptying the garbage, doing the laundry—and try slowing down as you do it, breathing and being in touch with your body and movement as you work. If it is difficult to do, increase the sense of difficulty; if it is easy to do, try and increase the sense of ease. Simply get in touch with your body's natural movement and rhythm. Repeat this exercise several times with different household tasks.

Other Ways to Get in Touch: Aches and Pains

The next time you have an ache, pain, or something troublesome in your body, exaggerate it, increase it, make it worse. Then, as you are doing this, say, "I am the headache, I am this pain, I am this ache." What begins to happen with the ache or pain?

How Do You Connect Your Mind and Body? The Senses

Sight—close your eyes for five minutes; try to get rid of any images that come before you. Then, open your eyes and look at the room as if you were seeing it for the first time. What do you see? What do the colors look like? What do the shapes look like? What do the textures look like? What do the spatial relationships look like? _____

_____

Do this in different environments. Try this exercise on the beach or while you are walking in the woods. See these environments as if for the first time.

Smell—close your eyes while outside and allow yourself to smell whatever is present. Concentrate on developing your sense of smell. You may choose to blindfold yourself, focusing only on your sense of smell. How does this make you feel? Have you been in touch with your sense of smell? When do you use your sense of smell? Could you ever smell the abuser before the abuse happened?

_____

Hearing—again, blindfold yourself and open your windows. Sit by them and listen to the sounds. What do you hear? Next, sit in a movie theater or some other public place (movie theaters are good because you can keep your eyes closed), listen to the conversation and sound. What do you hear? Continue to listen. You will become more aware of your sense of hearing.

_____

Touch—give yourself a Touch Party. Gather several objects of different textures from around the house: towels, spoons, books, flowers, tapes, plates, clothing, tablecloth, dog collar. Close your eyes and touch each object. Touch it as if for the first time. How do you know what it is? Is it pleasant or not? What memories come as you are touching?

_____

Taste—taste and smell are connected, so although you may be focusing on taste, you may also be involving your sense of smell. Go to the grocery store, gather four foods that you are familiar with and four foods that you may have tasted only occasionally or never at all. Note each taste. Pretend you are the food you are tasting. What do you like? Allow yourself to enjoy the sensation of taste.

_____

As you complete this chapter, you may want to repeat some of the exercises, particularly those you feel best put you in touch with your body and who you are. Any of these exercises can be adapted to be done with other people. The exercises that are most useful to do with others, however, will be discussed in chapter 10, *Relationships and Sexuality.*

You may also choose to practice these sense exercises in front of a mirror, getting a view of your acts and your image as you do them. Other variations for observing yourself are to use a video camera or to ask someone you trust to photograph you. Both could help you gain a sense of yourself as a moving, sensing person. Spend time now to record what you have learned in this chapter:

_____

_____

_____

_____

_____

_____

Make a plan to continue body exercises to keep increasing your sensitivity. Choose a form of exercise that involves body movement. Although exercises such as working in a gym or running can be very helpful in making you whole, other types of body movements, such as dancing, yoga, some of the martial arts—particularly the Tai Chi or classes that involve pantomime or body movement at a school that teaches theater—would be most helpful. Take classes outside your home because they involve other people. Understanding your own body is essential in recovery; connecting with others by watching, moving with, or touching is an important next step.

Stress Reduction

The grandfather of stress studies, Hans Selye, first identified stress as "the body's nonspecific response to any demand placed on it, whether or not that demand is pleasant." Essentially, the body reacts anytime there is a change or continuing need to defend and protect itself.

Stress can be either positive or negative. Too much stress can cause physical illness. Abused children have grown up in a land of stress. In chaotic families, stress reactions result from an emotional climate that changes on a daily basis. In the case of neglect, as well as in physical and sexual abuse, defending and protecting yourself produced continuing and chronic stress. Adaptation to stress is part of the body's biological fight or flight reaction. Reaction to stress has been examined by researchers in its three stages: (1) Alarm Reaction, (2) Resistance, and (3) Exhaustion.

If you think about what you endured during the active period of abuse, you can probably understand these three stages: (First Stage-Reaction) The body recognizes the stressor, be it physical or emotional, and the body prepares to respond. Essentially the body says, "Stay with it or leave" (fight or flight). (Second Stage-Resistance) The body adapts by trying to replenish energy. It tries to repair itself through rest, relaxation, and retuning hormones. (Third Stage-Exhaustion) Not all stresses reach the Third Stage. However, when too many stressors or a chronic stressor is present, the body cannot adapt quickly enough or keep up with a stress-related response, such as heart trouble, high blood pressure, gastrointestinal illnesses, emotional illness, and distress. Over a short term and in moderation, stress can be helpful by pushing a person to perform, work well, or react quickly and with ease to the world around.

In what ways did you go through these stages as you were experiencing the abuse?

_____

_____

_____

Today's News

In working through issues of abuse, remember that as you do, your body feels the stress as if it were today's news. In reliving and working through the abuse, your body feels the events as if they were happening. That is why this work must be taken slowly. Do not overstress yourself or those around you. When you are stressed, your response to others around you may be negative. The best way to cope with stress is to understand it, recognize it, and take charge of it.

Stress management is a learned skill that takes regular, active practice. You cannot bank it. The idea that, "I'll meditate today, hoping it will carry me through next week," does not work.

Since people are pattern-making and pattern-recognizing, it is important that when looking at your relationship to stress, you ascertain if your current stress response follows a direct pattern from your childhood. You may have become "addicted to stress" as a way of feeling present and alive, or you may be locked into a pattern of "anticipatory" stress. Anticipatory stress is the result of your brain reacting to certain environmental or sensory stimuli that remind your body of past pain.

Ending repetitive stress patterns will take a combination of three things: (1) your motivation to change; (2) your resolving the abuse memories; (3) reduction of painful stimulus (which re-establishes stress patterns), such as frequent contact with the abuser.

Stress-reducing Tips

1. Repeating negative or anxious thoughts keeps your brain in an alarm reaction state, ready to respond to the worry, fear, or urge to fight.

2. Indecision as well as unresolved feelings stay in your system, and they focus your nervous system on the problems. You are then constantly doing battle with them, eventually ending in an exhausted state.

3. Focused attention on tasks will relieve stress because your mind has less chance to wander and associate with other things or to anticipate anxiety-provoking situations. The prevalence of the "workaholic syndrome" is often an avoidance of anxiety.

4. To change stress patterns, be consistent with your interventions. Otherwise, you will continue in the old pattern—which dies hard!

5. Accepting, not judging, your perceptions and emotions will reduce your stress.

6. Increasing your awareness of stress-related behavior will help you control it.

7. Stress-related behavior is a reaction to underlying stressors.

For a complete discussion of stress-reduction techniques and the theory behind emotions and stress, read *Freedom from Stress: A Holistic Approach* by Phil Nuernberger, Ph.D., published by the Himalayan International Institute of Yoga. Stress-reduction techniques can be helpful in developing coping mechanisms as you work through abuse.

The best way to integrate stress reduction into your life is to do it slowly and one step at a time. Remember, change is an evolution, not a revolution. The more slowly and fully you integrate stress-reduction techniques, the more they will stick. Below is a series of stress-reduction techniques.

Awareness

The most important thing to note in the following stress checklist is recent change. Have you had any increased or decreased stress? Having one symptom does not mean you have elevated stress. However, if you find yourself clustering symptoms or having many of them, begin stress reduction as soon as possible. Some of these symptoms are also signs of increased depression or anxiety.

If the stress-reduction techniques do not seem to work or if your symptoms persist and interfere with home or work, you may want to get medical attention. You will increase your stressors as you work through your memories, so it is well to begin a stress-reduction plan as soon as you can.

	Have had previously	Bothered by now
• Any kind of habit or nervous tick such as shaking your leg, pulling on your hair, blinking, clearing your throat, or yawning.	❑	❑
• An internal feeling, as if a motor were running inside of you.	❑	❑
• Frequent headaches, backaches, or other pains.	❑	❑
• Increased tenseness in your muscles.	❑	❑
• Numbness in your feet, hands, or limbs and/or a hyperalertness in those areas.*	❑	❑
• Rapid heart beat or other unusual feelings in your heart or chest.	❑	❑
• A sudden weight gain or loss, or increase or decrease in appetite.	❑	❑
• Dramatic changes, either positive or negative, in your energy states.	❑	❑
• Changes in sleep, either increase or decrease, and in frequency of urination or defecation.	❑	❑
• Increased illness, such as frequency of colds or skin problems.	❑	❑
• Breathing problems: feeling unable to breathe, being out of breath, or being short of breath. If these persist, seek medical attention.	❑	❑
• Increased intake of caffeinated beverages or use of drugs or alcohol.	❑	❑
• Changes in voice, volume, tone, or pitch, or inability to speak, such as laryngitis.	❑	❑
• Increased negativity or sarcasm.	❑	❑
• Hostile jokes or language, gallows humor, or cynicism.	❑	❑
• Making mountains out of mole hills.	❑	❑
• Loss of temper or frequent blow-ups.	❑	❑
• Repeated lateness or forgetfulness.	❑	❑
• Rigid thinking, fear of changes, or increased need for perfectionism.	❑	❑
• Not caring or being concerned about things you once were concerned about.	❑	❑

* This may be caused by thyroid or other nervous system difficulties. If this condition persists, seek medical attention.

	Have had previously	Bothered by now
•Increased sense of competition or combative-ness.	❑	❑
•Increased misperceptions of reality.	❑	❑
•Increased irritability.	❑	❑
•Having small accidents or dropping things.	❑	❑
•Increased distraction.	❑	❑
•Deteriorating work performance or working harder and harder but accomplishing less.	❑	❑
•Chronic exhaustion.	❑	❑
•Too busy for normal routines of life.	❑	❑
•Feelings of disorientation or disconnection.	❑	❑

Any kind of tenseness (twitching or stomach upset, pounding of heart or increased rapid breathing) may be a signal that your body is experiencing increased stress. Work on tension reduction in those areas regularly. Remember, the best way to get rid of stress is to work on those areas of your life and your body that contain it. It won't go away on its own!

Working through Memories Slowly

Integration of memories and reduction of tension are the goals of memory work, not speed. Reducing stress will release more energy for your memory work and will decrease the stress on you and those around you.

Reduce Negativity/Develop Positive Attitudes

The body responds to its own thought processes. To cope with the extreme pain and negativity of abuse, you need positive thoughts about living and others. Stop yourself if you fall into a negative thought pattern.

To get in touch with your negative thought patterns, do two things: (1) Keep a pad with you for 24 hours; every time you have a thought about a person, place, or thing that is negative (include yourself in this), write it down. (2) Take a negativity inventory. See how long you can go without saying or thinking a single negative thought. If you feel up to it, ask some people you know and trust to give you a sense of how negative you are. Have them point out times when your thought processes seemed to be negative.

Next, talk to three people who you know have positive attitudes. Ask them if you can spend five minutes with them to ask what helps them get through stress and how they developed a positive attitude. Write the answers in your notebook.

Which of those things make sense for you? _____

_____

Which of those things do you think you can begin to do? _____

_____

Try a positive program for 30 days. Several audiocassette tapes on the market address the issue of relaxation and positive living. Buy one and play it, but, remember, you must practice consistently (30 days or more) for your attitude to undergo any kind of change.

Breathing and Breathing Techniques

Breathing and breathing techniques may provide immediate relaxation. To get in touch with your breathing, sit quietly or lie on the floor; watch your body inhale and exhale. Try breathing from your mouth, then your chest, deeper and deeper. As you breathe, notice any tension that is in your body. If you notice a tension spot, try to breathe the air into it so that the fresh breath and oxygen will cause the tension to go away.

Another breathing technique is to sit or stand and let yourself relax. Begin to inhale slowly through your nose and let your stomach and your chest expand as much as possible. Then, place your hands over your stomach. Feel how you are breathing. Hold your breath before exhaling. While your hands are on your stomach, exhale slowly, using your mouth and letting your lips control the flow of the exhale. Watch your stomach deflate and your diaphragm expand. When you feel that your lungs are empty, begin the cycle again. Slowly repeat this several times.

Stand with your back in a straightened position. Breathe in, and as you breathe out, let out a sound of deep relief. It should sound like "aah." Do not think about the next breath; your body will take care of that naturally. Continue inhaling and exhaling. Do it as many times as you feel it takes to get your body in a state of relaxation.

Stop the Movies in Your Head

One of the surest ways to maintain your stress is to continue thinking about your stressor. If one of your stresses relates to your boss or the abuser running through the scene, it is like having a movie in your mind. Your body will automatically re-experience or anticipate the stress. There are several steps you can take.

1. Deal with situations immediately. Do not hold on. Letting go does not necessarily mean, however, that it is permissible to release all anger, resentment, and annoyance whenever they arise. What letting go does

mean is that you deal with the situation as soon as possible in a way that enhances communication. If that is not possible, another way to get something out of your mind and allow yourself a certain period of time— one hour, two hours, a day—to think about the situation is to write down all your thoughts and feelings, all the things you want to say to the person, then put the list in an envelope, seal it, and just as you would with a time capsule, decide when you are going to open it to deal with it. If you were angry at your boss before he went on vacation and you cannot discuss an important matter with him, write it down, put it in a envelope, seal it, and open it the day he comes back.

2. Make a list of times you have held on to situations, neither discussing them nor dealing with them: _____

_____

3. List what might have happened had you taken care of the situations listed in (2) as soon as they happened: _____

_____

_____

4. What situations are your continuing in your mind, but not attending to?

_____

5. Make a plan for dealing with those situations.

_____

_____

Stress Tip: Minimize Change in the Unexpected

Whether change be positive or negative, it is a stressor. Too much change can cause illness or other stress symptoms. Think of a time during your life when you experienced many changes: a move, school change, relationships, illness, death, or childbirth. Describe the changes you went through in that year.

_____

_____

Reflect on that year. What stress symptoms did you have? Were you able to work? How did relationships go with others? Were you able to have fun and enjoy yourself? _____

_____

Think of the forthcoming 12 months. What changes have you planned? What changes can you minimize or decrease, particularly in light of old memories and feelings.

Planned Changes   Ways of Minimizing Change

_____   _____

_____   _____

_____   _____

_____   _____

Involve Yourself in a Regular Program of Exercise

Sedentary people initially may find exercise a painful experience. Find an experienced exercise physiologist or someone knowledgeable about the body and exercise. Devise a plan with that person. Do not plan more than you believe you can do. (Ten minutes of walking three times a week is better than an ambitious program of a half-hour run, plus racquetball, neither of which you will do.)

Stretching exercises can be helpful at any time of the day. A few examples: put your arms all the way up, stretching them over your head until they touch. Now stretch them to one side of your body, then to the other side. Stretch them in front of you and arch your back slightly, then stretch them in back. Now, stretch them toward your knees and/or toes without bouncing.

Next, while sitting, stretch forward until your head is near your lap. As you relax, let your hands move toward the floor. Hold and then slowly sit-up, repeating until you feel fully relaxed.

Move your neck from side-to-side, then from forward to back, letting your muscles stretch and relieve tension.

Another stretching exercise. Clasp your hands together, then move them slowly from side-to-side, over your head, back and in front of you, and then again from side-to-side. This exercise can be done several times a day during a break at work, at lunch, before you go to work, at your desk, or in your office.

Nutrition

Eating a balanced meal selected from the four basic food groups of dairy products, grains, fresh fruits, and vegetables is important. Limit use of salt, sugar, caffeine and alcohol. Write down a typical day's food for you—on a workday, a weekend, and a vacation day.

	Workday	Weekend	Vacation Day
Breakfast:	_____	_____	_____
	_____	_____	_____
Lunch:	_____	_____	_____
	_____	_____	_____
Dinner:	_____	_____	_____
	_____	_____	_____
Snacks:	_____	_____	_____
	_____	_____	_____

What is the first and easiest thing you can do to change your eating habits? Consult a dietician at a local hospital or clinic and work out a long-term dietary plan. There are many holistically-trained dieticians today. You may find several holistic resources in your area through food co-ops or the Yellow Pages of the telephone directory.

Boredom and frustration are some causes of overeating; anxiety and depression can cause undereating. Be sure that your eating habits do not reflect your moods. Eating slowly helps lessen stress on your digestive system. Nature designed it to help break down foods, but the liver does not have teeth and neither does the stomach. Chew slowly and completely before swallowing.

Humor

Finding humor and things you can laugh at or things that are humorous and enjoyable is an important part of stress reduction. If laughter is difficult for you, buy some joke books. Practice a few stories on your friends. Go to a humorous movie once a week or rent a tape from a video store. Make humor a daily part of your life.

In the space below, write the times in your life that you have laughed the most or you have enjoyed the most._____

_____

_____

What can you do to make those kinds of events continue to occur in your life?_____

_____

_____

Relaxation and Meditation Techniques

Relaxation and meditation techniques can be adapted to your needs. If you are uncomfortable performing relaxation exercises or meditation by yourself, you can purchase tapes in many bookstores. Relaxation is a progressive method of easing your body, and meditation is a way of improving your awareness and consciousness with the rest of the world and universe. Both can help you focus on positive, important matters and reduce stress.

Visualizations

Visualizations can help you handle stress by giving you an image of a safe, relaxing place, such as an ocean beach. Visualizations of a project or goal you have in mind are also helpful. Visualization can help you keep in a positive frame of mind. Develop your own visualizations if you can. You may see yourself smiling, walking along a wooded path, writing a book, or having a conversation with someone you always wanted to meet. You can also find a book in the library or a bookstore that can teach you how to practice visualization, such as *Creative Visualization*, by Shakti Gawain.

Establishing Routines

Reducing surprises and unexpected events is yet another way to minimize stress. The more routines you have, the more your body can adapt to stress. Establishing routines for getting up in the morning, going to sleep, and what you do when you arrive at work will help reduce stress. In the lines below, write on the left side, Routines I Follow Already, and on the right side, Routines I'd Like to Establish. Remember to permit yourself flexibility to change when necessary.

Routines I Follow Already   Routines I'd Like to Establish

_____   _____

_____   _____

_____   _____

_____   _____

On Vacations

A vacation does not necessarily mean a trip to an exotic place. A vacation is simply time-off, doing whatever helps you relax and unwind. For people who travel on their job, the best vacation can be to sit right at home. For others, taking a vacation means a day trip or taking a course for self-growth. What were your last three vacations like and when were they?

Write them here. What would your ideal vacation be like? Is it within your goal? Describe some mini-vacations that would help you relax and unwind.

_____

_____

_____

Lots of Sleep

Get proper sleep and rest without the help of alcohol or drugs such as tranquilizers that may initially help you sleep, but whose long-term effects can be addictive and devastating. Much better to learn to sleep by using relaxation techniques, music, or a glass of milk. Establishing a regular time for sleep without watching late night news or reading the newspaper can help you reduce your sources of stress. If you have sleep problems, try not to nap. Make the bedroom temperature comfortable, do not drink coffee, and keep noise to a minimum. If sleep problems persist, speak to a physician about being evaluated at a sleep clinic. Taking care of an on-going sleep problem can dramatically reduce stress.

Wellness

Focus on times when you were well. Most of us have enough symptoms on a daily basis to call ourselves either sick or well. Write down here the times you felt most healthy. Can you focus on those times and continue your feeling of wellness?

_____

_____

What do you need to continue that state of wellness? _____

_____

List environmental changes you need to make—in your office or your home— that will reduce stress. Pay special attention to lighting, noise, clutter, and orderliness. Write down changes you need to make, then rank order the ones you think you need to do now and what you will do later.

_____

_____

The best way to reduce stress is to treat others with respect. Treating others with respect will encourage them to treat you the same way. Think of times you have been most concerned, respectful, and caring of another person. Now, think of two people whom you like, and to whom you want to show more respect and caring.

_____

What is your plan for decreasing your stress?

_____

_____

_____

_____

_____

6
Feelings

In every abused person's process of recovery, reconstructing the ability to recognize feelings plays a critical role. Feelings help recovering people make sensible decisions. They work like a safety net that encourages people to take reasonable risks. At one time in their lives, abused people may have needed to shut off feelings, dissociate from them, or respond with a feeling they were not experiencing. In later years, it is not surprising that abused people find it hard to identify certain feelings or even to recognize their experience of them.

Some women and men go through entire lifetimes feeling very little or, if they do, feeling in a small range (an octave compared to a keyboard, a few bands of color instead of a rainbow). Usually they believed it was not safe for anyone to know what they were feeling, and, as a result, they became adults with a jumble of feelings difficult to identify.

Some people in recovery say that if they feel any more, they will all but die. Indeed, many people, as they heal from abuse and neglect, need to let feelings in slowly to prevent being overwhelmed by intense, unfamiliar emotions. Because many people have learned to control their feelings as a reaction to abuse, a rush of powerful and unfamiliar feelings may feel like loss of control.

This section will help readers identify, understand, and then use feelings at the level of intensity they want and need. Feelings are important not only because they color and enhance people's lives, but also because they give important, helpful information as rational decisions are made and appropriate actions are taken. Moreover, feelings can be the source of spirituality and creative energy. Feelings give recovering people the strength, courage, and joy to experience and share who they are.

There Are Many Kinds of Feelings

Feelings can be about:
1. situations, actions, and things
2. other persons
3. ourselves

97

Feeling Words

Affectionate	Deferential	Hopeless	Seductive
Aggressive	Defiant	Horrified	Self assured
Airy	Dependent	Humble	Sexy
Alarmed	Depressed	Immobilized	Silly
Angry	Determined	Impatient	Soft
Anxious	Dishonest	Inadequate	Spineless
Appealing	Distant	Independent	Strong
Arid	Dominant	Insecure	Submissive
Ashamed	Dull	Irritated	Sunshiny
Beaten	Ecstatic	Itchy	Surprised
Belligerent	Edgy	Jealous	Sweaty
Bewildered	Embarrassed	Joyful	Stretched
Bored	Empathetic	Light	Sympathetic
Breathless	Enraged	Locked in	Talkative
Burdened	Envious	Lonely	Taut
Bushed	Estranged	Loving	Tender
Calm	Evasive	Mixed up	Tense
Carefree	Excited	Nauseated	Terrified
Cautious	Fearful	Open	Thankful
Choked up	Firm	Panicky	Threatened
Close	Frisky	Paralyzed	Thrilled
Cold	Frustrated	Peaceful	Timid
Comforted	Giddy	Played out	Tolerant
Compassionate	Grateful	Pleased	Torn
Confident	Grief stricken	Powerless	Two-faced
Confused	Grumpy	Proud	Uptight
Contemptuous	Guilty	Quiet	Vacant
Contented	Gutless	Relaxed	Warm
Cooperative	Happy	Resentful	Weepy
Courageous	Hard	Respectful	
Dead eyed	Hopeful	Sad	

Feelings can be expressed in many ways:
- Words
- Body Movements
- Expressions
- Actions

Think how each of the following feelings might be expressed.

	Happiness	Anger	Sadness
Words:	_____	_____	_____
	_____	_____	_____

	Happiness	Anger	Sadness
Body Movements:	_____	_____	_____
	_____	_____	_____
Facial Expressions:	_____	_____	_____
	_____	_____	_____
Actions:	_____	_____	_____
	_____	_____	_____

Which feelings do you experience most often? _____

_____

Which feelings would you like to experience more frequently? _____

_____

Less frequently? _____

_____

Which feelings do you almost never experience? _____

_____

Which feeling are you most afraid of finding in yourself? _____

_____

Which feelings have you tried to avoid? (For example, by work or substance use to control anxiety)

_____

Which feelings do you have the most difficult time listening to in someone else?_____

Stuck or Frozen Feelings and Psychic Numbing

Abused and neglected children have difficulty letting feelings in and opening themselves to others' experiences. Because of the negative effects of having been violated, abused children must focus a large part of their emotional energy and skills development on struggling to survive. Their emotional resources are focused inward, not toward developing appropriate relationships with others. Abused children may have a rich fantasy life in which they are loved and rewarded as relief from the reality of a barren or hostile environment. Abused children often learn that depending on others usually brings disappointment. Their mistaken sense of independence comes from the repeated betrayal they have suffered, and many become emotionless or cynical long before they mature. Learning about social relationships, feelings, and interactions is a major task of socialization. However, with a focus on survival, learning to identify or communicate feelings is difficult.

The stuck feelings, frozen feelings, or "psychic numbing" are the all too frequent result of abuse and neglect. They are protective responses, and they can occur any time people become overwhelmed. In their emotional response to a traumatic situation, abused persons shut off feelings or they become numb. It is not that their bodies and minds are breaking down on them, rather, they are helping them cope with what they cannot tolerate. Unfortunately, as people are overwhelmed in any disaster—from an earthquake to a war—they deaden, dull, and blunt their feelings. They become spiritless. Overwhelming, powerful emotions, especially powerful feelings like fear and rage, eventually take a psychic toll.

Learning to re-experience "frozen feelings" takes time. But once old frozen feelings have been liberated, a new and fuller range can be explored. Interestingly, these new feelings are sometimes able to be identified first in someone else. Observing these feelings in others may be uncomfortable—they may accurately indicate what someone is afraid of experiencing or letting out.

Feelings can sometimes be recognized by specific body sensations. A tightening in the chest, a rapid heartbeat, or difficulty breathing may be a clear indication of anxiety. Some feelings may always register with the same intensity. Anger, for instance, may only be intense—or it may come with no bodily feeling at all. The following exercise will help you explore some common feelings, as well as a few that are unfamiliar.

Range of Intensity of Common Emotions

	Glad/ Happy	Mad/ Angry	Sad/ Inadequate/ Abandoned	Shame/ Embar- rassment	Fear/ Anxiety	Unsure/ Confused
High Intensity	Loved Excited Exuberant Terrific Jubilant Energized Enthusias- tic	Abused Enraged Seething Vengeful Hateful Repulsed Jealous Bitter Rabid	Dismal Defeated Lonely Hopeless Dejected Empty Miserable Worthless Depressed Crushed	Humiliated Demeaned Depreci- ated Mortified Ridiculed Disgraced Debased	Paniced Fearful Frank Shocked Over- whelmed Vulnerable Terrified	Ambiva- lent Trapped Immobi- lized Stagnant

	Glad/ Happy	Mad/ Angry	Sad/ Inadequate/ Abandoned	Shame/ Embar- rassment	Fear/ Anxiety	Unsure/ Confused
Medium Intensity	Tranquil Content Joyful Optimistic Confident Proud Accepted	Stifled Offended Agitated Irritated Frustrated Disgusted Resentful Smoth- ered	Drained Wounded Sorrowful Regretful Distraught Isolated Hurt	Scorned Disdained Numbed Embar- rassed Conde- scension Cheapened Re- proached Redressed	Distressed Scared Afraid Startled Tense Insecure Anxious	Troubled Tentative Disorgan- ized Awkward Flustered Nervous Foggy
Low Intensity	Pleased Calm Good Hopeful	Peeved Resigned Annoyed Perturbed	Upset Bad Sorry Lost	Scolded Put down Reduced Deflated	Shy Concerned Worried Reluctant Bothered	Unsure Undecided Muddled Puzzled

Range of Feelings Exercise

Go back to the list above and circle the emotions that you feel most often, then the ones that other people might use to describe you. Next, put them in the circle below.

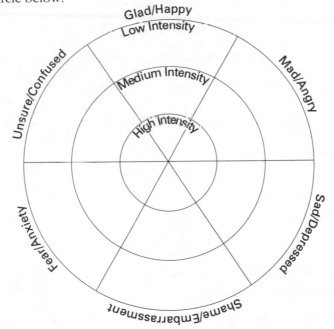

In what range of emotions do you usually spend your feeling time?

_____

On what level of intensity do you feel most of the time?_____

Compare your present response to that of your childhood. What percent of your time do/did you feel the following?

	Then	Now
Glad/Happy	_____	_____
Sad	_____	_____
Shame/Embarrassed	_____	_____
Mad/Angry	_____	_____
Unsure/Confused	_____	_____
Fear/Anxiety	_____	_____

Any change in the amount of time these feelings occur? Why do you think that has happened?

_____

Get feedback from friends: What percentage of time do your friends see you?

	Friend (name)	Friend (name)	Friend (name)
Glad/Happy	_____	_____	_____
Sad	_____	_____	_____
Shame/Embarrassed	_____	_____	_____
Mad/Angry	_____	_____	_____
Unsure/Confused	_____	_____	_____
Fear/Anxiety	_____	_____	_____

Are there differences in how you see yourself and how others see you? Why? Ask friends for feedback.

_____

Feelings simply exist. By themselves, feelings are neither good nor bad, and they do not make us good or bad people because we do or do not feel them. Although people may have been told they were good or bad for feelings they had, feelings are neither good nor bad. Everyone is allowed to have any feeling without having a *should* or *should not* attached to it.

In your notebook, list all the *shoulds* and *should nots* you were given regarding feelings when you were a child or an adolescent. *Example:* You *should* love your sister. Boys *shouldn't* cry.

Which of these shoulds and should nots have you carried into adulthood? Write them in your notebook and note how they may limit you. *Example:* Boys *shouldn't* cry. How this limits me: I don't express sadness

Remembering Films

Sometimes it is easier to learn about feelings by watching someone else express them. The following exercise will help you identify feelings. Watch two films, one comic and one dramatic, on separate days. Carry a notebook and record the following:

Sad/Dramatic Movie

1. Event/main characters in film _____

2. Body movements/facial expressions of character _____

3. My feelings/how my body felt _____

4. My memories of these feelings _____

Funny/Happy Movie

1. Event/main characters in film _____

2. Body movements/facial expressions of character _____

3. My feelings/how my body felt _____

4. My memories of these feelings _____

Do you have memories of movies you saw as a child? What were they?

_____

_____

_____

_____

What movies did you see?

Movies: _____   Age: _____

        _____   _____

        _____   _____

        _____   _____

Identifying Feelings

This is an exercise to help you identify feelings common to adolescence—feelings you may have blocked or discounted at that time. Because this exercise may bring up old feelings such as anger, sadness, or loss, it is important that you not do it alone. Ask a friend to be with you.

Visit a playground, watch both children and their parents, then identify their expressions. Are they happy? Sad? Scared? Excited?

Does your friend see what you see?

Types of Feelings/My Feelings

Describe the Child's Play	I See	My Friend Sees
Child 1		
Child 2		
Child 3		
Child 4		

Identifying feelings includes both showing and feeling them. Sit in front of a mirror and practice facial expressions for the following feelings: (If you have difficulty writing any of this down while it is happening, use a tape recorder and write it in your notebook later.)

Mirror Practice

Feeling	What my face and body did	What my body felt	When did I last feel this?
Pleased	My Head tilted. I smiled. My eyebrow went up.		

Feeling	What my face and body did	What my body felt	When did I last feel this?
Proud			
Hopeful			
Confident			
Excited			
Caring			
Energized			
Loving			
Loved			
Annoyed			
Frustrated			
Hateful			
Seething			
Upset			
Sorrowful			
Depressed			
Put down			
Humbled			
Mortified			
Shy			
Tense			
Scared			
Undecided			
Foggy			
Trapped			
Unsure			

Now, practice these feelings with your friend. See if your friend can guess the feeling you are showing. If you have trouble expressing these feelings, try to remember when you last felt the feeling or when you might have seen someone else express it. Ask your friend for help. Once you have practiced the feelings, have your friend take a photograph of you expressing each one. Post the pictures on your private poster board, and as you increase your range of expressions, add pictures to your board. Over the course of your work, you may notice changes in the expressions you use.

What have you learned about your feelings so far?

_____

_____

Anger

Anger tends to be felt and expressed in extremes by survivors of abuse, incest, and neglect. If anger is suppressed, it tends not to be expressed at all. Rarely do survivors learn to modulate their anger.

Acknowledging angry feelings and learning to express them is an important part of the recovery process. However, recent research has shown that repeated expression of anger can make a person even angrier. This section will help you identify the sources of your anger and place responsibility where it belongs—not on yourself or others who do not deserve it.

As you work through this section, you may be concerned about your level of anger. You may be frightened by the intensity of the anger, fearing that it will be destructive of self or of others.

It is important to make sure that you let your anger out, but at the same time, control it to the extent that you do not hurt yourself or others. Anger held in without resolution can wear you out and cause fatigue, exhaustion, and even physical illness. You may also fear that if you let go of your anger, you will become like the abuser. This feeling may be devastating since feeling like the abuser might mean feeling out of control. Remember that your feelings of anger toward the abuser are justified and need to be acknowledged. Take care, however, in expressing anger to others, so that it does not become destructive.

Anger can manifest itself in widely differing ways:
- explosive feelings when we know we are angry at someone;
- somatic responses in our bodies, such as ulcers;
- passive-aggressive behaviors;
- hidden anger—usually hidden even from ourselves.

If you do not feel angry, how do you know you are? There are several ways to discover anger, and most of what we discover will be hidden anger.

Anger can be hidden from both ourselves and others, but sometimes—much to our chagrin—it is hidden from ourselves but not from others.

First look at some common signs of hidden anger:
- nondirect communications; sideways confrontations
- enjoying humor that seems sadistic; telling jokes at the expense of others
- chronic lateness or forgetting appointments
- laughing or smiling when someone else is hurt or in trouble
- voicing sarcasm or cynicism, acting flippant
- monotone voice, overcontrolled speech
- forcing perfection: being upset when things are out of place
- procrastination
- dreams with angry themes; dreams with violence
- any sign of depression; depression is often anger turned against yourself
- clenched jaws or grinding of teeth
- falling asleep or yawning at inappropriate times
- being overly kind, polite, or always seeming cheerful
- quick bursts or temper at other drivers, service personnel, pets
- enduring irritability or impatience
- phobic avoidance of anger: never argue, never contradict, never explain
- being self-destructive and accident prone
- habitual stiffness, soreness and/or stomach ulcers or stomach problems.

Which hidden signs of anger have you exhibited? At what time in your life did you have them? In your notebook, list the hidden signs of anger that you have exhibited, when they occurred, and what you were angry about.

Think about other people who were present when you were growing up or are in your life now. How did they show hidden anger? Did you realize they were angry? In your notebook, list the various people in your life. For each one, list a hidden sign of anger, when it occurred, and how the behavior felt to you.

Were your patterns similar to those of people around you? Is your anger similar to theirs? Is it different?

_____

How is your anger similar to others' anger? _____

_____

How is your anger different from others' anger? _____

_____

Has your anger pattern changed over the years? Do you feel angry more or less of the time? Are there particular times when you feel angry more or less?

_____

Another type of anger is called passive-aggressive anger. Passive-aggressive anger can be very effective in that it gets the job done: it can make others uncomfortable without showing you to be angry. It is indirect and dishonest anger. Most people who use passive-aggressive anger are unaware of what they are doing or even that they are angry.

Examples of passive-aggressive anger are:
- A woman has a back injury. Her husband is angry because he has to care for her. She always asks him to close the door to the room so she will not get a chill, and he always "forgets."
- A mother and daughter argue in the morning. The mother remains angry and later, she "forgets" to pick up her daughter at school.
- Jane and Jill have a competitive but close relationship. Jane asked Jill what she wanted for her birthday, and Jane replied that she wanted a certain book. Jane got her a pair of earrings.
- Jack grudgingly agreed to help Sam with a special work project, but Jack always got sick on the day he was supposed to help. Sam finally found someone else.

At times, we all act passive-aggressively, usually by forgetting something or waiting until the last minute to cancel something we promised we would do. In the next exercise, look at times when you know you were not direct with your anger.

Direct Anger

Event	What I said I would do	What I did	Whom I was angry at
Example: At Work	Make train reservation for co-worker	Waited until the last minute	My co-worker for having the nerve to ask/ Myself for agreeing
_____	_____	_____	_____
_____	_____	_____	_____
_____	_____	_____	_____
_____	_____	_____	_____
_____	_____	_____	_____

You now know some ways to identify hidden anger. Try to keep a record of your anger and your responses to others' anger in a daily journal. You will notice, as you continue your journal, that your expression of anger will change. Noticing these changes will help you understand how you interact with people.

Choose one close friend and two not-so-close friends. Ask them the following questions:

- Do you see me as angry much of the time?
- When I get angry, how do you know it?
- Do I seem never to get angry?
- Tell them the signs of hidden anger, then ask if you show signs of hidden anger.

Is their view of you similar to yours? Does their description of you remind you of anyone in your family? _____

_____

If you have been abused, have experienced incest, or have a neglect history, anger can erupt when it is least expected. In some families, abused or neglected people may not have been allowed to express anger, although their parents or caretakers were allowed to show it. In other families, perhaps no one acknowledged being angry. If a parent showed anger by yelling, hitting, or penalizing a child, it was defined as punishment because the child had been bad. In these families, children were not allowed to have independent feelings like anger because adults found a child's anger threatening. If a child was angry, it might be an indication of unjust parental treatment.

Like other feelings, anger does not magically disappear. It remains and takes on other forms as months and years pass by. Children first feel frustration and anger when their needs are not met. They cry when they need something from an adult caretaker, and if the caretaker is responsive, their needs are met. If not, they quickly move from frustration to anger, eventually to despair. In later years, the trigger for anger can be feeling dependent on someone in either intimate or work relationships. Anger in such a situation can be most puzzling. A person might ask: "Why do I feel so angry with _____, since I have no reason to be, and I care for _____ so much?" A replay of early childhood experience may be occurring. Unresolved anger continues to circle in life until it is identified and resolved.

In job relationships, a worker can become angry with the boss for no reason, but on a closer look at the relationship, an employee may recognize a feeling of dependence on the boss for a sense of worth, promotion, or something else that is valued highly. In a sense, the employer has become a surrogate parent and is being asked for an inappropriate response.

On whom have you felt dependent in the past? _____

What happened when you felt dependent on them? _____

_____

Did you get angry at any of these people without good reason? _____

Do you now connect your angry feelings with dependent feelings? _____

Did you ever say how angry and frightened dependent feelings made you?

_____

   Some people do not find it comfortable to be angry about what they call "little things." Because everything is a little thing for them, they find it hard to show anger until they have stored up many little things. Transactional analysis therapists call this thinking "stamp collecting." Stamp collecting can be used with other emotions as well. People can collect jealousy stamps, sad stamps, or affection stamps.

   The process is a bit like receiving coupons for purchasing items in some grocery stores. For example, every time you have reason "to be a little angry," you collect "a right to feel angry stamp." When you have collected whatever number of "angry" stamps you require "to have the right" to show your anger, you cash them in and get really angry at one person. Cashing in "angry stamps" is unfair to the recipient of the anger. So often, that anger is greatly out of proportion to whatever caused the anger at the moment. The recipient of your anger seldom understands what is going on. As a result, there is no opportunity to discuss feelings, to clarify any misunderstanding, or to change any behavior.

   The best way to handle anger is to speak out when you first become angry. That way, anger will not build, and there is a chance to work out any real problem. For some people, unfortunately, stamp collecting and cashing are the only ways they can handle anger or other emotions that make them feel uncomfortable.

   As you work through this book, you may feel like cashing in all the stamps you now recognize as having come from your childhood. A word of caution: getting in touch with anger is crucial to overcoming the effects of abuse, incest, and neglect. However, do not spend too much time feeling angry. Let your anger out slowly. Over time, that will insure you do not embarrass yourself and alienate others as you work through angry feelings.

List two times you have held onto your anger, not telling anyone about it.

_____

_____

Write down an example of when you saved up your anger and used it later.

_____

_____

List recent examples of stamp collecting. _____

_____

How could you have let your anger out in the past? _____

_____

Did you ever feel anger stored in some part of your body? Do you feel it anywhere now?

_____

Now comes a difficult idea. Some people show anger by identifying with their aggressor. The rage these people feel is so intense that they are afraid to let it out. Because they are afraid of what they would do if they started showing anger, these persons take their anger, need for control, and rage inside themselves, and they remain very uncomfortable with their violent feelings. Only by imitating their aggressor can these abused persons discharge troubling emotions or work out feelings. Demonstrating anger in this way indicates that the abused person is taking blame for the abuse and does not recognize the difference between being an abused person and an abuser.

A well-known example of an abused person imitating an abuser is the case of Patty Hearst. After being held captive for some time, she first identified with her kidnappers, then began to act like the people who were abusing her. She so completely identified with her aggressors (her captors) that she finally joined them in a bank robbery and carried a gun.

Think about your anger. Is it like the anger of people who abused you?

_____

Vicarious anger is anger experienced while watching someone else express anger or violence. Why would an angry person settle for watching someone else be angry? Being angry often makes a person feel uncomfortable; watching someone else be angry makes it easier to handle. A person who becomes absorbed while watching violent sports or war movies may well be an angry person. For that person, the killing, burning, and pounding may be the next best thing to being there. The person in the neighborhood or the office who seems to be an expert at getting two people to fight and argue with each other is another anger suspect.

Think of some examples of vicarious anger:

Situation: Who:

_____   _____

_____   _____

_____   _____

_____   _____

Direct anger is anger that is felt, acknowledged, directly dealt with, and resolved. Direct anger is usually associated with recent events—perhaps it is recent anger being saved up—but it is not anger left from childhood. Direct anger has a quality different from old anger: most notably, it is both quicker to come and quicker to end.

Have you been able to be angry with someone and feel good about the way you handled the situation?

_____

What made you angry? How did you handle it? How did you feel about the way you handled it?

_____

Once anger has been acknowledged, it is important to work through it. Working through old anger feels different from working through recent anger. Old anger frequently lives inside your body, almost as if it has taken up residence. Old anger may manifest itself in headaches, stomach ailments, and muscle or joint problems. Basic body awareness can help you locate some body areas that may be sending you messages about your anger.

You can take several steps to get rid of old anger.
- Locate where it is in your body—begin to do appropriate body work to move it from inside to outside.
- Try to identify the sources of your anger. It may take some work and time. The usual sources will be people, places, and things from your childhood.

Example:

People: Aunt Jill—for trying to control everything about my childhood
Uncle Paul—for touching my breasts

Places: I am angry that I grew up in an isolated town, where I did not have anyone to talk to.

Things: I am angry that things in my parents home—vases, carpets, dishes—were more important than my feelings.

How to Resolve Old Anger

- *Let yourself feel that anger.* You have a right to it.
- *Work out your anger* by finding safe ways to rid yourself of it. Get a punching bag, some old dishes, or telephone books. Go into a room, and let it go. You can scream, cry, or yell, if that will help.
- *Make lists.* List each person with whom you are angry, and write down all the reasons for your anger. When you are finished, get an empty chair and imagine the person sitting there. Tell the person why you are angry. You might want to have a close friend available after you do this exercise because it can be a highly emotional experience, and you may need comfort or support.
- *Exercise regularly.* As you exercise, think of your old anger. Let the tennis ball you hit be the person with whom you are angry.
- *Review an old conversation or event,* preferably one from your childhood, when you knew you felt angry but were not allowed to express it. Re-imagine that situation now as an adult. You now have the power of a grown person. What would you now say to show your anger?

You may not feel ready for any of the above suggestions. If they seem too frightening or out of character for you, you can begin by just looking through the lists of words for anger on pages 100–101. Start with the easy ones and say them to yourself, then repeat them before a mirror, speaking more loudly and with feeling as you say them. As you grow more comfortable with them, speak them into a tape-recorder or in front of a friend. Do the words sound angry? Practice them until they sound angry.

Next, take crayons or paints and draw some of the feelings on the list. What color and shape are the words *annoyed, bitter, enraged?* (For those doing this exercise with someone else: compare your drawings. Does the other person think you have expressed anger?)

Continue to use the list:

1. What words applied to your parents as you were growing up?

_____

2. What words applied to other adults?

_____

3. Did all those adults show these emotions?

_____

4. In your notebook, draw a picture of them showing those feelings.

What have you learned about expressing your anger? _____

_____

What have you learned about the anger of those around you? _____

_____

What steps do you now want to take to help you let go of your anger? ____

_____

Guilt

There are several theories on the origin of guilt. In summary, they are:

Examples:

• *Repressed rage and anger;* holding anger in so long that it turns against you.

• "If I express my angry feelings, it will hurt them, so...I will have these feelings and then I will feel *guilty* because I have them."

• *Response to an internalized code of moral values;* regret when you have violated a personal value.

• "Why didn't I do it sooner?"
• "I feel bad spending so much money when there are so many homeless people."
• "I should not allow myself to be depressed."
• "I should have called her when she got sick."

• *Acting or feeling in ways disapproved by those you depend on.*

• "My mother would be angry for my dating this man."
• "I shouldn't be having a good time without my parents here."

Guilt may also be based on a strong tendency to feel responsible for the lives (including thoughts, feelings, and actions) of others. Guilt is an emotion that says "I must rescue" rather than "I must allow a person to be responsible to self."

To have *some* guilt means having a set of morals and values. It means having a personal code by which to measure actions and having the capacity and honesty to recognize occasional moral failures. People who do not feel any guilt lack a moral system. Those who lack a moral system hurt others and refuse to take responsibility for their own actions. Invariably superficial, their connections to the other people of the world are minimal.

Guilt, however, can *overwhelm* and *paralyze* a person, and except for being a reminder of our values and guide for moral action, it can destroy our ability to function. When guilt is responsive to a moral code other than our own (e.g., the code of a church or parents), it becomes a voice that need not be heeded. It is unnecessary to feel guilt about the codes or values of other people or social institutions. Responding to others' value systems is to unwittingly accept responsibility for other people's lives.

How was guilt used in your family? _____

_____

Was guilt used to make you behave in a certain way? _____

_____

Do you feel guilt about the abuse? In what ways? _____

_____

How do your current guilt feelings keep you stuck in behavior patterns?

_____

How has guilt kept you from growing and developing? _____

_____

Do you use guilt to control or influence others? _____

_____

Is this similar to the way guilt was used by the abuser? _____

_____

Now, if you feel safe enough, ask people you trust to explain how their guilt is not yours.

Guilt	Explanation
_____	_____
_____	_____
_____	_____

Were you surprised by their answers? _____

The next exercise will help clarify why a person feels guilty.

Feeling Guilty

How do you feel when you feel guilty? List five things you have felt guilty about in the last six months.

| I feel guilty about | I felt guilty because: | | | I felt this guilt before when |
	Repressed anger	Violation of personal values	Actions contrary to others	
1.				
2.				
3.				
4.				
5.				

Getting rid of guilt is important to recovery. You can get rid of your guilt by:
- Believing you are okay and have a right to live your own life
- Changing your actions that you do not like
- Apologizing when you cause someone pain
- Having people in your life that do not promote or encourage guilt
- Allowing others to grow and develop by not running their lives according to your guilt.

For each of the guilt feelings you listed, make a plan to get rid of the guilt. Show the plan to your friends. What do they suggest?

Guilt	Plan	Friends' input

Now think about the four people you interact with most often (work, friends, family). How do they use guilt?

How they use guilt	Where I have seen this pattern before

How do you feel about how they handle guilt? _____

_____

What can you do to change the patterns when you do not like the way they use guilt?_____

_____

Healthy guilt is guilt which you feel because you have violated your own code or values. Healthy guilt motivates you to take action. Healthy guilt goes away when you take a positive step toward achieving congruency between making your values match your actions.

List the guilt feelings you have had and done something positive to resolve.

Guilt	Resolution	How I Felt
_____	_____	_____
_____	_____	_____
_____	_____	_____
_____	_____	_____
_____	_____	_____

How can you continue to reduce guilt in your life? _____

_____

_____

How long must you feel guilty? _____

When will you have had enough of feeling guilty? _____

Are you filled with guilt? Are you looking for someone who takes advantage of guilty people? _____

How have your current guilt feelings affected your relationships?

	How I think guilt has affected these relationships	How they think guilt has affected these relationships
friends:	_____	_____
co-workers:	_____	_____
family:	_____	_____
intimate partner:	_____	_____

How would your life be different without guilt? _____

Shame

Shame is different from guilt. Guilt is the feeling that "I have done something wrong." Shame, however, says "There is something bad about me, about the person I am."

Shame is the emotion we feel when we have been degraded, when our dignity has been reduced or removed, or when we fail to act within perceived behavioral standards. Shame most often begins to occur in early childhood when children are humiliated in front of their parents, other children, or adults. In short, shame is a direct attack on one's personhood.

Fossum and Mason, in their authoritative book *Facing Shame*, define shame as an "inner sense of being completely diminished or insufficient as a person." This condition occurs when the self is judging the self. One moment of shame may be a humiliation so painful or an indignity so profound that a person feels stripped of dignity or exposed as bad, inadequate, worthy of rejection, or not valid as a full human being.

In the book *knots*, R.D. Laing wrote of the fundamental bind of feeling bad and living in shame:

"My mother does not love me.
 I feel bad.
I feel bad because she does not love me
 I am bad because I feel bad.
I feel bad because I am bad
I am bad because she does not love me
 She does not love me because I am bad."

A person whose whole being is based in shame feels like a person who does not belong to the human race. Shame can be found in individuals, families, and even in whole cultures and races. Abuse is a leading cause of the development of shame. Concentration camp survivors felt shame, slaves have felt shame. When anyone's dignity is taken away, the result is likely to be shame.

In *Shame*, Gershen Kaufman writes that shame occurs whenever our expectations of significant others are exposed as wrong, when someone we value unexpectedly betrays our trust. We say, "What a fool I was to trust." Kaufman describes shame as feeling that there is no way of reliving the matter, that one has failed as a human being.

One of the worst aspects of shame is its self-perpetuation. The cycle of abuse continues when abusers, overwhelmed with their own shame, pass it on in desperate attempts to rid themselves of it. Secrets hide shame and shame hides secrets. Families develop elaborate secrets to hide their shame; an individual's shame will prevent the secrets from being told.

If you have lived in a family whose dynamics are based in shame, you will have no sense of what is normal (non-shame-based). Environments that promote self-esteem and growth are entirely different from a family whose dynamics are shame-based. Shame does not promote growth. It encourages secrecy and is based on fear of exposure, debasement, and ridicule.

Two other emotions go hand in hand with shame: shyness and embarrassment.

Shyness is essentially the fear of exposure. Shyness is the self-scrutinizing of every detail of our being; it is not something that just happens. We learn self-scrutiny and self-consciousness from those around us. Children who grow up relatively free of shame rarely experience these feelings.

Embarrassment and the overwhelming fear of it is an extreme feeling of being ill-at-ease, vulnerable, or exposed. All of us feel embarrassed at times, but constant fears of embarrassment point to old and early feelings of shame.

Two Different Systems of Values

In a respectful system, the self is a separate part of a larger system. Rules of the system require accountability, and relationships require ongoing dialogue.

In a shame-bound system, boundaries are vague, and violation of the person leads to shame. Because the rules of the system require perfection, relationships—based on uneven power dynamics in which someone always wins and someone always loses—are always in jeopardy.

Fossum and Mason* discuss characteristics of the rules they found in shame-based families:

1. *Control.* There is control of all behavior and interaction. A particular family member often holds control in tyrannical fashion.

2. *Perfection.* There is need to be perfect and right, to be "more perfect than others, more right than others," and to be able to show perfection to the outside world. In this system, only perfection means that the family (and parent) are good.

3. *Blame.* Blame is fastened on someone else if things have not gone as planned. Shame-based families constantly transfer blame to others.

4. *Denial.* There is a denial of feelings, a pretending that events did not happen, and no acknowledgment of negative feelings.

5. *Unreliability.* There are changes in relationships, sudden appearances, disappearances, and mood swings.

6. *Incompleteness.* Decisions are not made, plans are not followed up, questions go unanswered, clarity of interaction is difficult if not impossible.

---

*Fossum, Merle A., and Mason, Marilyn J. (1986). *Facing shame: Families in recovery*, 86–104. New York: W. W. Norton.

7. *No Talk*. Situations are not talked about, family secrets are not discussed, reality is not acknowledged in words.

8. *Disqualification*. Abusive behavior is disqualified and explained away as something other than what it was. For example:

"Jack deserved the punishment..."

"Jane is a hard-to-handle kid..."

"Dick is just a bit oversexed. There are different ways of affection."

Shame in My Family

Shame characteristics in my family	Not much	Somewhat	Extreme
Example: Control	Always some control; allowed to make some choices.	Accepted most friends; wouldn't let me see two of them in high school. They were O.K.	Pressure to marry their choice—threatened to disown me if I didn't.
Control	_____	_____	_____
Unreality	_____	_____	_____
Incompleteness	_____	_____	_____
No Talk	_____	_____	_____
Disqualification	_____	_____	_____
Perfection	_____	_____	_____
Blame	_____	_____	_____
Denial	_____	_____	_____

Do you use these shame characteristics in your current relationships? With whom?

Person	Characteristic
_____	_____
_____	_____
_____	_____
_____	_____

How are these similar to or different from those used in your family?

_____

How have the shame characteristics affected your adult life?_____

_____

Ask people you trust for feedback. Do they see you as feeling shame? How?

_____

Do they see you as shaming others? _____

Do they have any suggestions how you might make changes? _____

_____

What strategies for change do you want to try? _____

_____

_____

Make a plan to get rid of shame. Write it here. _____

_____

_____

Guilt and shame invariably have their roots in childhood. Years later, adults often respond to both guilt and shame by attacking themselves. Attacks take the forms of depression and anxiety, physical illness, or self-harm and self-punishment. Guilt and shame are also indirectly expressed by persons who project their feelings onto someone else. Thus the cycle of abuse continues.

Feelings of Wanting to Hurt Yourself

Research on self-injurious behavior shows that people who have been abused suffer an extremely high level of self-punishment. Green (1978) found that 40.6 percent of his sample of physically abused children engaged in self-injurious behavior.

DeYoung showed that, among 45 women who had experienced father-daughter incest, 57.7 percent had engaged in self-bruising, attempts to break bones, or self-poisoning. Kosky, in a study of childhood suicidal behavior, found that two-thirds of children who had attempted suicide had been the target of physical abuse from a parent. Two-thirds of his sample of children who attempted suicide had witnessed arguments involving violence between their parents.

Substance abuse is one of today's most common acts of self-destruction. Besides substance abuse, self-destructive behavior can include the following:

- Picking up people (for sexual contact) who might hurt you
- Driving too fast
- Having frequent accidents:
  —breaking things
  —car accidents
  —cutting self while shaving
  —burning self while cooking or ironing
  —leaving iron on and starting a fire
- Walking or driving in dangerous areas
- Leaving the house unlocked
- Not watching while crossing the street
- Physically abusive behavior
  —sticking self with pins
  —giving self painful enemas
  —hitting/burning self
- Engaging in physical exercise or lifting that may cause injuries
- Letting self go—poor self-care, neglected appearance, dirty clothes

Some internal reasons for these shame-based behaviors may be:

- If I make myself ugly, no one else will hurt me.
- If I punish myself, I'm in control.
- Hurting myself lets me feel real.
- People who love me hurt me. To love myself I must hurt myself.
- I will not be noticed if I dress like a nobody.
- I'm bad. I deserve punishment.
- Accidents allow me to hurt myself without responsibility.
- Nothing is mine. I don't deserve anything.

Self-destructive Behavior

List all past destructive behavior.

Destructive behavior	Age(s)	Where?	Why?
Example: I picked-up street people and invited them in.	18	On street/ in my home	I felt nothing was mine; I couldn't have anything. Guilt.

Current self-destructive behaviors	Where do they take place?	Similarities to old self-destructive behaviors	Why I behave this way
_____	_____	_____	_____
_____	_____	_____	_____
_____	_____	_____	_____
_____	_____	_____	_____

Self-destructive urges and behaviors are often preceded by numbness, emptiness, a feeling of unreality, or a dream-like state. It is not uncommon for self-destructive persons to hurt themselves in front of a mirror. Write a contract with yourself to stop self-destructive behavior. Reward yourself if you keep to your agreement. Your contract will work best if you tell it to someone who cares about you.

My Contract for Stopping Self-destructive Behavior

_____

_____

_____

Sadness and Depression

Sadness is the feeling that responds to pain, hurt, abandonment, regret, sorrow, and loss. Sadness may be momentary — a child may feel sad after losing a piece of candy or saying goodbye to a favorite friend. Sadness may also continue, becoming in its extreme form depression and despair.

Sadness is a "vulnerable" emotion—when you feel sad, you usually feel vulnerable. Thus, you may have difficulty allowing yourself to feel sadness. Sadness is not an angry, outward emotion. Rather, it is a feeling that tends to bring you inward, that points you to look within. Most sadness is connected to a sense of loss or powerlessness. You might feel sad that you could not help someone in the way you wanted, that your abuse prevented you from having the self-confidence to do things other kids accomplished easily.

Sad feelings can have a wide range of causes—major or minor, some serious, some trivial. Sadness might be your response to another's misfortune or it might result from not having enough money to take a vacation or purchase a new car.

Whatever their source, feelings of sadness can make you question your world view, sense of self, and personal values. Sadness also has a significant, positive characteristic: it can help bring about an emotional release as you work through the abuse.

Soon after beginning the process of memory recovery, you are apt to find that your sad feelings increase. If you do not feel sadness at that time, it may be that you were not allowed to express sad feelings when you were young. Or, you might be concerned that once you begin to feel the sadness, you will not be able to stop a flood of feelings.

You might find that you are able to feel sad while watching a movie, play, or television news program, but you cannot feel sadness as you look at your own life. Or you might find that while minor events make you feel sad, you are left cold at moments of greater import.

Releasing sad feelings can begin a healing, letting-go process regarding abuse. Thus, if you can feel sadness, cry and release the emotion. Do not be concerned that the emotion does not initially seem connected to past abuse. Simply allow yourself the feeling of sadness. Connecting sadness to abuse memories will come about in time. It is most important to allow yourself to feel emotion at this time.

Sadness

Talk to some children between the ages of 4–12. Ask them what makes them feel sad and what they feel when they are sad. Write down what you learn.

_____

_____

Do you remember having any of these feelings as a child? _____

What does your body feel like when you are sad? _____

If you are afraid of being overwhelmed by sad feelings, you probably have adjusted your life to avoid sadness. Some typical ways to avoid sad feelings are:
1. Filling your life with people and activities so you do not have time to experience sadness
2. Purchasing, shopping
3. Inadvertently developing an addiction to cover the sad feelings

How have you avoided sad feelings? _____

_____

What do your fear most about being sad? _____

_____

List the times you have felt most sad in your life. What happened to make you feel sad?

Event	Age	Who else was there?	What I felt
_____	____	_____	_____
_____	____	_____	_____
_____	____	_____	_____

List some times when you think you were sad, but you were not able to express any feelings of sadness.

Event	Age	What I did instead of feeling sad
_____	____	_____
_____	____	_____
_____	____	_____
_____	____	_____

Telling other people about sad events may help you release the sadness. As you tell your story, you can watch others' reactions and emotions. Their feelings of sadness for you will encourage you to feel the sadness for yourself. Their compassion can help you focus your attention on your sad feelings. If you use the story-telling to help you get in touch with your feelings, be sure and tell the other person about your fears of vulnerability. Make sure you have the support you need to feel safe as you open up.

Depression is the continuation of sadness, loss—and sometimes anger—to the point where you first lose perspective on the issue, then, the ability to address the issue and let go of the feeling. Depression saps a person's energy. It affects your sense of self-worth, power, and ability to feel that you can have some control over your environment. Depression can become so dominant that you may not even recognize its presence or know what has triggered it.

"Learned Helplessness," discussed in relation to Post-Traumatic Stress Disorder, may accompany trauma. The ability to mobilize your body and mind to get yourself out of the depression cycle simply may be lacking. Depression can even sap the energy and will to live. Suicidal feelings and thoughts are not uncommon to abused people, as they sometimes provide the only sense of personal power an abused person can feel—the power to end the pain.

Once you begin to recognize your feelings, depression might be the first feeling you can name. John Bowlby's work has contributed greatly to understanding how loss experienced by youngsters in childhood can create extreme depression in children. Poverty and the perceived or real inability to make changes in one's environment can lead to depression.

If you think about the times you were depressed, you will find that depression has almost always deepened the sense of powerlessness to effect change.

Times of Depression

Write down the times in your life when you have felt most depressed.

Times I experienced depression	What was going on?	What I felt I could not change
_____	_____	_____
_____	_____	_____
_____	_____	_____

Review the times you noted. If the depression lifted, what helped it become less burdensome?

_____

Did the depression go away? _____ If so, when? _____

Did any specific thing happen to help the depression go away? _____

_____

Did your functioning and ability to cope change before depression set in?

_____

Did they change during the depression? _____

Did they change after the depression? _____

If you are still prone to depression, ask your friends for feedback. How do they know when you are depressed? _____

_____

Do they try to help you feel better? _____ If so, how? _____

_____

What suggestions do they have to help you get out of your depression?

_____

_____

Major depression—the kind that will not go away or that saps your energy, makes you feel suicidal, and stops activity—needs professional intervention immediately.

Allowing depression to bring activity to a halt, enclose one at home, or prevent one from working will only increase the depression. Keeping active, even if you are just going through the motions, does help. It is important not to use depression and abuse as an excuse to stop your life. If the depression continues, medical intervention in the form of medication may be needed. Current research seems to point in the direction that early trauma can affect both brain and body chemistry. Some antidepressants are effective in treating, greatly reducing, and even ending what might otherwise be years or even decades of depression.

Psychopharmacology is not an exact science, and it may take a lengthy trial period to determine the most effective medication for your depression. You can always choose to stop the medication. Because there may be a physiological cause of your depression, it is necessary to have a thorough medical examination with appropriate blood workup before beginning medication. Women should chart depression in relation to their menstrual cycle to watch for Premenstrual Syndrome. If you are alcoholic or drug addicted, you can still safely take many of the medications, but it is vitally important to check with a physician who is an addictionologist as to which medications can be used safely.

If you are depressed and choose not to accept medical intervention, ask yourself the following questions:

1. How is my depression affecting others around me? _____

_____

2. If I were not depressed, what might be different? _____

_____

3. Am I punishing myself or the abuser by staying depressed? _____

4. How will I know if I cannot handle life anymore? _____

Antidepressants will not impede your ability to work through your feelings or your depression. However, working through these feelings might temporarily increase your depression. As you reexperience old memories and feelings, you may respond as if the experiences and feelings were taking place again. If any feelings of sadness, helplessness, and depression do recur, rational thinking and feedback from others can transform those feelings into useful tools for working through the process of recovery.

To make sure that depression does not become overwhelming, write out a "Fire Drill" to use when symptoms of depression arise.

Some signs of depression are:

Changes in sleep patterns — insomnia, sleeping more, waking up early

Chronic exhaustion

Increased drinking (alcohol)

Decrease or increase of appetite

Decreased memory function and ability to concentrate

Frequent crying

Withdrawal from friends

Agitation

Loss of interest in sex

Increase in fear, anxiety, or phobias

Difficulty in making decisions or staying organized

Lack of energy

Loss of hope

Increase in physical symptoms

Difficulty getting to work

Difficulty in doing previously easy tasks

Suicidal thoughts

Fire Drill Worksheet

My symptoms of depression are:

_____

_____

I know I need to do something when:

_____

_____

The things that make depression worse are:

_____

_____

Things that have helped me work through depression in the past are:

_____

_____

People from whom I can ask help are:

_____

Grief and Grieving

A healthy resolution of grief is the beginning of the healing and recovery process. Unresolved grief may result in long-term (or even life-long) depression, and it may impair your overall ability to function.

Much has been written on the stages of grieving, both in anticipation of loss and after loss takes place.

In abuse, the steps of grieving are:
- Accepting the reality of the loss(es)
- Experiencing the grief
- Reinvesting the emotional energy in other areas of your life.

Step 1

Accepting the reality of the loss. This is a review step. It is the memory recall stage, and the way to get in touch with what you did not get, could not get, and will never get. It is the realization that there is no going back to an earlier time; that there is no possibility of having a childhood free from pain, neglect, and abuse.

This review is usually done in the bottoming out stage of your abuse work.

Lost years are irretrievable. What has passed cannot be undone. What you can do is to mourn the childhood that never was, the family that could not be there, the fun you could have had, the love you did not feel, and the person you believe you could have become had the abuse never happened.

Make a list of what you feel you have lost _____

_____

_____

How have you avoided feeling these losses? _____

_____

How can you arrange your current life to allow yourself to experience these losses? _____

_____

What supports will you need? _____

_____

What is your biggest fear in grieving your losses? _____

_____

What can you do to get through your fear so you can experience these feelings?_____

_____

Step 2

Experiencing the loss. Painting, drawing, and poetry are often the most direct ways to get in touch with loss feelings. Try the following:

- Go to the library and look through the poetry books. Find some that express feelings similar to yours. Copy the poem down and read it aloud. When you feel comfortable, share the poem with friends. Let them know that the poem speaks of your experience.
- Try writing your own poem. Just begin with words that represent the loss and grieving you feel. Let the words flow, not trying to make sense of the order. Look for words that describe your feeling.
- Get some paints. Focus on your feelings and let the brush take you with it. Let the brush portray your feelings. If painting the whole poem is difficult, focus on one word such as loss or sadness. What happens? What images do you get?_____

_____

- Write out your story, focusing on the pain, sadness, and loss you have experienced. As you are writing, focus on what you feel you have lost forever— that which you cannot get back. Try to be aware of the emptiness and anger you feel.

Experiencing Grief or Loss

Letting yourself feel loss is the next step in the grieving process. You may have spent months and years defending against and preventing yourself from feeling sad, lonely, and empty feelings. You can experience your loss by letting these feelings surface.

In re-experiencing your loss, you can master it and gain greater control over integrating it into your adult life. Ongoing and continuing depression (which may be unresolved grief and loss) is a barrier to full grieving, since it drains your energy and self-esteem. Without those two steps, you cannot fully work through your grief. If your depression has used up your energy or your will to live, consider medical intervention to enhance your ability to deal with your feelings and recoup your energy to continue your work.

You are beginning to experience this grieving process when your sadness and loss feel as if they are happening now. They will not feel like yesterday's news, but rather as if the pain is present again. Let yourself experience those feelings, encourage them, and affirm your right to feel them.

During this time, as in any other period of loss, grieving, or mourning, avoid decisions that will take away from your grieving. Think carefully before entering a new relationship, changing jobs or careers, or making a big purchase such as a house. During the grieving period, such actions have the power to stop the grieving process.

During the grieving period, it is important to affirm life and living. Two Jewish customs around mourning provide examples.

After a burial, the custom is to wash your hands (to symbolize the end of the burial and death process) and eat a whole egg (to symbolize the recognition of continuing life). At the same time, seven days of mourning take place. To underline the importance of continuing life, Jewish tradition says that even weddings must go on after a recent death.

Recognition of loss and grieving does not mean that your life affirming processes stop. Both grieving and celebration of life can occur simultaneously, although joy and fun may be difficult during this period.

Glen Davidson, in his book *Understanding Mourning,* says "Mourners must clean away the debris of their collapsed world in order to find the foundation on which to rebuild their lives to recover (or discover) their life orientation."

He suggests that this can be done by telling and retelling your story to those who will listen. In the telling, the story becomes yours, you integrate your feelings, and you can begin to think about people and activities that will help you renew your energy.

During your grieving process, you can reacquaint yourself with old friends, invite new people into your life, find new hobbies and interests, go on a trip, join local groups, or volunteer for charity.

Such activities will help you redevelop and refine a solid life orientation. By connecting yourself with others, you can regain a sense of hope and a fresh viewpoint.

What activities would you like to start?_____

_____

Whom would you like to meet? Whom would you like to bring into your life?

_____

_____

Without taking away the pain you need to experience in order to recover from abuse, list ways you can affirm your life while going through the grief process._____

_____

Ask your friends, counselor, or therapist to help you develop ways to keep your perspective while doing this work. Write their suggestions here.

_____

_____

Make a plan on how you are going to engage in life-affirming activities while progressing through grief. Write your plan here.

_____

_____

_____

Reinvesting Your Emotional Energy

You have put an incredible amount of emotional energy into coping with abuse and deflecting its effects. If you are now working on feeling the pain, sorrow, and sadness that are part of the grieving process, you know how much of your energy is taken up. Important, however, is to search out all your sadness and pain. Otherwise, investing energy in any activity will work as a defense against the grieving process. When the sadness is felt and the tears have flowed, that is the time to seek positive, life-affirming activities. List some positive activities where you can reinvest your emotional energy.

_____

_____

Fear and Anxiety

Fear and anxiety are experienced in different ways by the body and mind, but they are related emotions: anxiety is frequently a fear response. Fear is an emotion usually felt first in the body as a physiological, emergency response. Since the beginning of time, the body's first response to fear has been the fight-or-flight reaction. Sean Haldene, in his book *Emotional First Aid*, describes the fear process as follows:
  • Stage 1: Terror—(gasp of air inward)
  • Stage 2: Suspension motion—(momentary freezing)
  • Stage 3: Fight—(attack—breath let out) or Flight—(body leaves, flees, or goes to soft protections, such as into a mother's arms; emotion discharged through tears and comfort).
If fear was a common emotion in your family, you will most likely experience many fears and fear responses. Whether learned or genetic, fear seems to run in families. Babies show fear of separation, unexpected noises,

and sudden movements as well as of things that are new and strange. These reactions are basic biological responses designed by evolution to protect the body. Children commonly feel afraid of such things as water, carpet sweepers, and bathtub drains. Try to remember early fears that may or may not be related to early abuse, or recall the fears of other children with whom you grew up.

Write down any fears you remember having as a child.

_____

_____

If you lived with other children, write down some fears they had.

_____

_____

Did your parents or caretakers have the same fears? List them.

_____

_____

Fears with no assignable basis are irrational, but other fears are grounded in the possibility of physical or emotional hurt. Youngsters may develop fears of an object or person representative of a hidden fear. In these instances, the observable fear is a metaphor or rationalization for a deeper, larger fear.

Look again at the childhood fears you listed. For each fear of yours or your childhood friends, name what you think motivated the fear.

Fear	What the fear really represented:
Example: fear of bathroom drains	fear of not being safe, of being consumed by something else
_____	_____
_____	_____
_____	_____
_____	_____

How many of your fears have you transformed into other fears, with the underlying fears remaining?

_____

_____

Which of your fears do you relate to abuse, incest, or neglect experiences?

_____

_____

Many children who grow up with fear make fight-or-flight their standard response to fear. Because this response is both learned and environmental, violence toward others and self is often correctly interpreted as a distorted fear response.

By what fears might the violent and aggressive abuser have been motivated?

_____

_____

Do you use aggression or self-violence as a fear response? _____

_____

How does your body respond when you are fearful? Think of times when you were frightened. Try to remember exactly what happened. Write down the incidents you recall:

_____

_____

What did your body feel like? _____

_____

How did you feel at the beginning of the incident? _____

_____

During the incident? _____

_____

After the incident had passed? _____

_____

Understanding how your body reacts to fear can help you recognize when you are afraid. When your body is responding as if in fear, do you deny or dismiss what is happening? When do you do this? _____

_____

_____

Fear can be classified in two ways: fears over which you have no control (e.g., your own or someone else's death) and fears you can do something about. List some fears over which you have you have no control.

Fears I have no control over_____

_____

What fears can you reasonably take action on?_____

_____

Fears that can be quieted by taking action_____

_____

Susan Jeffers, in her book *Feel The Fear, And Do It Anyway*, describes two other fear states: fears that have to do with inner states (such as fears of rejection, success, and disapproval) and the overall fear of not being able to handle a particular situation.

List fears that correspond to your inner states:_____

_____

Do you have fears of not being able to handle things or situations?

_____

_____

Some ways of handling fears are:
- Change what you normally do when you are fearful. Do something different.
- Visualize the situation with yourself as a strong person, unafraid and able to handle the situation.
- Develop a set of fear mantras, for example.:
  "I can handle this situation."
  "I will do ___."
  "I will get through this."
- Discuss your fears with others. Ask your friends how they would handle the situations.
- Connect the fear to past abuse. By connecting your current fear to past experiences, you will put distance and perspective on the situation. Doing so will enable you to work through your fear.
- Make an "I will conquer the fear" plan. List specific strategies for conquering your fear.
- Set up a reward system for yourself as you make progress by conquering a specific fear.
- Recast your language of fear into language of personal power.

Example: "I cannot handle this…." could be translated into "I will not handle this…I choose not to handle this." Then remember: if you choose not to handle something, you can also choose to handle it.

Write down one of your major fears. _____

1. Write down what you could do when you feel this fear. _____

_____

2. Now, take yourself through the steps leading up to this fear and visualize yourself as unafraid and confident. Does anything happen? Does the situation change?

_____

_____

3. Write down your positive fear mantras. Repeat them several times a day. My positive fear mantras are:

_____

_____

4. Describe your fear to a few people you trust. What is their advice on how to handle it?_____

_____

5. How is your fear connected to your abuse experience? What is different about your life now? What strengths do you have to quell the fear?

_____

_____

6. What is your plan for conquering your fear? Be specific.

_____

_____

7. How would you like to reward yourself for handling even a small part of the fear?_____

_____

8. What language do you use when you talk about your fear? _____

_____

Can you change this language?_____

You have just made a fear reduction plan. Try it out! Anxiety (or panic) is a continuing fear response. It stays with you. It feels irrational and is usually less clearly defined than fear of a specific situation or thing. Anxiety is fear of the future, an anticipation that something bad will happen. In a sense, anxiety is the anticipation of fear.

Children who have been abused or neglected often develop anxiety to such a degree that it becomes a part of their body's physiological pattern. If you live in fear, never knowing what is going to happen next, and if you are not helped to feel safe and secure, your response to the surprising or unexpected could well be anxiety or panic.

Constant anxiety and panic will reduce a person's ability to cope with day-to-day or life challenges, make personality adaptations, and produce physiological reactions. Some symptoms of anxiety are:
- trembling, twitching, or feeling shaky
- muscle tension, aches, or soreness
- restlessness and fatigue
- shortness of breath or sensations of smothering
- palpitations or accelerated heart rate
- sweating or cold clammy hands
- dizziness or light-headedness
- nausea, diarrhea, or other abdominal distress
- hot flashes or chills
- need to urinate frequently
- trouble swallowing or feeling a lump in throat
- feeling keyed up or on edge
- exaggerated startle response
- difficulty concentrating or mind going blank
- trouble falling or staying asleep
- irritability.*

Panic and panic reactions are the most extreme form of anxiety. Panic is an overwhelming terror and feeling of fright. Phobias are a form of anxiety: they are fears specific to a thing or group of things (such as fear of heights, crowds, snakes).

Some anxiety is caused by physical problems such as thyroid disorders or Premenstrual Syndrome. If you have chronic anxiety, a good medical workup can determine if there is any physiological cause.

Current theory holds that anxiety is a complicated interaction of three factors:
- Biological—the chemistry and genetics that make you unique.
- Learning and conditioning—how events can lead to a learned anxiety response.

*Adapted from the American Psychiatric Association's *Diagnostic and Statistical Manual of Mental Disorders (3rd ed.)*.

• Stress—stress from the environment and actions of others.

Many people will go to great lengths to avoid feeling anxiety or panic. They may stay inside for weeks if going out frightens them, restrict their social life if they have fear of crowds, wash their hands compulsively if they have a fear of germs, or become addicted to substances such as drugs or alcohol to avoid feeling anxiety or panic.

Anxiety

List the times in your life when you have been most anxious.

_____

_____

How did that anxiety manifest itself in your thoughts? _____

_____

In your body?_____

_____

How long did the anxiety usually last? _____

What reduced the anxiety? _____

_____

What did you learn about coping with the anxiety? _____

_____

Who else in your family is anxious? _____

What symptoms do those persons show? _____

_____

Did the abuser show anxiety? _____

Are the abuser's patterns of anxiety the same or different from yours?

_____

Secondary Gains

A secondary gain results from an experience or situation that yields another important benefit. For example, for someone who is ill, a secondary gain might be seeing people who do not regularly visit. There is a possibility of a secondary gain in some anxiety and panic disorders. An agoraphobic, afraid to go out, might unconsciously manipulate family members into visiting. Another person might experience a secondary gain from an anxiety-provoking memory retrieval.

List any current anxieties and phobias you have.

_____

_____

What secondary gain might you get from them? _____

_____

How can you get what you want without having to experience anxiety or phobias?_____

Do you think that the abuser got a secondary gain from anxiety? How?

_____

How does anxiety or a phobia get in the way of your life now?

_____

Did anxiety or a phobia get in your way when you were a child?

_____

Are your childhood anxieties like/unlike those you experience as an adult?

_____

   Your anxiety today may be the same as you experienced in childhood abuse situations, albeit in a different form. Understanding and connecting your anxiety to childhood abuse may begin to reduce it. You may also reexperience your childhood anxiety as part of your recovery process. If anxiety or phobias persist, consider a psychiatric evaluation. Cognitive and behavior therapy can be useful. Excellent medications are available for the control of phobias, compulsiveness, panic, and anxiety.

   Recovery from abuse is difficult and painful, but you can reduce some of your most troubling symptoms to be free to do recovery work. There are several things you can do to reduce anxiety without resorting to medical treatment.

- List your automatic or distorted thoughts. Examples: "I would be better off dead" or "Harm will come to me if I go outside." Then write positive thoughts to replace the others.
- Try to accept your anxiety. Let yourself feel it. Battling with it is likely to create a greater internal struggle.
- Meditate and use relaxation techniques regularly. Use breathing exercises and engage in physical exercise at least three times a week.

- Cut down or give up caffeine, chocolate, and alcohol.
- Keep active. Plan your schedule and stick to it.
- Talk with others about your anxiety.
- Observe the things that trigger your anxiety. Write down your observations and try to change the situation.
- Avoid fantasies and thoughts that make you anxious. Replace them with other thoughts and visual aids.
- Visualize a positive future in which you handle fear, and anxiety is absent.

A Plan to Reduce Anxiety

I am most anxious about: _____

_____

My distorted thoughts are: _____

_____

I will replace these thoughts with these statements: _____

_____

I can accept my anxiety by: _____

_____

I will schedule meditation and relaxation for: _____

_____

Activities I will plan to reduce my anxiety are: _____

_____

I will share my anxiety with: _____

Anxiety triggers I can watch for are: _____

_____

Fantasies I often have are: _____

_____

_____

Thoughts and visual images I will use to replace the fantasies are: _____

_____

_____

A positive future without anxiety will look like: _____

_____

_____

My commitment to reducing anxiety is: _____

_____

Joy and Happiness

Joy and happiness are feelings everyone wants, but many people find them difficult to achieve. If you were promised joy at the end of working through your abuse, you might not have believed it would happen or simply not understood what happiness and joy feel like. Or, you might worry about feeling too happy or joyful because of the later let-down you anticipate. Letting yourself feel happy and close to someone in a relationship might bring similar feelings: "I dare not feel happy because there will be a subsequent let-down."

Those who have experienced abuse, incest, or neglect are often unusually aware that the experience of happiness and fun is followed by an emotional let-down, fighting, and abuse. Having too much fun might even be seen as bringing on the wrath of the abuser. Many children have learned that joy and happiness belong only to story books. Whatever pleasure they were able to experience, it was brief and transient.

Life does not have to be that way. You can experience joy and happiness. You can have fun without having to pay a later penalty. Try to remember the times you had fun as a child.

Times I had fun	Who was there?	What happened afterwards?	What made it fun?
_____	_____	_____	_____
_____	_____	_____	_____
_____	_____	_____	_____

Times I was happy	Who was there?	What happened afterwards?	What made it fun?happy?
_____	_____	_____	_____
_____	_____	_____	_____
_____	_____	_____	_____

Of the times listed, which ones gave you the greatest sense of joy/happiness?

_____

_____

Have you felt any of these feelings as an adult? _____ When? _____

_____

   The first step in experiencing happy, joyful feelings is to imagine that you can have those feelings without fear of punishment or let-down. Happiness and joy are within your grasp as an adult. As a child or adolescent, times when others controlled your food, home, and daily agenda, you had little power to change your environment. Now, however, you can make changes to directly affect your ability to experience positive feelings.

If you could change your environment to make way for feelings of happiness and joy, what would you change?

_____

_____

What prevents you from making these changes? _____

   Making small changes can modify your perspective enough to prepare the way for larger changes. Think about this simile: finding joy from these small pleasures is like making a necklace of pearls. Each pleasurable moment can be strung into a jewelled necklace of memories. Most people who experience happiness and joy describe special times or moments. They do not experience happiness and joy as constant or even conscious states.

Whom do you consider happy? Who do you believe experiences joy on a deep level?

_____

_____

Ask them how they are able to experience those feelings, and how much of the time they feel that way. Write down what they say.

_____

_____

What did you learn from them? _____

_____

You may expect to experience joy or happiness all the time or never.

How much of your time was fun as a child? _____

As an adolescent? _____

Now, as an adult? _____

Ask people who are well-grounded and who have not been abused about their experience of fun. How much of the time do they experience joyful and happy feelings?

_____

_____

Make time during the week to let yourself imagine what would allow you to feel joyful or happy. Do not fall into the trap of saying, "If the abuse hadn't happened" ... or "If I had only..." These negative, self-defeating thoughts will block positive possibilities.

Try thinking of small things that give you pleasure. Write them here:

_____

_____

Changing your expectations of people, of time, and most important, of yourself will have substantial effect on your ability to experience happiness and joy. Positive thoughts will help you think even more positively and reduce your expectations of negative outcomes.

Think of Positive Times

Think of four coming events at which there is a possibility of having fun.

Events	Expectations
_____	_____
_____	_____
_____	_____
_____	_____

What are your expectations of these events? _____

_____

Are any of your expectations negative? _____

_____

For each negative expectation, write a positive possibility.

_____

_____

What can you do ahead of time to make the positives more likely?

_____

Achieving joy and happiness is a step-by-step process during which you can work to achieve positive moments, then allow these moments to flow together. While working with this book, it will be important to remember that you can experience joy — you can have fun and you càn be happy. If you lose sight of this truth (and at times you might), return to activities that bring you pleasure and in which you can have fun.

Before going on, make a list of activities and people that bring you special, happy moments. Write your list here:

_____

_____

_____

Keep adding to your list, reviewing it when you forget that you and happiness both exist. Keep a chart and log of times you feel joy. You will discover that happy occasions increased over time, even if you cannot see that anything has changed generally. Your "happiness log" will help you keep perspective.

Share your happiness. When you feel good, include people you care about in your feelings. Most important, keep a list of positive possibilities in your wallet. When you feel good and think of additional ideas, add them. They will help you get through rough times. Remember, great joy is made up of small, happy moments.

You have just reviewed some of the major feeling states.

- Anger
- Shame
- Guilt

- Sadness and Depression
- Anxiety and Fear
- Joy and Happiness

As you read through these feelings and did the exercises, what did you learn?

_____

_____

_____

Would you like to change your range of feelings? _____

What would you like to experience more of? _____

_____

Less of? _____

_____

Expressing Feelings

Drawing or painting is a way to express feelings and let go of barriers. Try to assign each of the feelings a color:

Feeling	Color
Anger	_____
Shame	_____
Guilt	_____
Sadness and Depression	_____
Grieving	_____
Anxiety and Fear	_____
Joy and Happiness	_____

Draw two pictures. Use shapes and colors to represent the feelings. In one drawing, show how you are feeling now; in the other, draw how you want to feel. Place them side-by-side, labeling one "Now" and the other "Positive Possibilities."

7
Defenses as Coping

To cope with any form of abuse or neglect, a person must develop defense mechanisms. Defenses are ways that help you, first, survive the experience, and, second, make sense of what happened. Defenses are important and useful.

Someone has probably said to you, "You are being defensive," and perhaps you felt bad as a result. While it is true that defenses you have had since childhood might hinder adult relationships and communication patterns, you have needed them. However, defenses that worked when you were a child may not be well-suited to adulthood. Your task now is to recognize the defenses you use most often and to exercise control as to when, where, and with whom you use them.

The steps for controlling defenses are:
- Understanding what defenses are and why you have them;
- Recognizing defenses you needed to cope with abuse;
- Determining defenses that others have used in your family situations;
- Understanding how you use defenses currently;
- Determining which defenses you still need and planning how to modify or change others.

This chapter will help you develop tools for understanding and controlling your defenses.

Decompensation

Since defenses are coping strategies, it is important to understand the mechanism of decompensation, which is a complete falling apart of defenses. In some instances, decompensation could be helpful because coping skills can then be rearranged. However, decompensation may also be destructive of self-esteem, so defenses should be changed or modified slowly and carefully.

Defenses—Some Descriptions

Many defenses may sound familiar to you. As you read through the descriptions below, try to understand them before you think about how they apply to you or your family. A thoughtful approach will allow you to be more open to the ways you and others have adopted and used defense mechanisms. For ease, the defenses are listed in alphabetical order:

Anger/Aggression

Expressing anger or aggression can be a way of avoiding feelings such as hurt, sadness, or anxiety. People also use anger and aggression to prevent others from becoming emotionally close to them or to avoid feeling vulnerable. Expressions of this defense show up as acting out, defiance, shouting, provocative behavior, baiting, and intimidation.

Who uses or has used this defense? _____

How did I feel when they used this defense? _____

_____

Did I use this defense as I was growing up? _____

What feelings or actions was I defending against? _____

_____

How do I use this defense? _____

_____

Avoidance

Manifest in strategies such as procrastination, this defense is used to avoid unpleasant tasks or feelings. It is closely linked to denial: if I avoid an event or situation, it may never happen or I might never feel it.

Who uses or has used this defense? _____

How did I feel when they used this defense? _____

_____

Did I use this defense as I was growing up? _____

What feelings or actions was I defending against? _____

_____

How do I use this defense? _____

_____

Behavioral Constriction

This defense protects emotions and behavior. Since expressing feelings somehow increases vulnerability, the mind/body defends itself by narrowing the range of emotions that are shown or felt. People who use this defense never seem to react much to anything, or they appear to operate only in one or two modes. Their range of emotions is literally constricted.

Who uses or has used this defense? _____

How did I feel when they used this defense? _____

_____

Did I use this defense as I was growing up? _____

What feelings or actions was I defending against? _____

_____

How do I use this defense? _____

_____

Blaming

Blaming someone or something else for an action or feeling is another defense. A child is often blamed for the way an adult feels in emotionally abusive families. In physically abusive families, the abuser may find a reason to blame a child, although the reason may have little to do with the situation at hand. With sexually abusive families, blaming may take the form of saying that the child acted in such a way that the adult could not control his feelings. Blaming, which is closely related to displacement and projection, may include defenses and behaviors such as threatening, accusing, judging, attacking, and being hostile.

Who uses or has used this defense? _____

How did I feel when they used this defense? _____

_____

Did I use this defense as I was growing up? _____

What feelings or actions was I defending against? _____

_____

How do I use this defense? _____

_____

Blocking

In this defense, you are unable to remember what you have to do. Because of forgetfulness, a thought or action remembered a short while ago cannot be retrieved.

Who uses or has used this defense? _____

How did I feel when they used this defense? _____

_____

Did I use this defense as I was growing up? _____

What feelings or actions was I defending against?. _____

_____

How do I use this defense? _____

_____

Control

Controlling behavior can be related to one area (e.g., the family checkbook), or it may relate to a whole personality style, with someone needing control of everything in every detail.

Who uses or has used this defense? _____

How did I feel when they used this defense? _____

_____

Did I use this defense as I was growing up? _____

What feelings or actions was I defending against? _____

_____

How do I use this defense? _____

_____

Conversion

Conversion is the result of feelings (e.g., acute anxiety) that, too painful and frightening to feel, are converted into another form of expression. Examples of conversion range from loss of voice to temporary paralysis.

Who uses or has used this defense? _____

How did I feel when they used this defense? _____

_____

Did I use this defense as I was growing up? _____

What feelings or actions was I defending against? _____

_____

How do I use this defense? _____

_____

Denial

Denial, one of the most frequently used and discussed defenses, is disavowing or dismissing as untrue feelings, wishes, needs, behaviors, or other realities that are not tolerable. Denial allows a person to act out because there is no connection to or ownership of feelings and actions. Because denial is progressive, it may grow stronger in time and be activated by fear. Other defenses often accompany denial.

Who uses or has used this defense? _____

How did I feel when they used this defense? _____

_____

Did I use this defense as I was growing up? _____

What feelings or actions was I defending against? _____

_____

How do I use this defense? _____

_____

Delusional Thought

Fixed ideas unamenable to rational explanation are called delusional thoughts. Delusions remain firm in the face of contrary evidence. In abused people, a frequent example of delusional thought is that the abuser "may treat them different this time." Sometimes, holding on to a delusion may be a way of holding out hope of getting needs met.

Who uses or has used this defense? _____

How did I feel when they used this defense? _____

_____

Did I use this defense as I was growing up? _____

What feelings or actions was I defending against? _____

_____

How do I use this defense? _____

_____

Distancing from Affect

This defense is seldom seen by others. To the person using this defense, it is like watching a movie or seeing the world through a tinted pane of glass.

Who uses or has used this defense? _____

How did I feel when they used this defense? _____

_____

Did I use this defense as I was growing up? _____

What feelings or actions was I defending against? _____

_____

How do I use this defense? _____

_____

Displacement

Displacement transfers a feeling to someone or something else because the person with the feeling cannot accept its presence. Displacement is frequently used by families who have had contact with social service agencies. Negative feelings toward the abuser are directed onto the agency or helper instead. Displacement permits the discharge of feelings while keeping the family free from blame. This defense may also be used by adults in therapy. A variation of "killing the messenger," displacement is similar to the defense of projection.

Who uses or has used this defense? _____

How did I feel when they used this defense? _____

_____

Did I use this defense as I was growing up? _____

_____

What feelings or actions was I defending against? _____

_____

How do I use this defense? _____

_____

Dissociation

Dissociation is a significant coping mechanism found usually in instances of severe abuse. Dissociation is the body/mind's great supportive move to protect itself when no other defenses are available. It provides refuge when abuse exceeds human tolerance. Dissociation allowed concentration camp victims to survive and cope by allowing the mind/body to deal with information in a context other than abuse.

As a response to less extreme forms of abuse, dissociation can take the form of inattention to what is going on—mind-wandering or daydreaming. As a protective mechanism against more intense abuse, dissociation enables a person to go through an action or situation but not feel it. Men and women have suffered broken or severed legs, looked at the injury, and not felt pain. In extreme physical or mental trauma, entire thoughts, memories, and actions may be stored as separate memories, sometimes in the compartment of another personality. People with multiple personality manifest an extreme form of dissociation. Multiple personality indicates a serious clinical problem and requires professional help.

Who uses or has used this defense? _____

How did I feel when they used this defense? _____

_____

Did I use this defense as I was growing up? _____

What feelings or actions was I defending against? _____

_____

How do I use this defense? _____

_____

Distortion

This defense changes reality by misperceiving some of the original thought, feeling, or action. Distortions are usually related to specific events. A distorted style of thinking is not truly a defense, but rather the mind's adaptation to a particular world view. Aaron Beck and David Burns, two cognitive therapists, defined common manifestations of distorted thinking that they call "cognitive distortions."

Who uses or has used this defense? _____

How did I feel when they used this defense? _____

_____

Did I use this defense as I was growing up? _____

What feelings or actions was I defending against? _____

_____

How do I use this defense? _____

_____

Intellectualizing

Reasoning and explanation are used by abused people to defend themselves against feelings or actions. Related to this defense are explaining, generalizing, theorizing, and debating.

Who uses or has used this defense? _____

How did I feel when they used this defense? _____

_____

Did I use this defense as I was growing up? _____

What feelings or actions was I defending against? _____

_____

How do I use this defense? _____

_____

Identification, Incorporating, and Introjection

Identifiers unthinkingly pattern their lives after another's. At certain times, identification can be healthy—e.g., school children often identify with their teachers and adopt their behaviors. Incorporation is a kind of identification in which a person adopts a part of someone else's personality. Introjection is the symbolic taking of something into the self. A child who has been abused, then hurts him- or herself in the same way, is introjecting.

Who uses or has used this defense? _____

How did I feel when they used this defense? _____

_____

Did I use this defense as I was growing up? _____

What feelings or actions was I defending against? _____

_____

How do I use this defense? _____

_____

Minimizing

Some people trivialize or render unimportant things that happened or what they felt. Minimizing is a defense commonly used by abused people. "It didn't happen often," and "It didn't feel all that bad," are examples of minimizing. Evading and dodging are related defenses.

Who uses or has used this defense? _____

How did I feel when they used this defense? _____

_____

Did I use this defense as I was growing up? _____

What feelings or actions was I defending against? _____

_____

How do I use this defense? _____

Manic Behavior

Sometimes manic behaviors are called "high vibration" defenses. Talking quickly or nonstop, asking lots of questions, putting out a flurry of activities—are all examples of a manic defensive style. Like depression, manic behavior may indicate the need for immediate psychiatric help and medication. In their milder form, they may be treated as a defense mechanism.

Who uses or has used this defense? _____

How did I feel when they used this defense? _____

_____

Did I use this defense as I was growing up? _____

What feelings or actions was I defending against? _____

_____

How do I use this defense? _____

_____

Narcissism

Narcissists see the world only from their own view point, or they see people, places, and things only as they relate (or do not relate) to themselves. Narcissists are unable to see others' needs and wants.

Who uses or has used this defense? _____

How did I feel when they used this defense? _____

_____

Did I use this defense as I was growing up? _____

What feelings or actions was I defending against? _____

_____

How do I use this defense? _____

_____

Psychic Numbing

Psychic numbing has been described as the world's collective reaction to the threat of nuclear war. When people become so overwhelmed by the possibility of destruction or suffering, they can become numb. In that state of mind, feelings shut down and inaction is frequently the result.

Who uses or has used this defense? _____

How did I feel when they used this defense? _____

_____

Did I use this defense as I was growing up? _____

What feelings or actions was I defending against? _____

_____

How do I use this defense? _____

_____

Physiological Defenses

These defenses show up in the body as aches and pains. Getting sick and needing to go to bed can be defense mechanisms.

Who uses or has used this defense? _____

How did I feel when they used this defense? _____

_____

Did I use this defense as I was growing up? _____

What feelings or actions was I defending against? _____

_____

How do I use this defense? _____

_____

Projection

In projection, an unacceptable part of oneself is attributed to others. This mechanism is related to transference (see chapter 10).

Who uses or has used this defense? _____

How did I feel when they used this defense? _____

_____

Did I use this defense as I was growing up? _____

What feelings or actions was I defending against? _____

_____

How do I use this defense? _____

_____

Rationalization

Using reason as an intellectual defense, some persons try to explain away whatever happens. "But I deserved the punishment," is an example of rationalizing abuse. Justifying one's actions, thoughts, or feelings at length is another common variation of rationalizing.

Who uses or has used this defense? _____

How did I feel when they used this defense? _____

_____

Did I use this defense as I was growing up? _____

What feelings or actions was I defending against? _____

_____

How do I use this defense? _____

_____

Repression

Sometimes the mind is so pained by thoughts that it prevents unacceptable ideas, affects from consciousness, and violent urges from entering our awareness. However, repressed material may emerge in disguised forms: dreams, compulsive actions, or conversions. Repression is related to suppression.

Who uses or has used this defense? _____

How did I feel when they used this defense? _____

_____

Did I use this defense as I was growing up? _____

What feelings or actions was I defending against? _____

_____

How do I use this defense? _____

_____

_____

Sublimation

Unacceptable feelings or goals may be diverted into other feelings or goals. A workaholic may sublimate sexual life into work. People who feel ineffectual in their personal lives may strive for power in politics or corporate life.

Who uses or has used this defense? _____

How did I feel when they used this defense? _____

_____

Did I use this defense as I was growing up? _____

What feelings or actions was I defending against? _____

_____

How do I use this defense? _____

_____

Suppression

Suppression is a conscious effort to dismiss thoughts, feelings, or actions. It is related to repression.

Who uses or has used this defense? _____

How did I feel when they used this defense? _____

_____

Did I use this defense as I was growing up? _____

What feelings or actions was I defending against? _____

_____

How do I use this defense? _____

_____

Withdrawal

In its lesser form, withdrawal may simply mean a pulling away from a painful interaction or event. In its extreme form, it can be a complete avoidance of any activity, and it might manifest itself as agoraphobia or fear of being in public. Withdrawal is related to the defenses of shyness and silence.

Who uses or has used this defense? _____

How did I feel when they used this defense? _____

_____

Did I use this defense as I was growing up? _____

What feelings or actions was I defending against? _____

_____

How do I use this defense? _____

_____

The following are not technically categorized as defenses, but they operate in much the same ways.

Agreement/Compliance

Through this process, fulfilling others' expectations avoids disagreement, maintains peace and respect, and safeguards the love of family members. This particular behavior may range from agreeing to and complying on a specific event to molding a whole personality style that is always in compliance and agreement. The compliant person does not wish to stand out or cause negative reactions. Being compliant is sometimes called "people pleasing." The behavior may ultimately cause interpersonal problems because a people-pleasing person will try to accommodate everyone and never take an "I" stance.

Who uses or has used this defense? _____

How did I feel when they used this defense? _____

_____

Did I use this defense as I was growing up? _____

What feelings or actions was I defending against? _____

_____

How do I use this defense? _____

_____

Confusion

When overwhelmed with feelings or choices, people may feel confused. Sometimes they adopt confusion as a regular reaction whenever they are confronted with making a choice. As a defense, confusion is closely related to avoidance.

Who uses or has used this defense? _____

How did I feel when they used this defense? _____

_____

Did I use this defense as I was growing up? _____

What feelings or actions was I defending against? _____

_____

How do I use this defense? _____

_____

Conforming/Chameleon

The ability to cope with the environment by seeming to be a part of it is a useful skill. At times, it is safest to be indistinguishable from others in the same environment, even unwillingly. Victims of capture sometimes adapt chameleon behavior, as in the instance of Patty Hearst's participation in terroristic activities. This particular coping behavior is closely related to agreement/compliance.

Who uses or has used this defense? _____

How did I feel when they used this defense? _____

_____

Did I use this defense as I was growing up? _____

What feelings or actions was I defending against? _____

_____

How do I use this defense? _____

_____

Fantasy

People use fantasy as a coping mechanism to get what they want or need. Sometimes, people can develop a full set of fantasies to call on when a particular situation does not fulfill their desires. Abused children may have a particular fantasy they carry into adulthood. Some people develop fantasy to such a level that they do not feel real unless they are playing a role.

Who uses or has used this defense? _____

How did I feel when they used this defense? _____

_____

Did I use this defense as I was growing up? _____

What feelings or actions was I defending against? _____

_____

How do I use this defense? _____

_____

Fun

Most people do not think of fun as a defense, but it can be a very healthy way to cope with what would otherwise be a difficult and painful situation.

In *It's Always Something,* Gilda Radner makes excellent use of fun and humor as a coping technique in discussing her fight against cancer. Individuals may carry this behavior to an extreme by joking, smiling, or being humorous at inappropriate times.

Who uses or has used this defense? _____

How did I feel when they used this defense? _____

_____

Did I use this defense as I was growing up? _____

What feelings or actions was I defending against? _____

_____

How do I use this defense? _____

_____

Personalizing

Personalizing is a coping behavior usually learned in early childhood. Children relate the actions or feelings of virtually everyone else to themselves. For a child, personalizing is a way of filtering the world.

Who uses or has used this defense? _____

How did I feel when they used this defense? _____

_____

Did I use this defense as I was growing up? _____

What feelings or actions was I defending against? _____

_____

How do I use this defense? _____

_____

Rigidity

Many people have set ways of feeling, doing, or thinking that make openness to change difficult. For many reasons, change is frightening and spontaneity uncomfortable. Rigidity is related to compulsiveness and behavioral constriction, and it is often found in homes where set patterns are the norm. Rigidity may be accompanied by perfectionism.

Who uses or has used this defense? _____

How did I feel when they used this defense? _____

_____

Did I use this defense as I was growing up? _____

What feelings or actions was I defending against? _____

_____

How do I use this defense? _____

_____

In your notebook, make a list of the defenses or coping techniques most frequently used by your family members. For each item listed, write who used it and when.

Review the definitions and make a list of the defenses or coping actions you use and when you use them.

How many of your frequently used defensive moves are the same as those used by other members of your family?

My Defenses

Think of the defenses you use most. Then, on a large sheet of paper, draw or paint each defense. Take a break after you complete each one. What do your defenses look like?

_____

Is their texture rough, smooth, silky, or what? _____

What colors did you use? _____

Put the drawings on the wall. Label them. What do you feel as you look at them?_____

At a later time (perhaps in a day or two), repeat the exercise. Draw the defenses the abuser used. When you are finished, put the drawings on the wall next to the others. What do you feel as you look at this second set?

_____

Now look at them both. What are the differences? Are they similar? How are they the same?_____

_____

Think of the defenses that you use most often. If the defenses were animals, what would they look like? What color would they be? What texture? Would they be tall or short, fat or thin? List the defenses you use most often and the free associations you make with them._____

_____

_____

Think again of the defenses you use the most, and then think of different kinds of music: jazz, classical, country, rock, reggae. Write down the defenses, associating them with music you know._____

_____

_____

Listen to the music as you think of defenses you associate with it. What is your reaction as you listen to the music?

_____

Changing Defenses

If you are trying to change a defense, think of the associated musical tune in your head before you use that particular defense. Thinking will help you distance yourself from the defense. When you feel ready, show the list of defenses to a close friend (one who can be objective with you; rarely would a family member be an appropriate partner in this exercise). Ask your friend to be candid about the defenses you use. List the defenses your friend sees and instances when you used them.

Defense	How You Used It
_____	_____
_____	_____
_____	_____
_____	_____
_____	_____

What defenses do you want to change or modify? List them here.

_____

Now go back and examine your list. Which defense would be easiest to change?

_____

How would you or your behavior be different if you changed that defense?

_____

If you changed, would you like yourself better? _____

How could you change or modify this defense? _____

_____

Ask people who care about you (friends, professionals, or sympathetic family members) for ideas on how you might change or modify that defense. Be sure to explain to them what you are doing. What are their suggestions?

_____

_____

Taking their suggestions and your ideas, make a plan. Once you have made a plan, use it as a daily affirmation.

Affirmation	Example
1. "I wish to change or modify the defense I use of:	fantasy.
2. This defense has helped me:	cope with past abuse by allowing me to escape to a place where people were kind and nice to me.
3. I no longer need this defense because:	I am beginning to be nice to myself and have allowed others to be nice to me.
4. I will change this defense pattern by:	stopping myself when I begin to retreat to fantasy and remind myself that I can live in the present and have a good life with people who love me."

If you are comfortable, display your change affirmation in a place where you will frequently see it.

It may take weeks or months to change or modify a defense. With some defenses—such as fantasy—you may want to begin by reducing the amount of time you are using the defense before eliminating it all together. The Chinese character for change also means chaos. Be prepared to explore some feelings of internal chaos as you try to modify your defenses. A certain amount of anxiety will accompany any change. Be patient. If you become anxious, reassess whether you have chosen to work on the right defense or have the best timing. When you are ready, ask your friends for feedback.

Now, move on to the next defense you would like to change or modify, and repeat the process.

Distortions in Thinking

In families where there has been abuse, some members are apt to manifest faulty thought processes. Their faulty processes may conclude in abusive or neglectful behavior. David Burns and Aaron Beck, two cognitive therapists, have studied such families, and their work has been useful in identifying maladaptive thought processes. If the section below proves useful to you, consider reading *Feeling Good* by David Burns, M.D.

Dr. Burns' premise is that past experience influences a person to misinterpret current experience. Like a needle on a scratched record, thinking can get stuck in a pattern. Common forms of distorted thinking are:

All-or-Nothing Thinking

Seeing things in good or bad, black or white, success or failure. Using absolutes and not seeing shades of gray.

Who in the family thought that way?_____

Examples of when I think that way:_____

_____

How this thought process gets in the way:_____

_____

Overgeneralization

Seeing an event as a never-ending pattern, such as "I can't do it now, and I know I won't be able to."

Who in the family thought that way?_____

Examples of when I think that way: _____

_____

How this thought process gets in the way: _____

_____

Filtering

Magnifying a negative detail so that it becomes the "filter" by which you see an entire situation or person. For example, "My whole day was ruined by that traffic ticket."

Who in the family thought that way? _____

Examples of when I think that way: _____

_____

How this thought process gets in the way:_____

_____

Disqualifying the Positive

Rejecting feelings and positive experiences and feeling that they "don't count."

Who in the family thought that way?_____

Examples of when I think that way: _____

_____

How this thought process gets in the way: _____

Jumping to Conclusions by Mind Reading or Fortune Telling

Feeling you know what people think of you — without checking it out — or feeling that things will turn out badly.

Who in the family thought that way? _____

Examples of when I think that way: _____

_____

How this thought process gets in the way: _____

_____

Catastrophizing or Magnification

Making things more important or more of an emergency than they are, or expecting a disaster.

Who in the family thought that way? _____

Examples of when I think that way: _____

_____

How this thought process gets in the way: _____

Emotional Reasoning

Feelings, particularly negative ones, are taken as true. "I feel ugly so I must be ugly."

Who in the family thought that way? _____

Examples of when I think that way: _____

_____

How this thought process gets in the way: _____

_____

Should Statements

Statements that expect a certain type of behavior or emotion. "You shouldn't feel that way."

Who in the family thought that way? _____

Examples of when I think that way: _____

_____

How this thought process gets in the way: _____

_____

Labeling and Mislabeling

Extreme overgeneralization which is often emotionally loaded. "You are a ..." or "I am a ..." are indicators that labeling is taking place.

Who in the family thought that way? _____

Examples of when I think that way: _____

_____

How this thought process gets in the way: _____

_____

In addition, personalizing and minimizing are also identified by David Burns as distortions in thinking. They are found in the defenses part of this chapter.

To change your thought processes, concentrate on one type of thinking at a time. Use affirmations similar to the ones you used for defenses. Be tolerant of yourself. Change is evolution not revolution.

What feelings did you have as you worked on this chapter? _____

_____

_____

What did you learn from this chapter? _____

_____

_____

What surprised you most? _____

_____

What is your plan to continue to change? Write it in your notebook.

8
Communication

Abuse is unlikely to occur in families whose members communicate clearly, directly, and honestly with each other.

Research shows that communication is blocked or stopped in young abused children. Camras and fellow researchers described abused children as less skilled than nonabused children in identifying universal facial emotions. Other researchers have noted several interesting discoveries: facial expressions of abused children were difficult to interpret; battered children manifest a delay in language development and socialization; and abusive mothers are less likely to encourage curiosity in their children. One scholar, in reporting on communication styles of abused children, found them to range from aggressive and hostile to precociously adaptive. The same researcher found that no matter how much abused children talked, they avoided any real contact through conversation. These authors—among many others—have speculated that abused children who do not talk may be fearful of responding incorrectly or are anxious about "saying the wrong thing."

Other theories suggest that family members lack understanding about the true meaning of signals. Learning effective communication skills requires attention and the ability first to discern, then define emotions and signals, and a curiosity about others. Abuse damages communication skills.

Family communication and abuse are so intertwined that an adult recovering from abuse may find learning a healthy communication process as difficult as learning to speak a foreign language. The difficulty comes from the abused person's need to mask feelings, dissociate from the body, and defend the body in order to survive. So many mixed messages have been received, it is virtually impossible to determine if emotions, body movements, and words actually represent to others what they represent to the abused person. A parent who hits a child, then says "I love you" is not communicating the conventional meaning of "I love you." Becoming clear about actions, expressions, body movements, and words is one way of putting the abuse experience into proper perspective.

171

The goal of this chapter is to present ways of defining and categorizing communication, ways of responding to others' communications, and ways of helping you chose the language and communications style that express personal control and power. The beginning exercises are designed to increase your awareness of how people communicate by laying out some basic propositions of communication theory. Later, conflict resolution and assertive techniques will be discussed. While doing the exercises in this chapter, try to be aware of your communication patterns and where you learned them. To prepare for these exercises, give yourself some positive communication mantras (e.g., "I will develop my own style of communication," or "My communication will be different from my family's"). Write down your positive communication mantras.

_____

_____

_____

To communicate effectively, you need to learn how the communication process works. Communication is sending and receiving signals or messages. These signals comprise facial expressions, words, sounds, skin tone, and body movement. Babies communicate first with sounds and then develop patterns made up of gestures and sounds. Caretakers sometimes do not pick up or understand a baby's messages. When communication fails, a corresponding problem in learning how a message is sent or received develops. This problem may result from one or several of the caretaker's personal fears, such as preoccupation, fear that a child's demand cannot be met, unwillingness, or never having learned as a child the meaning of the sent messages. Wanting to tune out the "news" and cues given by the child are equally common additional reasons.

Thus begins a pattern of failed communication. If communication continues to fail, or if the caretaker continues to tune out, the child learns that signals do not work and stops sending. Feelings and thoughts do not stop, however, simply because the signals are not being sent or received. The family in which sex is a forbidden topic of discussion provides a good example of this situation. Sexual activity is not necessarily absent because sex is not discussed. Not talking about sex may make it more alluring. In a family that does not discuss sex, a child who is sexually abused and too frightened to tell anyone may suffer an additional pain since there is no easy way to ask for help.

Think for a moment about communication, about the process of sending and receiving signals. Review your recent experiences with television, radio, and movies. What in the program moves you to take an action, feel something, or think a new thought? _____

_____

What in the movies makes you respond? What makes you cry or laugh?

_____

_____

What upsets you when you read the newspaper? _____

_____

What makes you want to buy something? _____

_____

When does the sender's message get across? _____

_____

What makes you understand? _____

_____

Ask some friends these questions; then write their answers here:

_____

_____

_____

What did you learn about sending and receiving signals?

_____

_____

_____

From the above exercise, you probably began to understand that most communication is nonverbal. Research has shown that communication is 7 percent verbal, 38 percent vocal and 55 percent body movement. In his book *Manwatching*, Desmond Morris categorizes nonverbal communication in the following ways:

- *Actions that are innate or instinctive.* Inborn actions that we do not have to learn.
- *Discovered actions.* Actions we learned as we learned how our body works. Children who have been told their bodies are bad discover only a limited range of actions.

- *Absorbed actions*. Actions that are unconsciously copied—usually from caretakers or parents—will reflect their behaviors and communication patterns.
- *Trained actions*. Consciously learned actions that are acquired by teaching or observation and practice.

Some gestures described by Morris:*

- *Facial gestures*—facial expressions or movements used to communicate a generally understood message.
- *Mimic gestures*—"putting on a good face," e.g., smiling when sad or crying at a funeral when not truly upset.
- *Compound gestures*—acts similar to laughter with accompanying gestures that make the information understandable. Facial expression and other key elements (e.g., sound), do not have to be present; on their own, compound gestures such as crying can communicate feelings. An element of compound gestures that expands the meaning of a movement—e.g., a body position—is what Morris calls "amplifiers."
- *Relic gestures*—part of the individual's infantile action so that recurring moments of stress are treated as a re-experiencing of childhood.
- *Baton signals*—signals that emphasize speech. Fingerpointing and fistclenching are examples.
- *Tie signs*—signs that display personal bonds. They may be composed of shared expressions or gestures, proximity (space between people), or objects such as wedding rings.

Take Yourself on a Field Trip

Visit a park, restaurant, or department store. What signals do you see?

Write them here: _____

_____

_____

_____

_____

_____

* Note: Morris describes signals and gestures (actions that send information to someone else). Learning to distinguish among these gestures and signals is helpful in the recovery process. Everyone can learn to communicate with others and to scan others' messages; similarly, they can choose to remain close to positive, good communicators.

Description of Signals — Who and What Was Happening

	Park	Restaurant	Department Store
Signals I Saw	_____	_____	_____
Facial Gestures	_____	_____	_____
Compound Gestures	_____	_____	_____
Relic Gestures	_____	_____	_____
Baton Gestures	_____	_____	_____
Tie Signs	_____	_____	_____

Now think about your family. What were some of the ways the same gestures were expressed? What did the gestures communicate? What did you feel when they were being expressed? _____

_____

_____

_____

Family Signals/Gestures

How were these expressed?_____

What was communicated by them?_____

My feelings about them? _____

Memories?_____

Facial gestures?_____

Mimic gestures?_____

Relic gestures?_____

Baton gestures?_____

Tie sign?_____

Which of the gestures do you use today? _____

Which ones do you want to keep? _____

Which ones do you want to change? _____

Space and territory are major elements in our communications. Edward Hall, an anthropologist who focused on communication, described space distances as zones of communication. He divided space distances into four categories: Intimate, Personal, Social, and Public Distance

- *Intimate Distance*—up to 18 inches. Close intimate distance is for lovemaking, wrestling, comforting, and protecting. Each person is aware of the other at this distance.
- *Personal Distance*—from 18 to 30 inches. Another person can be held or grasped at this distance. Far personal distance ranges from two and one-half feet to four feet. Personal subjects can be discussed at this distance.
- *Social Distance*—close social distance runs from four to seven feet. Impersonal business occurs at this distance, and it is used by people who work together. Far social distance — seven to 12 feet — is usually the distance in which desks in offices are arranged and subordinates are held by employers.
- *Public Distance*—close public distance is 12 to 25 feet, and far public distance (beyond 25 feet) is often used by public speakers.

In your home, you are likely to use Intimate, Personal and Social Distance to define boundaries. As mentioned in the Boundaries chapter, David Kanter calls these space boundaries "architectural boundaries." Review the personal boundaries exercise on pages 54–55. See if your personal boundaries fit into Edward Hall's definitions.

To test whether people use these distances, observe a family at home, people at a party, and people at work. What kind of distances do they maintain? What messages do they communicate at the following distances?

	Home	Party	Work
Intimate: Close	_____	_____	_____
Far	_____	_____	_____
Personal: Close	_____	_____	_____
Far	_____	_____	_____
Social: Close	_____	_____	_____
Far	_____	_____	_____
Public: Close	_____	_____	_____
Far	_____	_____	_____

Other Forms of Nonverbal Communication

Gaze behavior, for example, refers to how people look at each other. Quick glances or staring are two ways we take in information as well as give out communication. These two specific behaviors can be comfortable or uncomfortable, depending on the who, when, and where of their use. Were quick glances or staring used in your family? _____

By the abuser? _____

Do you use them now? _____

In *Body Language*, Julius Fast observes that staring is often used for nonhuman objects. It is behavior we use for viewing art, animals in a zoo, or even pets, but not for persons we like and respect. Staring at a street person who is mentally ill or at a homeless person may give a message that we do not respect that person's feelings. If staring was used in your family, it probably made you feel self-conscious—certainly not like someone who deserved to be treated with dignity. Was staring used in your family?

All the behaviors listed, usually learned in childhood, may be carried into adult years since they tend to form a behavior pattern. Patterning seems to hold especially true of behaviors learned as defenses against abuse. In extreme cases of abuse, body protection gestures are not allowed, and abused children develop an open body language that may be read by others as a signal inviting abuse.

Actions Signifying Fear

Being threatened or verbally frightened elicits three possible reactions:
1. Backing away
2. Protecting your body
3. Attacking or grabbing the aggressor.

Children, because of their size, usually cannot ward off the abuser. Adults who were abused as children may find that their body language about coping reflects backing away and seeking protection. Does your body language reflect any of these three coping styles?

_____

_____

Morris says that preparatory action movements indicate that someone is about to take action. The action may or may not be carried out. Movements made by someone preparing to respond to another's action—such as fleeing motions—are also preparatory action moments. Preparatory actions may be striking signs directed at a person or an object. Think about the preparatory action movements of the abuser: how did you know something was going to happen?

_____

_____

When you knew something was going to happen, how did you respond? Did your response make the abuser more threatening or less?

_____

The abuser (who is giving and receiving communication) is unhealthy at best, and may interpret preparatory defensive movements—e.g., fleeing—as rejection. The abuser may react with even more anger. Other body behaviors can communicate messages between the abuser and the abused person that reinforce one person's status, the other's submissiveness. Parents may have children kneel, kiss hands, curtsy, or stand in a corner—all as reinforcement of the parent's power status. Were status reinforcements used in your family?_____

How did these status reinforcements make you feel?_____

Do you use any status reinforcements with other people?_____

Pacing and posturing are names for natural body displays, companionship, and agreement in communication. These nonverbal messages are natural to people in agreement during communication, and they can also be used to improve rapport and heighten communication. As a test, watch a meeting where two distinct sides or opinions are presented. One group of people will demonstrate pacing or posturing through one kind of body movement, the other group will use different body signals. The movements of both sides can be bodily movements, facial expressions, sound and voice qualities, as well as words and breath rate.

Listening

Communication with others means listening. In the chapter on forming a support network, we discussed some ways to listen and to be supportive of others. Reread the suggestions on pages 40–44. After you have reread those ideas, write down the names of people who were able to listen to you when you were growing up. Who listens to you now? _____

_____

How did (do) these people make you know they were (are) listening?

_____

Pick someone you would like to talk to about a topic of general interest—the newspaper headlines or a recent movie. After a few minutes of conversation, ask yourself: Was that person listening? How do you know? _____

_____

Switch places and repeat the exercise. How did you show that you were listening? Was it difficult? _____

_____

Depending on the type of abuse you suffered in your family, your listening skills were either finely honed (listening closely might have been necessary for survival) or poorly developed (communication shut out) in order to survive. What was your survival communication style? _____

How do you carry out that style currently? _____

Ask friends for feedback. When do you have a hard time listening? _____

_____

Do you listen and not risk giving feedback? _____

What would you like to change about your listening skills? _____

_____

Watching Communication

Go to any place where people are communicating by talking (restaurant, train, park), and watch their pacing. What did you notice about:

body movements _____

voice quality _____

facial expressions _____

breath rate _____

words _____

At the next family gathering (your's or someone else's), watch how the family does or does not pace each other. What did you notice about:

body movements _____

voice quality _____

facial expressions _____

breath rate _____

words _____

What did you learn about this family? _____

_____

Who connects to whom? Who has power? Who is left out? _____

_____

Body Language

People even communicate by breathing. When a person is excited, breathing grows faster; when sad or depressed, breathing grows slower. You may have been able to detect what the abuser was intending to do by the manner of breathing. Watch people as they breathe and speak. What do you notice about their breath rate? Does their breath rate seem to have anything to do with what they are speaking about? What do you remember about the abuser's breathing style?

Other body language worth observing is that which hides someone from current interaction. Such hiding may include:
- closed eyes
- hands over the face
- blinking
- clear inattention by daydreaming

Do you use any of these? _____

Did you use them as a child? _____

Were they protecting you from someone or something? _____

Do you use them now? _____

What do they communicate to others? _____

As you work through the exercises, you may observe a behavior that Desmond Morris calls *auto-contact*. Auto-contact is an unconscious self-touch that is a replacement for the touch of someone else. The function of auto-contact is to provide comfort. Common auto-contact includes: supporting your jaws with your hand, touching your mouth, or clasping your hair. For some badly abused children, these touches may have been one of the few sources of comfort they had.

What are your auto-contact gestures? _____

What self-comfort do you think you are performing? _____

Facial Expressions

Facial expression masks and appearance management (i.e., how we want others to see us) are other forms of nonverbal communication. We all engage in masking through use of facial expressions, voice, clothing, or the entire body movement. Appearance management is accomplished in the way we dress and our behavior in public places. In abusive families, appearance management may be manifest only through an elaborate set of rules and communications designed to provide the "appearance" of a normally functioning family to the outside world. Appearance management can also take the form of dress, household organization, behavior of children, and masks. People can relate, masks cannot. Therefore, masking prevents honest communication in families. Were masks used in your family? Who used them? _____

_____

What happened when the masks were dropped? _____

_____

Masks I Have Known

Buy a sketchbook and label it, "Masks I Have Known." As you think of a mask, draw it. It may be a mask that you use or one used by someone else. Draw in this book any mask image that comes to mind.

Did you develop masks as protections when you were young? _____

What masks do you still use? _____ _____

When do you use them? _____

Facial expressions are probably the most common form of nonverbal communication, telling much about what a person feels and thinks. Richard Bandler, known as the father of neuro-linguistic programming, has developed interesting concepts about eye and other facial movements, and Genie Laborde has refined them. Neuro-linguistic programming proposes that facial movement (eye and expression) can describe a person's thought process. Neuro-linguists categorize people as visual, auditory, or kinesthetic processors.

- *Visual processors* move their eyes in an upward direction, or, like people watching a movie, they look straight ahead without focusing when processing information. Visual processors tend to use visual images when they speak. Frequent word choices: graphic, see, outlook, illustrate, perspective, picture.

- *Auditory receivers* keep their eyes at midpoint in left and right movements. They appear to be listening, and they use words with sound images when they speak: tune-in, hear, note, key-in, sound.
- *Kinesthetic (feeling-oriented) people* move their eyes down right; some move their eyes down left. They use words with feeling images: impact, irate, shock, move, throw, hit.

Are you primarily a visual, auditory, or kinesthetic communicator? _____

List each member of your family. What kind of communicators are they? If you don't know, guess. Next time you see them, check out your guess.

_____

Try using words and images used by someone else. What happens? _____

_____

How did the varying communication patterns affect your family communications?_____

Facial Clues

You can improve your ability to communicate with others by using techniques that are not part of your natural communication style. Practice giving and receiving information in these ways.

By watching another's face, you can discover much about the emotions behind it. In their book, *Unmasking the Face*, Paul Ekman and Wallace Friesen, two great facial communication researchers, say that the face provides three types of signals:

- *static*—permanent personal aspects such as skin, color, shape of face, bone structure, and where features are placed
- *slow*—gradual changes over time, such as wrinkles and crow's feet
- *rapid*—expression.

Six Emotions and Their Characteristics*

Surprise—Usually a brief emotion often followed quickly by another emotion. Some people go so far as to organize a life of facial expressions around surprise: eyebrows are raised, curved and high; eyes are opened wide; jaws drop open; lips and teeth part, and wrinkles cross the forehead. A startled expression—related to surprise—comes with eyes blinking, head moving back, and lips retracting.

Fear—Always a terrible experience, it endures longer than surprise. In fear, the skin is likely to become pale and hands may tremble. The forehead wrinkles in the center, eyebrows rise and draw together, eyes open, and the

*Adapted from Ekman, Paul, and Friesen, Wallace V. (1984). *Unmasking the face: A guide to recognizing emotions from facial expressions*, 34–128. Palo Alto, Calif.: Consulting Psychologists Press.

lower lip tenses. Lips stretch back. The same facial expressions may also occur with feelings of sadness and disgust.

Disgust—Somewhat like aversion, disgust is related facially to contempt and scorn. Disgust is often communicated by a pursed mouth and wrinkled nose. The upper lip is raised, the lower eyelid is pushed up, the eyebrow is lowered. It feels like having a bad taste in the mouth. With contempt, a variation of disgust, lips are usually closed and cheeks are raised.

Anger—Brows are lowered and drawn together, and vertical lines appear between them. With both eyelids tensed, the lower raised and the upper lowered, the eyes have a hard stare. Lips may be pressed together or opened, and nostrils may be flared.

Happiness—Corners of the lips are drawn back and up, and the lips may be parted. A wrinkle runs down from the nose to the outer edge of the lip corners, and wrinkles appear below the lower eyelid (it may be raised, but there is no tension). Crow's feet and wrinkles go outward from the outer corners.

Sadness—Inner corner of the eyebrows are drawn up, cheekbone to eyebrow triangulated with inner corner up. The eyebrow may be raised; the corners of the lips are down, usually trembling.

Expressing Emotions

Think back to times corresponding to each of the emotions described above. Then, simulate an emotion and ask a friend to guess which one you are expressing. If you can, have your friend photograph you as you demonstrate these emotions.

Are the expressions clear to you? _____

Observe other people. Can you tell what emotions they express?_____

People can lie with their facial expression, but their body language often gives them away. Morris and Ekman and Friesen call such communication "leakage." You may or may not be able to tell by an expression if someone is lying, but you can be quite sure that something is going on if you observe increased body shifts, flash expressions, hands placed over the mouth, and increased hand motions. You may know people you believe to be less than honest. Do their communications to you feel different from those of your friends? Write the names of these people and their relationship to you:

_____

_____

What signals make you feel they may not be truthful?_____

Do they remind you of anyone in your family? _____

Whom? _____

Who in your family was not honest with their expressions? _____

What clues did or do you have? _____

    Nonverbal and verbal language are connected just as body language and spoken language depend on each other. In communicating feelings, we all use words descriptive of our bodies. Some examples of verbal body expressions are:

- pain in the neck
- get off my back
- makes my heart flutter

Can you think of more? _____

_____

What phrases did you hear when you were growing up? _____

_____

What do these phrases say about your body? _____

_____

Additional Nonverbal Exercises

Review what you have learned about nonverbal communication. How could small children send nonverbal requests for help to adults such as teachers, family, or physicians without verbalizing their secrets? _____

_____

Ask your friends for some ideas. Write them here. _____

_____

_____

What is a nonverbal way to say, "I've had enough; go away"? _____

_____

What is a nonverbal way to tell acquaintances you would like to know them better?_____

Place chairs back to back for a friend and yourself; then have a conversation. What happens? _____

_____

Early Verbal Communication

Verbal communication reflects what children hear as well as how their thought processes are developing. Children use words to communicate and to make sense of the world. In an unpublished paper, Grace Smith classified children's early language into basic developmental categories:

- *Classification and discrimination.* "The crane looks like a rocket; the smell is grass growing."
- *Taking old ideas to construct a sense of time and number.* "I'm not four anymore." "This is tomorrow—No, this is today."
- *Using imagery to make sense.* "The water is pretty like a tree."
- *Symbols take on new meanings.* "My daddy's name is Joseph. Joseph means daddy."
- *Can only understand one kind of classification at a time.* "I'm not thinking, I'm talking."
- *Defines self by words and images.* "This is my breast; it's going to be a bosom when I grow up."
- *Personification of objects.* "The ball loves me."
- *Magical thinking.* "If I'm good, Santa will bring me presents."
- *Linking causality and events to personal activity.* "When I'm with you, you're a nice person; when I'm not with you, you're not." "If I close my eyes, you're not here." "The only safe place is next to me."

As you look at the above examples, you may begin to remember ways you first looked at the world and first verbalized your thoughts.

Imagination

For each of the verbal processes above, try to remember an association or connection you might have made. Do not be concerned about making conscious associations now or judging what was most important.

Close your eyes. Then, imagine yourself as a small child about three or four years old and let your imagination take you on a tour. Things to think of are games or activities you enjoyed — riding in a car, going to a playground, or feeling safe in your room.

Associations, Classifications, and Discriminations

Constructing time and number _____

Using images to make sense _____

Giving symbols new meanings _____

One classification at a time _____

Define self by images _____

Personification of objects _____

Magical thinking _____

Linking causality and events to personal activity _____

What was happening in the family when you were beginning to learn language?

_____

Review each classification and your associations with them. How do you think you might have talked about your parents or the abuser? If the abuse was taking place at the age you are reviewing, describe your feelings about the situation._____

_____

What associations became part of your adult ways of thought and speech?

_____

Think of as Many Value Words as You Can

Very early on, children learn value words such as: *good, bad, nice, mean.* If, parents or caretakers see the world in these narrow, moralizing ways, children will be hindered in developing more complex ways of expressing themselves.

Worthless	Evil	Best	Smartest	Stupid	Dumb
_____	_____	_____	_____	_____	_____
_____	_____	_____	_____	_____	_____
_____	_____	_____	_____	_____	_____
_____	_____	_____	_____	_____	_____

How many of those value words are negative? _____

Go back to the list. Circle words you heard from your family. Now, go back and put an asterisk by any word that you use in speech or that you use internally.

Killer Words

Killer words literally stop communication. These words hurt someone, put someone down, or show disinterest. Some common killer words and phrases:

Words	Used in family by whom	Used by me
Not Now	_____	_____
Later	_____	_____
That's Stupid	_____	_____
_____	_____	_____
_____	_____	_____
_____	_____	_____

How do you feel when people use killer words on you?

_____

Do you work or live with people who use killer words that you heard in your family?

_____

In an excellent book, *Messages: The Communication Skills Book*, Matthew McKay, Martha Davis, and Patrick Fanning note that other words, e.g., *always* and *never,* reflect an absolute position for the speaker. The hearer, in order to get to a moderate, nonabsolute, "sometimes" position, is put on the defensive by the generalized accusation.

Who used absolutes when you were growing up?_____

Do you use them now? When?_____

There are other words that modify the meaning of a statement: for example, *again, certainly, merely, now, of course,* and *naturally.* What kind of response do you get when you use these words? What are you usually feeling when you use them?

_____

Change of meaning can be made by inflection and tone of voice. To "hear" how these modifying words work (or do not work), take time to tune into the ways people use modifiers. In abusive households, words usually become "loaded," i.e., they take on negative meanings. Negative loading gives these words a specific meaning and the unconscious mind continues to process that word in its negative meaning. For example: "There you go again!" Although some people may give these words a positive meaning, most hear them as a negative.

As you listen to others use modifying words, get a sense as to whether the connotation is positive or negative. If you do not understand the meaning of the message, ask for clarification. Ask what a specific word or phrase means.

What did you learn from listening for modifiers? _____

Were the modifiers you heard similar to or different from what you heard in your family? _____

Voice

Your view of yourself as an abused person will be reflected in your voice and your use of words, according to the authors of *Messages*.

Pitch. Pitch is directly expressive of some emotions. Higher pitch generally represents intensity of emotion, and a lowered pitch represents a calm or depressed feeling.

Articulation. How clearly do you enunciate? Children who grew up in abusive homes may find articulation difficult. Clear speech might have made you stand out from your siblings, and, therefore, made you a more noticeable target for abuse. Articulation difficulties frequently surface in counseling or therapy. Difficulty in articulation could be the body's signal that articulation was used as a defense from abuse.

Resonances. Thickness or thinness of voice may reflect how well-grounded you are feeling, although heavy or authoritative people may have a thick resonance (obviously for different reasons). People who have settled into a victim stance may have acquired a thinner resonance in their voices.

Tempo. How fast do you speak? Fast or slow speech is often a reflection of region. Compared to Northerners, Southerners speak more slowly. Tempo may also reflect mood, particularly in people who manifest manic-depressives illness or a similar disorder. If you grew up in a home where the abuser suffered an affective illness, you may have learned that voice changes were clues to coming abuse.

Some parents with mood disorders leave children with caretakers while they pursue their own interests for either hours or weeks. Very young children may become sensitized to when a parent is preparing to leave by noticing changes in the parent's voice tempo. Obviously, parents who have self-medicated a depression or anxiety state by drinking or drugging are likely to give cues by their behavior, body language, and tempo. A person can even connect with another by matching that other's tempo. Try it and see what happens to communication.

Rhythm. Each person's speech has its own rhythm. Depressed or anxious people may have dull rhythm, while people in good spirits may have a lilting rhythm. In rhythm, certain words may be emphasized, or they might be spoken in a flat drone.

Volume. How loud is your voice? Think about kinds of abuse in terms of voice volume. Emotional and physical abuse usually are accompanied by loudness, while sexual abuse (often done in secret) and neglect usually occur in quietness and whispers. Your voice volume may reflect the type of abuse you experienced.

Listening to Voices

Select people you do not know (in a restaurant, on a bus, at school) and listen to their voices. What did you observe about:

	Person 1	2	3	4
Articulation				
Resonance				
Tempo				
Rhythm				
Volume				

Listen to family member's voices. What do you hear?

Articulation _____   Rhythm _____

Resonance _____   Volume _____

Tempo _____

How does your voice sound? _____

Record yourself speaking or reading out loud. What do you hear in your voice? _____

What do you remember about the abuser's voice? _____

Word Choice

Your choice of words reflects what you feel about yourself. If you feel like a "victim", your words will reflect that. Two things happen when you use a "victim vocabulary."

- You reprogram your unconscious mind to keep you in a "victim" state.
- You give others the message that you are a "victim," and thereby pass on the message that you can be victimized. Think of it in this way: we

choose "dance partners" for ourselves. "Victim" vocabulary attracts victimizers. They become partners in a painful, repetitive dance.

Some examples of "victim" vocabulary :

"Victim" Statements	Examples of Healthy Statements
I'm crazy.	I'm feeling out of sorts.
I need to be taken care of.	I need your support now.
I can't change.	I have choices now.
It's always my fault.	I'm responsible for my own mistakes; I'm not responsible for your behavior.
I can never trust anyone. I can't trust you when you behave…	I can take risks.
I give up.	I'm going to fight it. Can you help?
I can try that, but….	I will try. Thanks for encouraging me.
You are always so much better than I.	We have different skills.

Try writing some healthy statement responses to replace the "victim" statements:

I'll never find anyone
who loves me.   _____

I can't do anything right.   _____

No one really cares about me.   _____

You made me…(do or feel).   _____

I guess I'll try.   _____

The world would be better
off without me.   _____

I shouldn't feel…   _____

I'm really weak. I really messed up
again.   _____

Communication Styles

In their book, *Messages,* McKay, Davis, and Fanning identify the three basic styles of communication as passive, hostile or aggressive, and assertive.

Passive communications reflect a downtrodden attitude. People who speak in a passive style may have developed it as a way to maintain peace, get love or attention for being quiet or good, deflect criticism, and avoid rocking the boat. Passive communicators agree with others and rarely state their own opinions. In a sense, passive communicators have "given up the ranch," obtaining peace and nonconfrontation at the expense of not being authentic with themselves or with those whom they care about.

Hostile or aggressive communications project a "don't tread on me" attitude. The communicator aims to prevent being controlled by others, and the hostile stance effectively stops communications. It is the ultimate defense shield. Hostile communicators put others on the defensive, attempt to induce guilt, ignore feedback, and make demands. Much of their humor reflects anger.

Assertive communications take on a "I" position. Assertive communicators know where they stand, and so do the people with whom they communicate. They do not tailor their positions merely to fit people who have more power. Assertive communicators keep themselves in mind as well as the persons receiving the communication. They recognize the equal rights of both receiver and sender and that both parties have an equal stake in the outcome of the communication.

Passive-aggressive communications contain words that may look and sound like passive words, but they are really words and acts of aggression.

Someone who ends an argument by saying, "It's just fine," but who acts to the contrary is communicating passive-aggressively. One cannot argue with the response, "That's fine." Passive-aggressive people communicate agreement by saying they will do something and then not do it, or, like so many witnesses before congressional investigative committees, they simply "forget." Some people have developed passive-aggressive communication into an entire personality style, and rigorously avoid directness in their communications; others—the more fortunate—use this style only occasionally.

Mixed messages contain conflicting messages, and they use a tone of voice or a word with another known meaning to the receiver. Mixed messages can be sent with words alone or through body language with a verbal communication. An example: "I care about you," with a nonverbal hand motion that means "Go away."

Common Styles

Think of people in your day-to-day life. Identify the communication style they use primarily and any other ways (any of the styles discussed above) in which they use verbal communication.

Person	Communication Style	Examples
_____	_____	_____
_____	_____	_____
_____	_____	_____

Now, think of your family members — what primary style does each use?

Person	Communication Style	Examples
_____	_____	_____
_____	_____	_____
_____	_____	_____

What style do you use now? _____

What style did you use as a child? _____

Has it changed? When? _____

Would you like to change your style? In what ways? _____

_____

Other Blocks to Communication

Phrasing a statement as a question is a direct and manipulative way of communicating. "Don't you think you would look better in a dress rather than slacks for the party . . ." is an indirect way of saying, "I want you to wear the dress, not the slacks."

Holding back communication is another way of indirect communication. Although at times it is best to withhold communication (to avoid embarrassing someone in front of others), holding back communication impedes an honest response.

Timing is an important but often forgotten element in successful communication. So much of what is said will be heard better if a time when the receiver can listen is chosen. Poor timing will cloud good communication at best. It can turn a difficult statement into a passive aggressive stand-off or, worse, into a hostile act.

Giving and Receiving

In the chapter 2, basic rules of listening and giving feedback are listed on pages 40–44. Review them.

Children who have been neglected and abused have not had good listeners. Their cries, pain, and words themselves have been discounted or ignored. If you come from a family where communication was not attended to, you may never have learned to attend to others. You cannot listen to someone else if you are preparing your response, trying to do another task, or attempting to manipulate members of the group so that you will be listened to next.

As with any communication change, learning to listen is a process that slows the integration of changes so that they are more likely to become permanent within you. Work on a single listening block at a time. If you spend a lot of time daydreaming, bring yourself back to the conversation when you find yourself doing it. Say (and mean it), for example, "I will be here now!" to yourself. Pay attention to what you are feeling when you are not listening. Active listening is an effective way to let the speaker know you are attentive, that the speaker is communicating with you.

Marks of Active Listening

Encouraging the speaker can usually be done by short phrases such as "Yes, I see," or "Uh-huh." Encouragements can be verbal or nonverbal (leaning forward attentively is a nonverbal encouragement).

Restating what the speaker has said shows that you are listening carefully. Restating can be exact or in paraphrase (for example, "If I understand you correctly, you are saying… ").

Reflecting means letting someone know that you are hearing the feeling in their message. An example: "You sound really happy about that!"

Summarizing is listening by restating and pulling the communication together. Example: "It sounds like your points are…."

If no one in your home was an active listener, you probably never learned how to let someone else know that you were listening and tracking as you were communicating. You can learn to be an active listener by practicing for one week, spending two days each (a total of six days) for encouraging, restating, and reflecting. On the seventh day, try summarizing. What are your observations?

Encouraging _____

Restating _____

Reflecting _____

Summarizing_____

Responding to Others

Spineless responses (sometimes called "people pleasing") to communications are based on fear. People who are abused and neglected live in fear, unable to make statements that reflect how they feel and think. If you have been abused, you may give a spineless response because you fear:
- making a mistake
- having someone think you are wrong
- someone might not like it
- you will be criticized
- someone will laugh at you
- you have nothing worthwhile to say
- that someone will leave you
- you are interfering.

When you are having a difficult time saying what you feel, look at this fear list. Is your fear realistic? _____

To whom are you giving power by responding from fear? _____
_____

On occasion, everyone gives a spineless response. However, such a response reduces your self-esteem because it takes power from you and gives it to another. Think of some of your spineless responses.

Example of spineless response	To whom?	What I wanted to say
_____	_____	_____
_____	_____	_____
_____	_____	_____
_____	_____	_____

Becoming aware of what you really want to say is the first step in overcoming spineless responses. When you are aware of what you want to say, take risks with some people. With practice, you will find it easier to take more risks and say what you feel.

Change Relationships by Changing Communication

You can change a relationship by changing the communication pattern. Often, the very process of changing or advancing a stuck process can change the entire dynamics of the relationship. Sometimes, changing one thing—such as voice tempo—can make communication more positive. Moving from a "victim vocabulary" to an assertive style is almost certain to change the way others treat you. That, in turn, will change your internal programming to one that builds greater self-esteem. Assertive communication is the ability to make "I" statements. "I" statements reflect your feelings but do not trample someone else.

Before you can be assertive, you need to decide on what you want, then plan how you are going to get it. Without a goal, you will find it hard to communicate your needs to others. You have basic rights of assertion, and expressing them will help you achieve your goal. You have a right:.

- to change your mind
- to say no
- to state what you feel
- to not respond
- to ask for help or support
- to make your own decisions
- to make up your own mind

- to disagree
- to ask for information or clarification
- to be treated seriously and respectfully
- to negotiate.

Common Rights

For each of these "rights," think of a time in childhood when you could not use your rights; then think of a time when you could have as an adult but did not. Finally, think of a response you could have made as an adult.

Right to	Response as a child	Response as an adult	Assertive adult response
change your mind	_____	_____	_____
say no	_____	_____	_____
ask for help or support	_____	_____	_____
state what you feel	_____	_____	_____
make your own decisions	_____	_____	_____
make up your own mind	_____	_____	_____
disagree	_____	_____	_____
ask for information or clarification	_____	_____	_____
be treated seriously and respectfully	_____	_____	_____
negotiate	_____	_____	_____

Assertive Techniques

Assertive techniques can be learned. You can take an assertive communications course or read either *Your Perfect Right,* by Robert Alberti and Michael Emmons, or *When I Say No, I Feel Guilty,* by Manuel Smith.

Before you practice assertive techniques, observe other people. Do they use them? _____ Do they have any problems in doing so?_____

What do you observe? _____

_____

_____

In the situations you observed, were there ways that assertive techniques could have been useful? Which ones? _____
Think of times when you did not get what you wanted from a communication. List them. _____

_____

What were your goals? What assertive techniques could have helped you get what you wanted?

Situation	Goal	What I said	What I could have said to get my goal
_____	_____	_____	_____
_____	_____	_____	_____
_____	_____	_____	_____
_____	_____	_____	_____

Conflict Resolution

When you are communicating and you find someone else's behavior troublesome, a procedure called "conflict resolution" may help. In conflict resolution, you

- Identify the behaviors or words you do not like or that you find disturbing.
- Determine if you are being reasonable and are responding to what is being said or done. Possibly you are responding to a transference you have made.
- Decide the goal of the communication. Anticipate some possible responses. Prepare an assertive response for each possibility.
- Discuss with the other person. Tell that person what you would find acceptable. Be prepared to offer alternatives.

During conflict resolution, pay attention to your body's reactions to what you and the other person are saying. If you do not feel comfortable, you can amiably disagree and discontinue communication that is damaging to your self-esteem.

How was conflict handled in your family? _____

Note some recent conflicts you have had. _____

What did you do? How did you handle them? _____

Choose a specific conflict. Write it here _____

What did you feel? How did you say what you felt? _____

What was your goal? _____

What happened?_____

What could you have done differently? _____

Does this model of conflict resolution differ from what you usually do?

_____

Now, think about this chapter. What have you learned about communication? _____

What have you done that is different from what your family did? _____

_____

List three skills you want to build on to improve your communication.

_____

_____

Write your plan to continue working on positive communication here.

_____

_____

_____

_____

Communication with others is essential to the process of recovery. At the time of the abuse, neglect, or incest, communication almost certainly became muddled and misleading. Words that were spoken did not always bear their meaning. *Mommie Dearest*, the now-notorious phrase Joan Crawford forced upon her children, clearly had a meaning to her children far different from the common understanding of those words. Parents who said they loved their children, but then neglected or beat them, gave confusing messages to the children. Did the word *love* mean a beating? When words are misused over and over, they lose their meaning, possibly taking on a new and opposite one.

Communication Patterns While You Were Growing Up

Now turn your attention to communication patterns you used while growing up. Review the following tools that can enhance communication, making it direct, positive, and immediately useful.

Communication Meanings — Frequent Expressions

Expressions you heard while growing up. Who said them?

_____

_____

_____

Expressions you frequently use now. Where did you first hear them?

_____

_____

_____

Which ones are the same? Write them here:_____

_____

What do you think your expressions mean to others? _____

_____

Ask your friends if they have noticed other expressions you use regularly and what they mean to them. Do these expressions make them feel comfortable?

Expressions	Feeling/Meaning
_____	_____
_____	_____
_____	_____
_____	_____

Are there any expressions you want to keep?

_____

_____

Are there any expressions that have a message you dislike or want to change?

Expressions	Meaning
_____	_____
_____	_____
_____	_____
_____	_____

What expressions have lost meaning for you? What messages make you uncomfortable or distrustful when you hear them? (Examples: "I love you," or, "I have a bone to pick with you.")

_____

_____

When you have completed the above, you will have a pretty good idea of how certain words influenced your interpretation of a communication when you were growing up, and how certain expressions reflected faulty communication patterns in your family.

What expressions make you react? Write them down.

_____

_____

Tell a friend how these expressions make you feel, and then discuss them. Say those expressions, change the way you say them, and change your facial expression as you say them. The changes you make will begin to modify the meaning of the phrases.

What changes do you want to make in your pattern of communication?

_____

_____

9
Memories

Exploring memories of childhood and adolescence can be rewarding; it can also be quite painful, sometimes even causing anxiety and depression. This chapter, primarily composed of memory-reconstructing exercises, will work to your benefit if you go slowly and do only as much as you feel comfortable doing at any one time. Memory reconstruction should bring on a feeling of being better integrated. If you begin to feel uncomfortable while doing these exercises, stop the memory work and switch over to building up your support network or self-esteem. Return to memory work only when you feel ready.

If these exercises begin to interfere with work, relationships, or other responsibilities, that is an indication you are going too fast or that you are flooding your inner coping abilities. Memory work may make you feel as if you are reliving the experience. Take care to protect yourself from negative memories that are sure to arise.

Working through Memories

I know that I need to stop exploring my memories when _____

_____

My greatest fear in exploring memories is _____

_____

I will seek additional support if _____

_____

Memory, your personal record of what happened, may be unavailable to your conscious mind for several reasons:
- The abuse happened too early in life for you to remember;
- To help yourself cope, you have used repression or suppression;
- You did not perceive what happened as abuse because it was an ordinary part of your family life;

201

- Some children experienced abuse or neglect so early in their lives that they have no clear memories of it. Vague discomfort or a persistent sense of danger is likely to remain, however;
- Repression and suppression are two defense mechanisms that keep memories away. Repression operates unconsciously and banishes unacceptable ideas and feelings from consciousness, or it keeps them from ever reaching consciousness. Repressed memories may emerge in our lives in disguised form, e.g., through dreams or compulsive behavior. Suppression is a conscious effort to control and conceal unacceptable thoughts, feelings, or acts.

Both suppression and repression operate to help people cope with overwhelming events in childhood. If repression or suppression is operating in your memory, you will be able to remember events only when it is safe to do so. Both repression and suppression drain a person's energy. These two memory guards exact a cost: they frequently are accompanied by physical symptoms of anxiety or illness.

One common cause of memory suppression is that the abused person does not, for some reason, register the action as abuse (example: "Every kid gets spanked") or because the person has made the following judgments: (1) it happened, but it was not important and has no consequences; (2) it happened, but I provoked it (i.e., I deserved it); (3) it happened, but it was not abusive. This kind of memory suppression is also called rationalizing. The defense mechanism of rationalizing is the act of attributing an unwarranted explanation, cause, or motive to an action that has a high emotional content. The damage done by rationalizing can be great. While a victim may face and accept intellectually what has happened, negative feelings connected to the action are totally ignored and may continue to influence the victim.

Alice Miller, a Swiss psychoanalyst, discussing why memories are sometimes suppressed or repressed, writes that child abuse usually takes place in secret, and the child is taught to be obedient to the abuser at the risk of loss of affection, punishment, or even the threat of death. The child accepts the order to keep the secret and tries to hold the parent's affection in order to live on unharmed. The child may then place a "shield" over this secret, hiding it from memory over a lifetime.

Another method of suppressing feelings "teaches" the child self-control by making sure that feelings, wants, and desires are not expressed; to the contrary, feelings, wants, and desires are rewarded when they are kept in check. The child quickly learns that suppression not only draws parental approval, it also may be a life-time survival technique.

Miller's work makes clear that not only the most painful memories are suppressed and repressed. Ordinary feelings and thoughts may also be repressed and suppressed if they run contrary to the desires of authority figures who are very important to the child.

You may not remember an event, either because you were too young to register the experience or because something else was going on at the time (e.g., physical illness or extreme trauma). Judith Herman has found that women whose abuse either began in or continued through adolescence had the most clear memories, while women whose abuse began in preschool years and ended before adolescence had the most memory deficits. Women who experienced violence or sadism had the most difficulty with recall. Memory recall for traumatic events may take years, with many months elapsing between the recall of one memory and another.

No matter what you do, you cannot avoid the consequences of your actions. Memories and feelings do not just go away. They always go somewhere, usually deep into our minds and feelings, and if they remain unresolved, they may manifest themselves as physical or emotional problems rather than as memories.

Expectations of Memories

Be clear about expectations of your memories: what do you want to learn from them? If you are expecting a lightning bolt of change, rethink your expectations. My expectations of remembering are:

Signs and Signals of Memories

All of the following may be signals from your unconscious and preconscious of unexplored memories and feelings:

1. *Fantasies*. Examine your fantasies for recurrent themes: punishment, sexual encounters, verbal abuse, or being left alone and neglected are strong indicators of unremembered events. Fantasies of being taken care of, being a small child or baby, or being rescued may be signals of emotional abuse and neglect.

2. *Dreams*. Dreams containing the themes listed above, violence, or recurring chase and abandonment episodes may be an unconscious signaling of repressed memories.

3. *Workaholism and Other Addictions*. Any form of compulsive activity—substance abuse, eating, exercise, or working may be your attempt at suppression. Ask your inner self what you may be avoiding by the activity or compulsion.

4. *Recurrent Behavior Patterns*. Behavior patterns you do not under-

stand, particularly patterns that are self-destructive or that prevent positive relationships, may provide a clue to a memory regarding someone else's behavior or to a pattern you established in coping with abuse or neglect.

5. *Quick Glimpses.* Memories sometimes first appear as a quick flash or glimpse, leaving as quickly as they come. You may feel some vague familiarity but not know why. These short scenes may be like a dream that you remember upon waking, but forget as the day goes on. Consider these flashes as puzzle pieces—write them down, and when you are ready, they will fit together for a whole memory.

6. *Sensory Perceptions.* Sometimes memories begin as sensory perception: a recognizable feeling on your skin or a distinct odor. Such perceptions are called kinetic memories, and they are the work of your unconscious reminding you of a feeling. Write down these kinetic memories and try to fit a time and place to them. Like quick flashes, they may arrive in small, unattached bits. You might remember where a bit happened, but not your age at the time.

7. *Voices, Sounds, and Visual Images.* You may hear a person's voice or a sound, or you may see an image. These perceptions are not hallucinations in a classic sense, but they may be a dissociated part of you lodged in your unconscious. Do not panic. You are only gaining access to your unconscious in an unfamiliar way.

8. *Positive and Pleasant Memories.* Not all suppressed and repressed memories are abusive or painful—some are pleasant—but because of the whole mechanism of memory repression, they may be unavailable to you. To help keep memories from your conscious memory, you may be excluding large sections or years of your life as well. Later in this chapter, some exercises will help you remember these periods.

Safety and Memory Work

You may have different kinds of safety needs for remembering. Who and what you need as support for one memory may be entirely different from the support and safety you need for a memory that recalls a different time and place. You may choose to work on a certain memory with an old friend or a loved one. Another memory may be best worked on with a therapist, a third with a spiritual guide or member of the clergy.

It is important to trust your sense of what best reduces anxiety, panic, or depression. As you begin to glimpse a memory, take time to determine what feels most safe and nurturing for your memory exploration. Find ways to reorient yourself to the present. For each memory, write an emergency plan that might include the following in your notebook:

Safe Memory Work

I think this memory is about _____

I believe I was _____ (age) when this memory took place.

My needs at that age/time were: _____

If I need to direct myself back to the present while I am having this memory, I think that I will need _____

I will ask the following people for what I need:

Person	What I am asking for
_____	_____

If I begin to panic, become anxious, or feel like falling apart, I will: _____

_____

My greatest fear about this memory is: _____

After remembering this, I hope I will learn and understand: _____

Do the above exercises for each memory or time period you want to explore.

Using and Accessing Dreams

Although there is debate about what dreams reflect and whether they are but images to which we later give meaning, dreams do provide us access to our memories. To increase your dream awareness, you can do the following:

- Tell yourself throughout the day that you want to remember your dreams.
- Before you go to bed, put a pad of paper and pencil by your bed.
- Say out loud, "I will remember my dreams."
- If there is a question or certain memory you want to address, speak your question or theme out loud. Speaking to yourself out loud will help you gain access to it.
- When you awaken, write down any images you have had—the remembered images may produce other images and give clues to the content of your dream.
- Write your dreams while you are still in bed—with your eyes closed.
- Recreating body positions you had while sleeping may help you remember your dreams.
- Tell your dreams to others if they will listen. The act of telling may increase your memory of the dream as well as validate the feelings in the dreams.

- Have a routine ready to handle a disturbing dream or nightmare. Can you wake someone up? Can you listen to soothing music or a meditation tape?
- If your dreams carry frightening content you think is not related to a memory, avoid reading newspapers, mysteries, thrillers, or watching the evening news before you go to bed.
- If you experience night terrors, sleep walking, or nightmares, you may want to consult a sleep clinic.
- Chronic sleep difficulties can impede your physical and emotional coping abilities.

Memory Exercises

The following section will help you activate your memories. The exercises begin with less painful topics and proceed to those that may cause troubling feelings. Experiences with the memory exercises will, no doubt, differ from person to person. The exercises may be done alone, with a counselor or therapist, or with a support group. You may want to return to a given exercise as you remember more or as you receive new information.

Most of the exercises are designed to jog the memory and to provide a framework for remembering. It is wise to start with memory exercises that will produce a minimum of anxiety, depression, or fear, and gradually move into the exercises that may be more frightening. Checking hospital data or school records may provide you a reliable framework and could be a good way to begin. Part of the recovery process from abuse is reliving and refeeling the memories in order to gain mastery over them.

As you prepare to search your memory, focus on the following image: you are in a video store called "This Is Your Life." Walk around this imaginary store and name the sections of your life as you see them.

_____

_____

_____

For each section make a list of the tapes that should be included (example: my first day in kindergarten) and then practice telling yourself— "I will watch the tape—'My First Day in Kindergarten.'" Imagine what might be in that video movie and get yourself ready to watch it; sounds, images, and memories should begin to return. For each memory section, ask trusted individuals who were present at the time of the occurrence for their recollections; their memories may not match yours, but they might be able to give you confirmation—or even hints of events you may have forgotten.

Time Line

To put your memory into perspective, take a large sheet of paper (shelf paper or construction paper works well). Draw the chart below, using "0" to mark the day you were born. Above the line, note events that happened to you or what you did (e.g., took your first steps). Below the line, mark world events or events that happened to others.

1949

	first steps		talked	
Birth	1	2	2½	3
		Father went to Korean War		Aunt Jill married Uncle Bob in Kansas

On the time line, place memories and facts about you, your family, and your friends. Keep your time line chart available and add to it during your recovery process. A time line can be very helpful in keeping perspective as well as reminding you about the sequence of events. Add pictures, objects, stories, and memories to your time line. If you fail to come up with any memories, fill in the chart with world and family events. These external events have relationship to events in your own life. Encyclopedias, almanacs, old magazines, museums, libraries, and antique stores that specialize in "your era" will be useful.

Toy Store Visit and Comic Books

Recall toys and games from your growing years. Many of the toys you played with are still popular; some are not. Spend an afternoon in the public library looking at the yearly update of World Book, Colliers, or Encyclopedia Britannica. Fad toys are frequently mentioned or pictured in these works. Before your toy store visit, complete the following exercise.

What toys and games were available when you were small?_____

_____

Whom did you play with? _____

Your age when you played with that person? _____

Did you have your own toys and games? Did you share most or all of them?

_____

Who gave you your toys and games? Who bought them? Did you have new ones? _____

Ask a family member to remember what toys and games you played with; write them down. _____

Trip To The Library

Go to the children's section of the local library and locate some books you read as a young child in elementary school.

Some old-time children's favorites:

Early years: Good Night Moon • Blueberries For Sal • Grimm's Fairy Tales • Bartholomew's Hats • The Cat In The Hat • The Velveteen Rabbit

Elementary/later years: National Velvet • Nancy Drew mysteries • Mr. Popper's Penguins • Mrs. Piggle Wiggle • The Hardy Boys

Take your notebook and complete the following:

Book	Who read it	Age when I read it	Feelings I have rereading	Memories and feelings
Example: Good Night Moon	Self	6	nostalgia	happy

School

This exercise includes several word associations. Do only one or two associations at a sitting. Take your time and free associate to any memories you have from school. Write each word listed below on a separate sheet of paper, then note any thoughts, images, smells, tastes, or body feelings you have after each of the listed word: Teachers • Classes • Projects • Parties • Assignments • Rules and Punishments • Most Embarrassing Moment • Principal • Songs/Music • Most Fun • Scouts • Most Dreaded Time • Recess • Parents Visiting • Other Kids • Work Habits • Games/ Athletics • After School Activities/Lessons • Grades/Report Cards • School Bus • Learning Problems

Grade	Memories	Feelings
Nursery School	_____	_____
1st Grade	_____	_____
2nd Grade	_____	_____
3rd Grade	_____	_____

Grade	Memories	Feelings
4th Grade	_____	_____
5th Grade	_____	_____
6th Grade	_____	_____
7th Grade	_____	_____
8th Grade	_____	_____
9th Grade	_____	_____
10th Grade	_____	_____
11thGrade	_____	_____
12th Grade	_____	_____

Leaving School: A Walk/Ride Home

How did you get to and from school? _____

What did you pass on your walk or ride home? _____

Did you walk/ride alone or with friends? _____

Did you talk to yourself? _____

What feelings did you have about returning home? _____

_____

Friend Map

Your age	Grade	Who were your friends?	How long did you keep them as friends?	Feelings/ memories about friends
0–4		_____	_____	_____
5–7	K–2	_____	_____	_____
8–10	3–5	_____	_____	_____
11–13	6–8	_____	_____	_____
13–15	9–10	_____	_____	_____
15+	11–12	_____	_____	_____

Who were the most popular kids? Why? Did you like them? _____

_____

Who were the least popular kids? Why? Did you like them? _____

_____

Childhood Clubs/Games/Secrets

Did you have sleepovers? At your house? At friends' houses? _____

Did anyone in school have secret clubs or get togethers? Did you go? Were you invited? _____

Did you start the clubs (were you a leader?) _____

Did you participate in varsity or intramural sports? In sandlot games? _____

Were you picked to participate? _____

Did you play games in which you picked on or teased others? _____

What secrets did you share with other kids? _____

What secrets did you not share with anyone? _____

Did your school life mirror your home life or was it different? If so, why?

_____

What feelings and sensations do you have as you answer these questions?

_____

Kids are often mean and cruel to each other: sisters and brothers play tricks on one another; friends say cruel things; and classmates sometimes develop a pecking order. Write your memories and feelings about these times in your notebook.

Do recent memories and feelings reflect your feelings of the past experience?_____

Songs/TV and Radio Shows

Locate materials that were current in your childhood: visit a library, golden oldies record store, or video store.

After your visit, answer the following questions. What songs did you hear? What TV or radio shows were available? Watch them, listen to them, and free associate to them. More memories and free associations will come if you share these tapes and records with trusted family members or friends of your own age.

	Records/TV Shows	My Associations, My Memories and Feelings
Pre-School (ages 0-5)	_____	_____
Elementary (ages 5-11)	_____	_____
Junior Years (ages 12-14)	_____	_____

High School/Belonging

All kids need to feel they belong, that they are part of a group. It does not matter whether the group is a family, school, friends, church, or even a neighborhood gang of kids. Some neglected children never find a place where they have that feeling of belonging. Did you feel that you belonged somewhere when you were growing up? Who or what gave you that feeling?

In early childhood? _____

Elementary school?_____

Middle school or junior high? _____

Senior high school? _____

Sometimes people create a sense of belonging in a fantasy world. There, they are members; they are needed and accepted. Write down some fantasies you may have had. How did/do those fantasies create a feeling of belonging? _____

_____

Remembering How You Were

Circle any of the words below that describe you as a young child. Put a star next to words that describe you as an adolescent.

ugly	happy	competitive	unhappy
lonely	rebel	scared	compliant
depressed	reasonable	happy-go-lucky	unreasonable
mischievous	disorganized	procrastinator	neat
adaptable	clean	scared of change	dirty
frightened	nervous	friendly	calm
predictable	angry	moody	poor attention
distractible	shy	embarrassed	organized
dumb	pretty	able to concentrate	crazy

How would you have liked to be? _____

_____

When you were a child, did you have any favorite older people? Aunts? Uncles? Grandparents? Neighbors?

_____

Name some people you looked forward to seeing.

Person	Ages when I knew them	Why I liked seeing them	People I know who remind me of them
_____	_____	_____	_____
_____	_____	_____	_____
_____	_____	_____	_____

Day-to-Day "Family" Life

1. *Pets*

Were you allowed to have a pet?_____

List any pets you or your family had:

Pet	Age you were	Memories of pet
_____	_____	_____
_____	_____	_____
_____	_____	_____

Who took care of the pet? Who fed it? _____

How was the pet treated? Where did it sleep? _____

Did you or someone else get angry at the pet? _____

Did you ever talk to the pet? What did you say? _____

Did anything bad happen to the pet? How did you feel? _____

_____

Put pet memories on your time line.

2. *Clothing*

Try another free association with the following words or terms:

Clothes _____

Dress code _____

Buying and choosing clothes _____

Sizes _____

Shopping _____

Hand-me-downs _____

Colors _____

Fabrics _____

Do you still think and feel the same thoughts and feelings about clothes?

_____

3. *Birthdays*

Try to remember each birthday you had (most people cannot, so just write down anything you remember about birthdays).

My Birthday Memories	Birthdays of Others in Family	My Feelings	My Age
_____	_____	_____	_____
_____	_____	_____	_____
_____	_____	_____	_____
_____	_____	_____	_____
_____	_____	_____	_____
_____	_____	_____	_____
_____	_____	_____	_____

Did you get the birthday gifts you wanted?_____

Did someone make birthday cakes?_____

Were they bought? _____

Were birthdays used for punishment? _____

Were they ignored?_____

Did some kids have more special birthdays than you did? _____

How do you feel about your birthday now?_____

4. *Halloween*

Were you allowed to celebrate Halloween? How?_____

What costumes did you wear?	**Who picked/made them?**	**Age/Grade**
_____	_____	_____
_____	_____	_____
_____	_____	_____

What themes did the costumes have?_____

_____

Halloween memories and feelings_____

_____

5. *Holidays*

List all the holidays you celebrated (excluding Halloween and birthdays).

Holiday	Who was there?	Where did it take place?	What food did you eat?	Incidents, problems/ Between whom?
_____	_____	_____	_____	_____
_____	_____	_____	_____	_____
_____	_____	_____	_____	_____
_____	_____	_____	_____	_____

6. *Rewards*

Do you remember any time when you did something well? Where was it? Home, school, church, camp? _____

What was said about it? _____

What words were used?_____

How did your family react? Did they compliment you? _____

Positive times	Age	What happened	Feelings and memories
With mother	_____	_____	_____
With father	_____	_____	_____
With other caretaker	_____	_____	_____

Positive times	Age	What happened	Feelings and memories
With relatives	_____	_____	_____
With brothers	_____	_____	_____
With sisters	_____	_____	_____

7. *My Summer Vacation*

At the beginning of each school year, you may have been asked to write an essay titled "My Summer Vacation." A boring assignment. What was really important to you or what you were really feeling was most likely left out. You may even have lied to make your summer look or sound different.

Choose a summer when you were between 6–16, and, using your notebook, write an essay: "My Summer Vacation." Think hard about activities, family members, alone times, games, boring times, and any trips. Write your feelings and experiences as they really were and or what you wished you could have shared when you were younger.

8. *Tasks I Learned*

	How/when did you learn	Who taught you	Memories
To use the telephone?	_____	_____	_____
To tie your shoes?	_____	_____	_____
To wash yourself/ take baths?	_____	_____	_____
To tell time?	_____	_____	_____
To cross the street?	_____	_____	_____
To dress yourself?	_____	_____	_____
To clean or cook?	_____	_____	_____
To share your toys?	_____	_____	_____
The alphabet?	_____	_____	_____
To drive?	_____	_____	_____
To write?	_____	_____	_____
To read?	_____	_____	_____
To ride a bike?	_____	_____	_____

9. *Fun*

In all families and in all growing-up situations, there are happy times and funny times. Either may happen only rarely or they may happen often. Write down anything that was fun or funny you can remember. _____

_____

Were any of the above times entertaining at the "expense" of someone else? How?_____

Do you have fun today as you did then? _____

_____

10. *Food*

From the stone age until the present, families and communities have organized themselves around food and eating. Mealtime—or its absence—is often symbolic of family life. Family structure around food and eating often points to power issues, feelings of emptiness, and issues about exclusion from family life. For some families, mealtime is a "together" time, a time when laughter and story telling take place. For others, it is a "together" time when family battles resume and are rehashed over and over without resolution. Some parents, for example, may use mealtimes to criticize or tyrannize their children. In some families, parents eat without children, and some families rely upon television or radio to connect them. In some families, children who are abused are left out of meals or are not allowed to eat at the table with the family. They may even be forced to eat over the sink or alone in their rooms. The following exercises will help evoke memories around food.

Remembering Mealtime

Remember mealtime in your house? _____

Who bought food? _____

Did your parents regularly eat food different from the kids'?_____

When? _____

Why? _____

How did that make you feel? _____

What foods were cooked/eaten regularly?

    Meats/poultry:_____

    Fish:_____

Casseroles:_____

Breakfast foods:_____

Fruits: _____

Vegetables:_____

Desserts: _____

Bread/pasta/rice:_____

Feelings

Did you have to eat everything? _____

Did you have a favorite food? _____

Was there enough food? _____

Were you forced to eat foods you did not like? _____

Were you forced to eat too much food? _____

What foods do you eat now when you are depressed and anxious? _____

_____

Were they foods you ate as a child? Did someone else in your family eat them when depressed or anxious? _____

On your time line, mark when you were over- or underweight. At the bottom of your time line page, list family members who were over- or underweight

The Family Meal

Draw a picture of the family meal when you were young (age 4-10). Be sure to note the age you were in the drawing.

Who sat where? _____

Who taught/talked about discipline? _____

How? _____

What topics were discussed? _____

Who talked about them? _____

Were wine, beer, or other alcoholic drinks served? _____

Who drank? When? (Before, during, or after dinner?) _____

_____

How did mealtimes end? (Did someone generally leave the table crying?)

_____

Were children allowed to talk? _____

Next, describe meals in your teenage years. How did they change? How do you eat meals now? Do you eat alone? _____

_____

Will you eat in a restaurant alone? Why or why not? _____

_____

11. Illness/Bedtime

	Memory	Feelings I have as I write this
Childhood illnesses/ accidents?	_____	_____
Were any caused by abuse or neglect?	_____	_____
Were you in the hospital?	_____	_____
Did you like going to bed?	_____	_____
Was bed used as punishment?	_____	_____
Were you read stories?	_____	_____
With whom did you sleep?	_____	_____
Until what age did you wet the bed?	_____	_____
How was this handled?	_____	_____
What did you wish for at bedtime?	_____	_____
Can you give it to yourself now?	_____	_____
Were you ever abused in your bed?	_____	_____
Did you have fears/dreams/ anxieties at night?	_____	_____
Do you have sleeping problems or night-time fears now?	_____	_____

	Memory	Feelings I have as I write this
How are they the same or different?	_____	_____
What did you think of before you fell asleep?	_____	_____

12. *What I Was Taught*

How I felt about:	My feelings	Who told me?	Age	What/how were you told?
God/religion	_____	_____	_____	_____
Where babies come from	_____	_____	_____	_____
Being male/ female and your gender role	_____	_____	_____	_____
When you walked, talked, ate by yourself, and other milestones	_____	_____	_____	_____
When you became a member of your family	_____	_____	_____	_____
Were you adopted?	_____	_____	_____	_____
Was your conception wanted? Planned? Unplanned and unavoided?	_____	_____	_____	_____
Family secrets you were told	_____	_____	_____	_____
Your parents' meeting	_____	_____	_____	_____
Your parents' marriage	_____	_____	_____	_____
Sex	_____	_____	_____	_____

13. Accidents

What happened in your family when something was broken or spilled?
What happened when there was a serious accident?

Memory/Incident	Feelings Then	Feelings Now
_____	_____	_____
_____	_____	_____
_____	_____	_____

14. Behavior Problems

Do you still have behavior patterns you started as a youngster? Examples
include:
- compulsive neatness
- angry outbursts
- fear of authority
- hurting yourself
- procrastination

_____

_____

_____

15. Fears

List the times in your life you have been most frightened:

Event/age what happened	Who was there/ should have been	How could this have been stopped/prevented?
_____	_____	_____
_____	_____	_____

Put these events on your time line.

What fears did you have? Examples: elevators, planes, electricity, germs:

Then	Age	Now
_____	_____	_____
_____	_____	_____
_____	_____	_____

How did you cope with these fears? _____

_____

16. Punishments

List all the punishments used in your family or at school. Think about what provoked or started the punishment. Did punishments just happen at times with no reason? Include threatened punishments that never occurred.

Punishment and/or physical abuse	To whom? Me/other family members/kids	Feelings /memory/ thoughts of it
_____	_____	_____
_____	_____	_____
_____	_____	_____
_____	_____	_____

What words, scoldings, or nonverbal threats were used when you were growing up? _____

_____

17. Getting Help for Abuse or Neglect

Try to think of ways you asked for help. Could anyone rescue you? Did you attempt to tell someone what was going on?

_____

_____

Did you feel as if you were marooned on an island?_____

Think back to those times. If you had sent a message in a bottle, what would you have written? _____

_____

Could you have convinced someone to come? _____

If you received a request from a child for help today, what would convince you help was needed? _____

_____

Do you remember losing hope? When? _____

_____

18. Embarrassment

List the occasions when you were most embarrassed as you grew up. Who was there? Could these occasions have been prevented? Did someone make fun of you?

Incident memories	Feelings then	Feelings as I write this
_____	_____	_____
_____	_____	_____
_____	_____	_____
_____	_____	_____

19. Sexuality

If you are concerned that others may see your book, write this section on a sheet of paper and keep it in a private place.

Briefly describe your first sexual experience _____

_____

_____

Did you want it to happen? _____

Was it an act of abuse? _____

At that time, who was allowed to touch you? Where? _____

_____

Who was not allowed to touch you, but did anyhow? _____

_____ _____

When you were small, who bathed you? Where did that person touch you? Did it feel safe or did it bother you?

_____

_____

What were you told about your body? _____

_____

_____

_____

20. *Verbal Abuse*

	Who said it?	How did I feel?
Have you ever been verbally abused?	_____	_____
Did anyone swear at you?	_____	_____
Call you names?	_____	_____
Say that you were stupid or dumb?	_____	_____
Say you were ugly?	_____	_____
That you were no good?	_____	_____
Other verbal abuse?	_____	_____
Did someone constantly yell at you or shame you?	_____	_____
Tell you that you were not wanted?	_____	_____
Were you ever forbidden to talk or speak?	_____	_____

21. *Abandonment and Neglect*

Were you ever left alone before you reached the age of

5? _____   10? _____   15? _____

Did people other than your parents take care of you? Were you threatened with abandonment? _____

Were you made to go to school with improper clothing (e.g., dirty or torn clothes) or inappropriate (e.g., flimsy jacket in icy, mid-winter temperature) clothing?

_____

Were meals prepared for you? _____

Were you ever shut up in a room for long periods of time? _____

Tied up and left? _____

Left in a dangerous or life-threatening situation? _____

_____

_____

22. *Other Memories*

If you were to write a movie of your life, what would the main scenes be about?

List them _____

_____

_____

_____

Who are the major characters? _____

_____

What are the most emotional scenes? The least emotional scenes? _____

_____

_____

23. *Putting the Memories Together*

Review this chapter when you are ready. Begin to tell your own story year-by-year; do not hurry. Take your time and write your own life story in your notebook.

10
Relationships and Sexuality

Good relationships with your family, friends, and intimate partner can be the most healing and stabilizing element in your life, and they are a cornerstone of recovery. In this chapter, you will first review your relationships, then look at difficulties you may encounter in establishing positive ones.

All relationships that promote growth and are positive forces in recovery from abuse share certain characteristics.

Principles of Positive Relationships:
1. *Be Accountable*—Be responsible and understand that what you do affects other people.
2. *Negotiate*—Be a person who can stand up for yourself while appreciating the value and beauty of compromise.
3. *Be Honest and Direct*—Abused people have been taught not to be honest or direct, and they have developed indirectness as a survival technique.
4. *Get Off the See-Saw*—Abused or neglected people often enter relationships that are abusive to others, to self, or both.
5. *Move to a Positive Stance*—Recognize positive aspects in the relationship, other life events, and circumstances.

In looking back on these relationships, you may notice that one person strongly reminds you of a family member or someone who was a force in your life. That person may have seemed quite different from anyone you had ever known. Then, you discovered qualities in that person that affected the way you viewed the person. You began to treat that person as you treated highly-valued persons in your past. This process—usually unconscious—is called transference, and it is the foundation of many relationships. Transference is a projection of feelings, thoughts, and impressions about one person to another.

Transference answers the question, "Who are you in my life?" We all make transferences in daily interactions and long-term adult relationships. Why? Our minds are associative: we recognize associations and then search for

225

more associations. We search for associations until we find something that fits or the pattern breaks.

Our minds work hard to make sense of patterns. We even take little associations to fit them into a larger pattern, and we tend to see others in terms of how they fit into our world view. How often, upon meeting, do we begin to speak and react to someone in a certain way because something about them reminds us of another person? Many patterns are set at an early age, just as our brains are developing pathways. If abuse occurs then, our brains are "taught" to recognize and respond to certain cues. Later, those cues will invariably elicit a similar response.

Transference reactions do not occur with everyone you know, but you can learn to recognize those occasions when strong transferences take place so that you can monitor or change your behavior. Transferences can also be reasonable and harmless responses, but it is always helpful to be aware of them.

A colleague dresses like your mother and has a similar voice.Your response to this woman may include some actions and feelings that formed parts of your response to your mother. Having recognized a pattern, you respond with a patterned behavioral response. That is how the mechanics of transference work: making patterns and then recognizing them.

Transferences can occur when you first meet someone. A handshake, a smile, a voice, or a mannerism may activate pattern recognition and you may "know" that a person is loving and caring. What you see in the person may relate to what you recognize—or what you want. In this way, many relationships turn out like previous ones: the brain recognizes a pattern and pursues it.

Transferences can be illogical. The woman at work who reminds you of your mother may have a completely different personality and worldview, despite those similaities of voice, dress, or manner. And everyone knows someone who has come home from work frustrated and angry and who then yells at the kids and kicks the dog. That is an example of transferring anger toward a boss onto family members and pets—subordinate beings who happen to be close.

Abuse, in a similar way, is confusion of "who you are in my life." Abusers transfer feelings and thoughts for someone else onto their victims. Frequently, anger at a partner or close friend is really unchecked transference made manifest. Left unacknowledged, it can destroy a positive relationship.

If any current relationship seems abusive, you are either choosing people similar to your abusers, or you are transferring negative thoughts, feelings, and fantasies from previous relationships.

People make transferences to another person, to a place, or to an object.

Similarities in Relationships

Person	List some qualities or what they look like	Family members who have similar characteristics
1. _____	_____	_____
2. _____	_____	_____
3. _____	_____	_____
4. _____	_____	_____
5. _____	_____	_____
6. _____	_____	_____

Has your response to those people in your past been similar to your response to people in your life now? _____

Does some family member have these qualities or looks? _____

_____

It is likely that you have invested one or more persons on your list with some kind of transference. Whom? _____

What would you like to get from that relationship? _____

What would you like to change in that relationship? _____

Exploring Transferences

Transferences—particularly negative ones—are often inconsistent. A split or ambivalent transference may flip-flop, sometimes on the slightest provocation. Split transferences can closely resemble relationships surrounding abuse and incest. Separating present emotions from past feelings about the abusive relationship can create a feeling of ambivalence. Ambivalent feelings do not necessarily mean that the person you currently relate to is not healthy; rather, ambivalence indicates something in the interaction is affected by transference.

Think of relationships in which you have felt ambivalent.

With whom have you had those relationships? _____

_____

What was the beginning of those relationships like? _____

_____

What was the ending of those relationships like? _____

_____

Could those relationships involve transferences? From whom? _____

_____

Do you now have any relationships affected by transferences? _____

_____

What past relationships do they mirror? _____

_____

It is not always easy to discontinue the transference process. You can, however, change your reactions and relationship patterns. Read on.

Stopping Transferences

To end a transference to another person, you can take several steps:
1. Think about the transference. Write down specific behaviors and characteristics of the person from whom the transference is being made.
2. List behaviors you find troublesome. Would they trouble most people?
3. Identify your contribution to the transference. Are your behaviors and thought patterns similar to those of the person from whom you are transferring?
4. Change old behaviors if you can. Modify the way you act toward the person to whom you are making the transference.
5. Visualize the person. See the person doing or saying something that is contrary to the transference.
6. List ways the person is different from the person in your past. Remind yourself of these differences before any interaction.

If others make a transference to you, remember that it is usually an unconscious process. Even healthy people make transferences (e.g., a man who calls his daughter by his sister's name). Most people are unaware of making transferences.

You can take several measures that will help you change a person's transference to you:
1. Look for the behaviors that engender a particular reaction.
2. If you can, modify these behaviors.
3. Practice some of the "pacing" methods outlined on pages 178–180. Practice will help you be sensitive to other persons' needs.

4. Consider asking if you remind the person of someone.
5. Ask how you might change the person's view of you.
6. Do not let the person abuse you or put you on a pedestal. Doing either will only continue the transference.
7. Appreciate the person's efforts to change. Changes take time.

Some people make psychotic transferences, and they are unlikely to respond to rational discussion. Psychotic transferences can be threatening. If you feel you might be the object of such a potentially dangerous transference, immediately seek professional advice on how to handle it.

Finding Transferences

Think of people in your family or someone else's that you know well.

Was anyone named after someone living or dead? _____

_____

Were nicknames used in the family? _____

Were these names based on transferences? _____

_____

Expectations and Transferences

Think of a time when you held a first impression or stereotype of someone. Then think of your later impression of that person. How accurate were you?

	First impression/ stereotype	As I later knew them
Person 1	_____	_____
Person 2	_____	_____
Person 3	_____	_____

How did your transferences and expectations influence your feelings and actions toward them?

_____

What were your fantasies, good or bad, about the other person?

_____

Were your fantasies related to your behavior toward the other person?

_____

Did you overcome or change your reaction?

_____

Keep transferences in mind when talking about intimate relationships. If you are scanning a group of people and say, "They aren't my type," what are you really saying? Are you looking for a certain person to play a part in a complicated transference? Try to identify your "type."

Your Type

What is your "type?" What characteristics are in your "type?" _____

_____

Are these characteristics the same as the abuser's? _____

When you were growing up, who had these characteristics? _____

When you were younger, you may have fantasized a "rescuer," a kind person who was the polar opposite of the abuser. You may have held onto a "fantasy transference" from that time, searching for your type in reaction to the abuse.

Are any of your characteristics a product of fantasy transference? _____

_____

Which characteristics? _____

_____

Think about people or types whom you have not considered for friends or intimates. What about them does not interest you?

_____

Are there some indications that a relationship with them would be positive?

_____

Dr. George Weinberg and Dianne Rowe offer more valuable information on transference in their book, *The Projection Principle*.

Make a plan for meeting a new friend, companion, or partner. Write your plan.

_____

_____

_____

Positivity and Relationships

Another way to change old patterns and reduce transferences in relationships is to become more positive and find ways to enhance your relationships. There are times when all of us harp on others, but, remember: negative thoughts will keep your mind looking for defects and maintain an abusive, nongrowth pattern.

Becoming positive does not mean looking at abuse or hurt in a positive way: that would be denial and only serve to continue the abuse. Being positive means:

- trying to find good both in others and in situations;
- looking at past relationships and not seeing them as all or nothing, good or bad, but as contributors to your learning and growth;
- understanding that a positive outlook does not call for reframing abuse as a positive or even as a learning experience.

By itself, abuse was not a positive experience. How you handle recovery from abuse can be both. Developing a positive frame of mind can open yourself to present and future possibilities. It is a way of opening yourself to other people and new experiences that are not connected to the abuse experience.

Learning from Relationships

Think of five relationships (friendships or intimate relationships) that were sad or painful.

	Relationship	Description	What I learned	How I grew from it
1.				
2.				
3.				
4.				
5.				

Negative Thought Patterns

A positive thought process can change your way of reacting and relating to others. Negative people attract negative people; positive people are likely to find positive people. Think about people you know who are "up" people.

Who are they?_____

How do you react to them? _____

How do others react to them? _____

Day-to-day negative thought patterns will keep you stuck in your relation-ships. Think of your more frequent negative thoughts. Write them down. (Examples: I'll never find anyone wholesome. I always get myself into the same situation.)

Situation	Logical Thought
_____	_____
_____	_____
_____	_____
_____	_____
_____	_____
_____	_____

For each thought, find a reason why it is not fact. If you have trouble, ask friends to help. Stop yourself each time you think negative thoughts, replac-ing a negative thought with a positive one. Remember, thinking can become mired in negative patterns.

Are these negative patterns the same as the abuser's? _____

Which family members have had successful, loving relationships? _____

_____

Who has had ambivalent, stormy relationships? _____

_____

Who has had angry, abusive relationships? _____

_____

Who of these people have been your models? _____

How do your relationships reflect these models? _____

What new positive models would you like to adopt? _____

_____

Once you become rutted in negative thinking, the only way to change is to revise what you think about.

Patterns of Relating and Communicating

As you explore different ways of relating to people and change your thoughts and communication patterns to become more positive, you will be able to look at family relationships and select what you want from them and what you want to change in the patterns you learned.

The more emotional distance you have from family relationships, the more you will be able to look at them realistically and learn from them. It is usually possible to gain perspective on how brothers, sisters, and cousins have managed their friendships and intimate relationships. Think about the kind of adult relationships your brothers, sisters, and cousins have.

What kind of friends do they have?_____

_____

Are they long-term friendships?_____

_____

As you look at your relatives, think about the communication styles in your family. These have served as road maps for modes of relating. Think about the abuser in your family. How did that person communicate in intimate relationships?

_____

Triangles and Fusion

Triangles form when a person in an intimate relationship becomes more focused on something or someone else to the detriment of the relationship. Triangles are formed to meet needs by engaging a third person or activity. Examples of triangles:
- work becomes more important than the relationship
- a child becomes allied with one parent
- an affair or close friend replaces the intimate partner

In fused relationships, feelings, thoughts, or actions of the partners virtually become one. We speak of people in fused relationships as "joined at the hip." Although these relationships can last, they make individual growth difficult, and outsiders feel as if they are relating to a team, not to individuals.

What relationships in your family became triangled?_____

_____

_____

How did they affect you? _____

How did they affect others? _____

_____

Have you been involved in an adult triangle? _____

_____

How did forming the triangle affect your primary relationship?_____

_____

Which relationships in your family were fused? _____

_____

How did they affect you?_____

_____

How did they affect others? _____

_____

Have adult relationships been fused?_____

_____

How did this affect you? _____

_____

How did this affect others? _____

_____

Identification in Relationships

Some relationships seem to replicate past relationships. Replication is usually a form of identification in which one member of a relationship takes on characteristics of someone from the past. Intentionally or not, you may have incorporated so much of what you, as a child, saw and heard from the abuser that you now act in your adult relationships much the way he or she did. Think of how you act in adult relationships. Are those ways similar to the abuser's or to the ways of other adults in your family?

_____

_____

_____

Have your tried to change any ways of acting?_____

_____

What changes would you want to make in this identification?_____

_____

Doing something different is a way to change an identification pattern. Try changing what you say or do. List ideas on how you can change your pattern identification.

_____

_____

_____

Ask friends for their ideas. What do they think might be different and unexpected for you?_____

Make a plan, selecting the best idea for making a change from the behaviors that represent your old pattern of identification.

Behavior	Change idea
_____	_____
_____	_____
_____	_____

Are there ways in which you act like the abuser in your relationships?

_____

Are there ways you act like the partner of the abuser in your relationship?

_____

What could you do that might help you change those patterns? _____

_____

Allocation of Resources

Money, space, and time are resources that most adults need to factor into a relationship. Only rarely do these issues fail to play major roles. How you and those close to you allocate these resources reflects the nature of your relationship. Think of relationships you saw as you were growing up. How were resources allocated between the partners?

Money_____

Space_____

Time_____

Were there conflicts around any of the resources? _____

In your adult relationships, how have you or your close and intimate partners and friends allocated these resources?_____
_____

List patterns that are the same as those you grew up with._____
_____

List patterns that are different from those you grew up with._____
_____

Who made decisions about these resources? _____

Then? _____

Now? _____

Would you like to change the allocation of money, space, and time in your relationships?_____

What steps can you take to make those changes?_____
_____

Relationship Rules

Every relationship has a set of rules, spoken or implied, that govern it. Many rules reflect gender roles (what "men" are "supposed" to do, and what "women" are "supposed" to do). Same-sex relationships are not exempt from "rules," but they are played out differently. In your notebook, write down as many "rules" as you can remember from your childhood. Keep a running list of rules and add to it as you remember more.

Example:
- Men put out the garbage
- Women set the table
- Kiss each other at night, even if you are angry.

What rules have you continued in your adult relationships? _____
_____
_____

What relationship rules did the abuser have? _____

_____

_____

Are these rules reflected in your behavior or your close friends' or partner's?

_____

Which rules do you want to change? _____

_____

Which rules have worked for you? _____

_____

Which have not? _____

_____

Conflict Resolution

Most families that experienced abuse have little if any ability for conflict resolution. Seldom in these families is there accountability, negotiation, directness, or honesty. Typically present, however, are volcanic eruptions of anger. In some families where there is sexual abuse or neglect, an overall calm might seem to prevail, but there is often an undercurrent of anger, disappointment, and violence.

Failure to resolve conflict means that issues can fester for years or never go away. In his book, *When Caring Is Not Enough*, David Augsburger defines unfair fighting techniques that continue conflict. Some of these techniques may temporarily stop a disagreement or conflict, but they do not end it. To the contrary, they may even initiate a cycle difficult to end. In the list below, check the techniques used by the abuser, others in your family, your partner, and yourself.

Unfair Fighting Techniques*

	Used by abuser	Used in family	I use	My partner uses
Catching the other off guard	❑	❑	❑	❑
Stepping up anxiety through timing, place	❑	❑	❑	❑
Always yielding or being a martyr	❑	❑	❑	❑

*Adapted from Augsburger, David. (1983). *When caring is not enough: Resolving conflicts through fair fighting*. Ventura, Calif.: Regal Books.

	Used by abuser	Used in family	I use	My partner uses
Being unclear, rambling, or purposefully confusing	❏	❏	❏	❏
Generalizing, exaggerating	❏	❏	❏	❏
Intellectualizing, analyzing, and questioning	❏	❏	❏	❏
Activity, ambivalence	❏	❏	❏	❏
Hiding anger or other feelings	❏	❏	❏	❏
Using rumors or "they said"	❏	❏	❏	❏
Blaming or shaming	❏	❏	❏	❏
Playing "Who's right?"	❏	❏	❏	❏
Walking out or clamming up	❏	❏	❏	❏
Being sarcastic	❏	❏	❏	❏
Pitting people against each other ("Let's have you and them fight.")	❏	❏	❏	❏
Attacking or undermining someone's self-esteem	❏	❏	❏	❏
Controlling by threat or manipulation	❏	❏	❏	❏
Using bribes to pacify the other person	❏	❏	❏	❏
Postponing or delaying	❏	❏	❏	❏
Mind-reading but not listening	❏	❏	❏	❏
Using "you" instead of "I"	❏	❏	❏	❏
Going for the jugular	❏	❏	❏	❏
Demanding or being jealous	❏	❏	❏	❏

For each of the techniques you use, think of a positive, fair conflict substitute.

Conflict Resolution

Poor method   Positive method

_____   _____

_____   _____

Poor method	Positive method

In your notebook, write down word for word the dialog of a recent conflict.

Next change what you said into fair negotiation, accountability, honesty, and directness.

How do the changes affect the discussion? _____

As with any other behavior skill, conflict resolution takes practice and time. To make conflict resolution last, make the changes slowly and systematically. Begin working with what is easiest to change, and be sure to let others know what you are doing to bring about changes. Ask those close to you for feedback.

Dissociation in Relationships

Relationships in which one person has experienced abuse may be troubled by transference and dissociation. Dissociation can work in two ways: it enables a person to relate positively, without feeling pain from the abuse; or to suppress the memory of angry and cruel words or actions.

You may have been the recipient of dissociated words or acts while you were young, but you may not have remembered what happened. Dissociation that previously allowed positive interaction with others may later dissipate as you become more aware of your feelings. People close to you may not understand why you are becoming aware of anger, sadness, and disappointment. Let others know that you are taking responsibility for your behavior, even if you do not feel that the behavior belongs to you.

Other Pitfalls in Relationships

Three common relationship pitfalls for abused people are:
- Fear of being alone
- Choosing a beauty, but not seeing the beast
- Feeling sorry for the other

Fear of Being Alone

If you had a family history of neglect or fear of being alone, loneliness may lead you into making poor relationship choices simply to avoid being by yourself. It seems better to some to continue putting up with abusive behavior than feeling the pain of loneliness. If you find being alone

terrifying, think how to increase your interaction with people so you avoid making desperate choices. Some ways to deal with the fear of being alone:
- Live with friends or relatives whom you like
- Become active in community organizations
- Join socially-oriented groups, such a hobby club, a church group, or an outdoor organization
- Get a pet
- Plan activities or short trips with others at which you can meet people
- Join a sports and health club
- Volunteer for a political organization or candidate.

Participation in any of these activities will reduce your immediate need to jump into an unhealthy relationship to avoid loneliness.

Choosing a Beauty and Not Seeing the Beast

It is important to understand that it is impossible to experience trauma and abuse but not be angry. Suppose, however, that you meet someone who has been abused and now appears to have life put together—to have come through abuse or trauma without anger. Remember, it is not possible. If things fit together too well, it is wise to look deeper into that other person who has experienced abuse and trauma. There is always a "beast" (of hidden anger) behind the beauty. Acknowledgment of anger is important to anyone seeking to become an integrated person. Be careful of people you meet who seem too good to be true. They probably are.

Feeling Sorry for the Other

It is not unusual for persons to stay in an abusive or unsatisfactory relationship because they feel sorry for or pity the partner. Even while the person is abusing you, you might rationalize staying because "the person needs you." If you are doing anything like that, remember that you are meeting that person's sick needs at the expense of your own growth. Staying with someone who is attempting to avoid reality hampers both that person and yourself.

A good relationship is also a good friendship. Some of the most important characteristics of friendship are:
- Is my partner there for me? Can my partner catch me if I fall while pursuing my need for self-esteem?
- Will my partner honestly talk about feelings without being hurtful?
- Can my partner help me feel safe? Will my partner take risks (e.g., by refusing to let me drive after I've been drinking) for my safety?
- Will my partner look out for my interests? How far will my partner go to avoid hurting me?

- Does my partner have a caring-curiosity about my life?
- Is my partner really interested in what I do, feel, or think?
- Will my partner go out of the way for me? How does my partner "give" of emotions, time, energy, and interests to me?

Choosing Relationships

Look at the above criteria. How have you chosen relationships? _____

_____

In your notebook, write down under each category what happened in previous relationships, then contract with yourself to make positive choices, such as:

- Paying attention to the first meeting and confronting uncomfortable "gut" feelings and power dynamics.
- Trusting your friends for feedback.
- Not expecting change.
- Acknowledging your fantasies.
- Choosing someone to be a friend.
- What clues have you gotten about why relationships haven't worked?

If you are not in a satisfactory relationship, contract with yourself how you will handle future relationships. Write your ideas in your notebook.

Check out your ideas with friends. Can they help you? _____

Communication in Relationships

Most successful relationships have special words, phrases, and signals. These help people feel close and attached, as well as reflect the nature of the relationship. Sometimes, it is necessary to change the language of how people talk to and about each other. Think of relationships you have had and relationships you saw when you were growing up. What words, phrases, and signals did you observe?_____

_____

How did those words or signals reflect what was happening in the relationship? _____

What words and signals do you use in your relationship? _____

_____

Do they reflect the state of the relationship? _____

What words and signals would you like to keep or change? _____

_____

Could words and signals increase your connectedness to others? _____

_____

Developing Rituals

Rituals hold people together by establishing a pattern, a sense of consistency, and belonging. Past rituals may have seemed negative or meaningless, particularly if any aspect of the abuse was repetitive or connected to rituals and events. You may also associate meaningless ritual with long religious services or particular events that you were pressured to attend. Rituals—if they have meaning for you and if you participate in developing them—can be a binding force in a relationship, and they can increase a sense of connectedness to others.

What rituals did you like when you were a child? _____

_____

Do you have any rituals in your life now? _____

_____

Which rituals would you like to keep? _____

_____

Think about developing some rituals for the following:
  • Holidays—civil, popular, or religious
  • Birthdays
  • Coming home after a long separation
  • Getting together for special occasions with friends

Plan to develop some rituals and feel free to drop ones you do not like or that do not work well for you.

Valuing and Cherishing Behaviors

Part of what makes any close relationship work is the ability to value and cherish the other person. Valuing and cherishing can only be done by giving in some manner to the other person. Giving does not mean things or activities that cost money or take a lot of time. Giving (oftentimes the best of gifts) can take the form of small actions, e.g., bringing in the newspaper or arranging a birthday party.

Giving on a regular basis is important to a relationship. Ask two friends and your partner what you could do to make them feel cared for, valued, and cherished. List them here:

Friend　　　　　　　　Friend　　　　　　　　Partner

_____　　_____　　_____

_____　　_____　　_____

_____　　_____　　_____

_____　　_____　　_____

_____　　_____　　_____

Choose one or two acts a week and do them for these people you care about. What happens?

_____

_____

Make a list of things you like that others do for you. Tell them what they are. Write them below.

_____

_____

Developing Sexuality

All abuse, even emotional abuse, affects how you feel about your body. Physical and sexual abuse are direct assaults on your body. Neglect—of the body or the person—and emotional abuse affect how you feel about yourself. Those feelings about yourself will show in your body, and, therefore, project your sense of self as a sexual person. Each kind of abuse affects the kind of sexually responding human being you are. Resolving your guilt, shame, embarrassment, and poor sexual- and self-image is one of the most difficult tasks in recovering from the abuse. You may experience many different feelings. Examples of some feelings common to abused people are:

  •I have no right to pleasure
  •Anyone can have access to my body
  •I am too disgusting to touch
  •The only part of me that is any good is my sexuality
  •I have been spoiled, ruined. No one will want me
  •I can only get sexual pleasure from pain or fantasies of pain
  •The only way I can feel alive is when someone touches me sexually.

These are only examples of a wide range of feelings that abused people may have about sexuality. To help you get in touch with your feelings about sexuality, complete the following statements. Do not try to think out your answers; just write the first response that comes into your mind.

Feelings About Sexuality

I first began sexual acts at age _____

Love means _____

Dating means _____

Masturbation is _____

My body _____

When someone touches me _____

Pleasure is _____

Men are _____

Women are _____

Sexual pleasure means _____

My fears of sex are _____

Touch is _____

I like _____

My fantasies _____

Affection is _____

Orgasm _____

I am aroused _____

What did you learn from completing the sentences above? _____

_____

What areas do you most want to work on? _____

_____

What areas are most uncomfortable? _____

_____

Are there areas of sexuality that you feel a need to say "No" to? _____

_____

How can you say "No" so that you feel safe and others know you mean it?

_____

Becoming positive about your sexuality means developing a strong sense of self-acceptance and learning to like your body. A positive attitude may be difficult to have because the abuse, in effect, denied your existence, shamed you, used you to help someone else feel powerful, or made you an extension of someone else. Becoming comfortable with your own sexuality is a process, and it is best taken step-by-step. The first step is to define areas of discomfort so that you can work on one area at a time.

Comfort and Discomfort

For each of the following words or phrases, put a mark in the appropriate column:

	Comfortable	Uncomfortable
Hugging	❏	❏
Being held	❏	❏
Being kissed on your mouth	❏	❏
Being kissed in your mouth	❏	❏
Being touched on your face	❏	❏
Being touched on your hands or legs	❏	❏
Being kissed on your hair/head	❏	❏
Being touched on your chest or breast	❏	❏
Being touched on your stomach	❏	❏
Taking a bath or shaving with your partner	❏	❏
Being touched on your genitals	❏	❏
Being touched on your back	❏	❏
Being touched on your buttocks	❏	❏
Insertion of a finger, penis, or toy	❏	❏
Your partner becoming excited	❏	❏
Your becoming excited	❏	❏
Your partner's orgasm	❏	❏
Your orgasm	❏	❏
Being touched on your feet	❏	❏

	Comfortable	Uncomfortable
Oral sex	❏	❏
Mutual masturbation	❏	❏
Masturbation	❏	❏

What is your favorite sexual position? _____

Which words or statements above do you feel most comfortable with?

_____

Least comfortable?_____

_____

As your review these, what memories come back to you? _____

_____

Memories of the abuse _____

_____

Memories of seeing others being sexual _____

_____

Memories of your own sexual experiences _____

_____

   Three things that contribute to sexual difficulties for abused people are memories, flashbacks, and fantasies. Memories and flashbacks may occur before, during, and after sexual contact. They can be triggered by a variety of stimuli.

   Not all the triggers of sexual discomfort are related to sexual abuse. Some triggers may directly remind one about experiences of physical or emotional abuse and neglect. But because sexuality is a human process related to human feelings, memories of physical and emotional abuse or neglect may be stirred by these triggers and subconsciously interfere with sexual activity. If you experience difficulty in being sexual, try to clarify the sequence of the actions and words as they happen. Talk about them with your partner. Discuss what is happening, then make changes in the environment, sequence, or words and actions.

   Try being sexual in a different, less intense way until the triggers no longer interfere. Most important, keep talking about your feelings and memories to your partner and those close to you with whom you feel safe.

Fantasies

Fantasies are the other area that can get in the way of being sexual. Some fantasies can enhance sexuality, but generally, fantasies that remind you of past abuse get in the way of closeness and sexuality, even if the fantasy results in orgasm. Sometimes, a nonsexual fantasy that recreates the abuse— a memory or fantasy of being beaten by a parent—can stimulate a sexual response or orgasm. The problem with fantasy is that it also recreates guilt and shame.

If your fantasies are disturbing you, you can begin to change them by focusing on other images. The new images might not be as sexually exciting, but creating new images will help you respond to stimuli free of guilt, shame, or memories of abuse.

Positive Fantasies

Write down images, thoughts, smells, and other stimuli that you might find exciting and pleasurable.

_____

_____

How can you use these fantasies in your sexuality?

_____

_____

Touch

Becoming comfortable with intimate touch generally poses some difficulty for everyone, even those who come from families where there has been no abuse. Many people say they are comfortable with sex, but intimate, close touch is usually hard to sustain. As a society, we are used to quick fixes, and sexuality is no exception. A paradox for people who have experienced abuse is that even though genital sexuality may be difficult, nonsexual touching—e.g., hugging, bathing or showering together—may be easier than they are for people who have no difficulty with sex.

As you become more comfortable with your own sexuality, increasing your self-touch and touching your partner will make it easier for you to connect and increase intimacy.Creating an environment where touching is safe is important. The bedroom may feel like the least safe place. A walk in the woods or on a beach, a shared bath, or even quiet time in your living room might feel safest. Think about the kind of environment that makes you feel most safe.

Write down your thoughts:

_____

_____

Self-touch may help you become open to someone else's touch. Some exercises in the relaxation chapter can help you become intimate with yourself. Meditation and breathing exercises will help develop increased body awareness. Masturbation and sexual self-pleasuring take time and focused energy, but in them you can begin with touches that feel comfortable, gradually working up to what feels least comfortable or most scary.

If you have dissociation or multiple personality, you may need to work with each personality or part of you, so that each can become comfortable and feel safe. Likewise, if you work with a partner, that person will need to understand the parts and personalities that are safe with touch and parts and personalities that are frightened.

Feelings I Had—What Will Be Safe?*

1. Select a part of your body that feels safe—perhaps hands or legs. Tell your partner how you want to be touched. Let yourself be touched. Now, after checking with your partner, touch him or her in the same way you were touched.

Feeling _____

_____

2. Allowing some space between the two of you, stand back-to-back with your partner. Close your eyes and allow yourself to fall backwards, allowing your partner to fall backwards.

Feeling _____

_____

3. Play a version of "Simon Says." Say to your partner, "Simon says, "Touch my wrist," or "Simon says, "Stroke my hand." You can maintain control over the touch that way. Ask your partner to switch roles with you.

Feeling _____

_____

_____

* Some of the following touch exercises can be done with friends or intimate partners. Other touch exercises are meant to be done only with intimate partners. After each part of the exercise, write down your feelings.

4. Experiment with different kinds of hugging. Discuss different ways you want to be hugged and let your partner hug you. Write down your feeling.

Feeling _____

_____

5. Let your partner give you a nonsexual massage. Before beginning, be clear on how and where you want to be touched, how you will let your partner know what you feel, when you want to stop, and any other information you want to give. Then, after determining what your partner wants, give your partner a massage.

Feeling _____

_____

6. Try touching each other in the bathtub or a shower. Light candles and put on music. Discuss any discomfort you might have before beginning.

Feeling _____

_____

7. When you feel ready, have your partner touch you in a sexual manner. Put your hand on top of your partner's and gently guide your partner's touch where and how you want.

Feeling _____

_____

If you go through a period where sexuality is extremely difficult, touching and snuggling may be satisfying to both you and your partner as well as alleviate feelings of frustration your partner may have. Keep trying actions that feel safe. Gradually increase the intensity and level of sexual activity. Most important, do not give up. Strike a balance between saying "No" and feeling like you are giving in. Keep a channel open in which to continue working toward mutually satisfying sexual activity.

Some couples have deepened their sexual bond by reading books on intimacy and body work together, discussing them, and then working on suggested exercises. If you never seem to find the time, make appointments with each other. Begin those times doing only what feels safe.

If you have developed a high degree of sexual activity as a way of coping with abuse, you may want to define the difference between intimacy and sexuality. Sexuality may be a way you connect with some people, but it may not bring long-lasting closeness. When you begin to feel more closely connected, you may also feel more frightened and vulnerable. Those feelings may be indicators of how you use your sexuality to keep people away.

How have I used sexuality to deny my feelings? _____

_____

How have I used sexuality to prevent intimacy with someone else? _____

_____

How does sexuality affect my anxiety level? _____

_____

Does sexuality make me feel powerful? _____

Do I connect sexuality and violence? _____

What fantasies do I have that disturb me? _____

_____

Does being sexual make me feel alive? _____

What do you feel when you can't get your sexual needs met? _____

_____

Does my use of sexuality mirror the abuse, incest, or neglect I experienced?

_____

If you feel you have used sexuality as a defensive pattern or as a way to avoid intimacy, consider making changes in the frequency, environment, speed, and method of sexual contact. If you feel you are compulsively sexual or sexuality acts on you like a drug, find a 12-Step group (e.g., Sex and Love Addicts Anonymous) and attend regularly.

Gender

Gender identification is simply what sex you feel you are. In our Western culture, identifying as male or female is important. Frequently in familial abuse, one member's gender identification has become confused. Parents who wished for a child of the opposite sex may have made that known. They may even have dressed a child as the opposite sex, called that child by names of the opposite sex, or made the child do things customary for the other sex.

Your gender identification is who you feel you are inside. For children who have been abused, gender identification may be confusing at times. Further, if you dissociate or have multiple personalty, a "part" of you may have an opposite sex identification. It is most important that you try to accept all male and female parts as worthwhile components of your being.

Try to understand that what you might view as "male" or "female" is defined by society—and society's ideas change with time.

Gender Identification

Find a place where you feel comfortable, relaxed, safe, and unhurried. Think back on all the activities, feelings, thoughts, and language you used to have about sexuality. Do your memories make you feel more male or more female?

		Male	Female
Activities	_____	❏	❏
	_____	❏	❏
	_____	❏	❏
Feelings	_____	❏	❏
	_____	❏	❏
	_____	❏	❏
Thoughts	_____	❏	❏
	_____	❏	❏
	_____	❏	❏
Language	_____	❏	❏
	_____	❏	❏
	_____	❏	❏

What do you find comfortable? _____

_____

What do you find uncomfortable? _____

_____

What did your family and teachers tell you about being male or female?

_____

Do you feel the abuse would have been different if you had been the other sex?_____

_____

Has abuse changed your feeling about your gender? _____

Do you like being the sex you are? _____

Do you ever fantasize being the opposite sex while having sex with a partner?_____ _____

How can you make yourself feel more comfortable with who you are?

_____

Talk to friends. How did they become comfortable with their gender identification? _____

_____

Sexual Identity

Sexual identity is the category in which you place yourself as an intimate sexual person—homosexual, bisexual, or heterosexual. There is a popular belief that sexual abuse changes a person's sexual identity. There has been no clear research demonstrating how sexual identification comes about, nor is there any research as to whether sexual identification is the definite result of learning, environment, genetics, or any combination of these.

Being abused by someone of the opposite or same sex can create identity confusion for some people who recognize that they did receive pleasure-able physical feeling from an abusive act. This is true for both heterosexuals and homosexuals. Confused people are usually unaware of Alfred Kinsey's suggestion that all of us have the potential of acting bisexually. However, no one easily moves from one category to another. It often happens that many people are abused by family members because their family perceives or knows them as homosexual. It is important for your comfort with yourself and others to feel good about who you are, and that you not view one sexual identification as better or worse than another.

You may find your sexual identity changing as you work through abuse experiences. Feeling more free to take on a homosexual, heterosexual, or bisexual identity can be a major way of making an "I" statement, as well as of increasing your self-esteem and sense of personal power.

What do you feel your sexual identity is? _____

Do you believe that your abuse experience is related to your sexual identity?

_____

How does your current life help or hinder your sense of peace about your sexual identity? _____

_____

In what ways? _____

_____

What can you do to help make yourself feel more positive about your sexual identify? _____

_____

Putting It All Together

1. To chart your progress around touch and sexuality, *have a friend draw the outline of your body on a large piece of paper* (shelf paper or the white side of wrapping paper is best). Tape the outline to the back of a door. Then, as you grow comfortable with touch and pleasure on various areas of your body, color in those parts. As you color in different parts, you will gain a sense of integration and oneness with yourself.

2. *Write sexuality mantras.* Say them regularly. *Example:* I can enjoy my body. I want to let some others be close to me.

3. *Be clear about your "no" areas.* It is okay to say no regarding any area, but be sure to re-evaluate your "no" areas as you become more comfortable with your sexuality.

4. As you become comfortable with yourself as an attractive person, *choose clothes and colors that make you look your best.* If you are unsure of your ensemble, photograph yourself wearing it before you purchase it and ask your friends' opinion, or take someone along when you shop.

5. *Visualize yourself enjoying sex.* If this is frightening, visualize yourself feeling comfortable with touch a little bit at a time. Keep working with an image until you feel that you are enjoying it.

6. *Draw a picture of yourself as a person who is comfortable with sexuality.* Hang it up. Keep the image in your mind. Show the drawing to someone you trust.

How to Keep an Intimate Relationship Alive

Keeping a relationship alive takes constant, consistent work. Abusive families seldom have a working model for healthy relationships, and often, in their struggle to gain such relationships, they did not achieve either closeness or intimacy.

One good way to look at a relationship is to see it as a third person, with its own needs, joys, and idiosyncrasies. A relationship is something that each person needs to give to, pay attention to, and nurture. Just as children and adults will not remain healthy if they are neglected, a relationship will not remain healthy without care and attention.

Below are 16 ways that help keep an existing relationship healthy:
1. Work hard at fair fighting and conflict resolution.
2. Develop and continue caring and loving behaviors: do things for the other person that make the person feel special.
3. Keep anger in check, especially when it is not appropriate to the situation.
4. Develop language specific to the culture of your relationship. This means making language changes that reflect how you both want your relationship to be (such as use of nonsexist language or adding personal, loving phrases).
5. Ask yourself how important little annoyances are, then let them go.
6. Do what you can to be good friends as well as lovers.
7. Make regular times to talk and share with each other in an honest, direct manner.
8. Allocate money, space, and time in a manner that is fair to both.
9. Do not involve third persons in difficult matters.
10. Be the best person you can be and continue to nurture your own personal growth.
11. Develop rules and boundaries for your relationship.
12. Develop sexual activities that make both of you feel safe and satisfied.
13. Develop a sense of spiritual togetherness and give to others who are in need.
14. Develop special rituals together.
15. Stay positive.
16. Allow the other person to grow and develop.

Study these 16 ways. What can you strengthen or use to keep your relationship strong? _____

_____

What areas can you improve? _____

_____

Whom do you know whose relationship has these qualities? _____

_____

Talk with them. Ask them how they are able to maintain a strong, healthy relationship. Ask them to give you their best advice on how to maintain positive relationships. Write down advice that seems to fit you._____

_____

_____

What about their advice makes sense? What do you want to try? _____

_____

_____

How will you know if your relationship is working? What would be positive signs?_____

_____

Write some positive relationship mantras. Say them regularly. If you are in a relationship, write them with your partner and say them together. Doing so may begin a ritual, and rituals help hold people together.

Relationship Mantras _____

_____

_____

_____

_____

Important!

People who were sexually abused as children may find themselves fantasizing about doing to children the things that were done to them. Although such a fantasy is not unusual and does not make a person bad, if there is any possibility that you will carry out your fantasy, seek help immediately from a professional who specializes in treating adult abusers and exhibitionists. The abused can cross the line and become abusers. Reacting to child abuse fantasies by seeking help can prevent the self-punishing act of getting caught for an event from your childhood that was not your fault, as well as prevent abuse of another young human being.

11
The Abuser*

This chapter aims to help you acknowledge to yourself what you already know and understand about the abuser. You may, in working through this chapter, decide to confront the abuser directly or you may decide that direct confrontation may be more harmful to you. In either case, by learning more about the abuser, you will be able to make better decisions about confrontation.

Deborah Daro's summary of research conducted on abusers indicates that, as a group, abusing parents and adults show the following characteristics: mental illness or severe personality disorder; difficulty dealing with aggressive impulses and anger; rigid and domineering behavior; low self-esteem; depression; alcoholism or drug addiction; poor self-understanding; history of abuse as a child or observation of physical abuse as a child; adolescent parenthood; lack of attachment to their own child; social isolation; lack of parenting skills; inconsistent use of discipline; lack of knowledge regarding child development; and sole responsibility for all parenting tasks.

Other qualities of this group include: lack of ability to empathize; outside forces being seen as responsible for the abuse; perceiving the child as an extension of self; a need for nurturing.

Review the above list. Which characteristics did the abuser have at the time of the abuse? _____

_____

How many of these characteristics could you see at the time of the abuse?

_____

_____

---

*Note: The word *abuser* should be understood in a broad sense. The abuser can be either a man or a woman, adult or young person. Two or more people can also work together as abusers of the same person.

Describe the abuser's behavior at the time of the abuse.

_____

_____

   Now consider stress factors that research has found to be contributory to child abuse. Personal stress experiences include: birth of a baby; loss of a job; divorce or separation; death of a close friend or family member; sudden illness or chronic health problem; loss of housing; and sudden financial burdens.

   Social and cultural stress factors include: a culture of poverty; tolerance for physical punishment; holding sexual stereotypes about child rearing; isolation from the community; violence in the media; and strongly held notions about individual rights and family privacy.

   Some household characteristics of stress include: a large number of children; children born less than one year apart; chaotic family conditions; and overcrowded or inadequate housing.

Did any of these factors occur in your family?

_____

Were any other events going on at the time of the abuse?

_____

   Go to your time line in the Memory chapter and add stress factors along with other characteristics of your family that may have contributed to the abuse. Make sure to note the year in which it happened.

How did the abuser manifest the above characteristics?

with you_____

with his or her parents_____

with his or her partner_____

with other family members_____

with your siblings_____

at work or the job_____

The Abuser's Developmental Stage

   Child and adult development takes place in stages and phases. Phases generally refer to times in life that everyone experiences, such as childhood, early adulthood, and middle age. Not everyone, however, has the same experience in each of these phases. Some people are able to move through these phases, learning and accumulating experiences, while others seem stuck in a thought pattern, unable to learn or grow.

Stages of development generally take place during a certain age period, but may not be completed in a specific time frame. Some developmental stages defined by Jane Loevinger are not age-specific, but rather depend on situations and life experiences to help advance a person to a higher stage.

As you review the following diagrams, think about your own developmental stage at the time of the abuse. You will find that you could not have stopped the abuse or fully understood it when you were a child. Study the diagrams on pages 259–262. Try to get a sense of what your thought process was at the time the abuse was happening.

Piaget's Stages of Cognitive Development

Sensorimotor Stage
(birth–2 years)

Awareness of self as separate from rest of world. Understand that an object is still there even if hidden from view.

Preoperational Stage
(2–7 years)

Language acquisition but often egocentric. Prelogical and magical thinking. Conclusions and thought processes are not step-by-step. The concept of time is not understood.

Concrete Operations Stage
(7–11 years)

The beginning of cooperation with others and logical thinking. Sometimes leads to rigid thinking. Problems can be looked at from different viewpoints.

Formal Operations Stage
(12 years and up)

Abstract logic and thought begins as does the concept of thinking about the future or values. Problem-solving and options are available.

Some Milestones of Ego Development
by Jane Loevinger*

Stage	Impulse control, character development	Interpersonal style	
Presocial		Autistic	
Symbiotic		Symbiotic	
Impulsive	Impulsive, fear of retaliation	Receiving,dependent exploitive	
Self-protective	Fear of being caught, externalizing blame, opportunistic	Wary, manipulative, exploitive	
Conformist	Conformity to external rules, shame, guilt for niceness	Belonging, helping, superficial breaking rules	
Conscientious	Self-evaluated standards, self-criticism, guilt for consequences, long-term goals and ideals	Intensive, responsible, mutual, concern for communication	
Autonomous	Add:** Coping with conflicting inner needs, toleration	Add: Respect for autonomy	
Integrated	Add: Reconciling inner conflicts, renunciation of unattainable	Add: Cherishing of individuality	

*Adapted from Loevinger, J. *Ego development: Conceptions and theories*, 24–25. (1976). San Francisco: Jossey-Bass. Used with permission of the publisher.

**Note. "Add" means in addition to the description applying to the previous level.

Conscious preoccupations	Cognitive style
Self vs nonself	
Bodily feelings, especially sexual and aggressive	Stereotypes, conceptual confusion
Self-protection, wishes, things, advantage, control	
Appearance, social acceptability, banal feelings, behavior	Conceptual simplicity, stereo-types, cliches
Differentiated feelings, motives for behavior, self-respect, achievements, traits, expression	Conceptual complexity, idea of patterning
Vividly conveyed feelings, integration of physiological and psychological, psychological causation of behavior, development, role conception, self-fufillment, self in social context Add: Identity	Increased conceptual com-plexity, complex patterns, toleration for ambiguity, broad scope, objectivity

Erikson's Stages of Emotional Development

Approximate age	Developmental crises to be resolved
Infancy	*Trust vs Mistrust* This stage forms a basis for trust of others as well as self-esteem and a sense of being all right.
Toddlers	*Autonomy vs Shame, Doubt* Children learn to hold on and let go. Learn to stand on their own without shame and self-doubt.
Ages 3–7	*Initiative vs Guilt* Guilt over initiating acts and fantasies. Wanting to explore vs guilt about those wishes, actions, and thoughts.
Ages 7–puberty	*Industry vs Inferiority* Winning recognition, developing a sense of industry vs the sense of inadequacy and inferiority.
Puberty and adolescence	*Identity vs Role Confusion* How adolescents appear to others and their sense of self vs the inability to settle on an indentity or comfortable role in society.
Young adulthood	*Intimacy vs Isolation* Becoming ready for intimacy and commitment to others vs becoming distant, territorial, competitive and combative.
Adulthood	*Generativity vs Stagnation* Productivity, creativity, and guiding the next generation vs stagnation.
Maturity	*Ego Integrity vs Despair* Defending the dignity of one's own life vs despair about one's life and choices.

Now look at the diagrams again and think about the stage the abuser was in at the time of the abuse.

An abuser stuck at Loevinger's Impulsive Stage will personalize morality and feel that what is personally good is good for everyone. At this stage, the abuser's world is split into good and bad. Abusers who remain in the Impulsive Stage have a limited ability to learn from past or present mistakes. Those persons are, in a sense, stuck in their development.

Loevinger's Self-protective Stage describes people who manipulate rules to meet their own needs, and who have very little internalized sense of guilt or remorse. Persons in the Self-protective Stage are motivated by short-term outcomes of their actions and by assessments, often quite skewed, of their ability to get away with unacceptable behavior, and they externalize the concept of responsibility. According to Anna C. Salter, author of *Treating Child Sex Offenders and Victims*, "An abuser might say, 'I beat my children because they don't do what I say.'" Loevinger describes this stage as "a zero-sum game." What one person gains, someone else loses. Erikson's most closely correponding stage is Autonomy vs Shame and Doubt. According to Erikson, a person who is not self-directed is still trying to live by someone else's beliefs or code, and failure to live up to those rules leads to shame and self-doubt.

Loevinger describes the next level as the Conformist Stage. There, a person identifies with a larger group and is motivated by group norms and by what members of the group-of-choice will think. The abuser who is stuck in the Conformist Stage is trying to conform. Abusers use group norms to define both good and bad, and they may feel guilty if they break a convention important to their peer group.

Stuck in one stage, the abuser may have developed other qualities and thought processes typical of either a less or more advanced stage. In blocking out memories of their own abuse or distress, abusers may revert to an earlier stage of development, acting as if they were still in that stage.

Which stage do you believe the abuser was in when the abuse occurred?

_____

Did the abuser ever manifest stages indicating more advanced development? _____

When was that? _____

Have you observed the abuser recently? _____

Has any change occurred in the abuser's development? _____

_____

Has the abuser seemed to have matured since the abuse happened? _____

Do you feel that the abuser was more or less cruel, depending on whether the victims were males or females? _____

What makes you think that? _____

_____

Do you believe that, had you been the opposite sex, you would have been abused?

_____

Salter states that the abuser's negative feelings toward the child may be one possible cause for abuse.

"Often the child is scapegoated or negative feelings are placed on him/her. For example, the parent may believe the child looks like a hated ex-spouse. Perhaps the child is blamed for the breakup of the family. Negative behavior may be cited as proof that an ex-spouse's visits, however infrequent, are the cause of a child being impossible. Simply being male or female can be enough to generate a negative affect (feeling). A mother may see a youngster as a competitor or displace her self-loathing onto a child of the same sex.

Conversely, all males may be seen as 'bad,' and the child is merely an example of his gender…. An active or temperamentally difficult child may trigger a fragile parent's sense of helplessness and become a target of the parent's rage about feeling helpless. The child may even be blamed for being dependent and immature and for not nurturing the parent. This process may be intensified if the parent has a developmental incapacity to experience ambivalence. That incapacity will cause the parent to exaggerate the dominant emotion toward the child and to perceive the child as all good or all bad."

What do you feel when you read the above paragraph? _____

_____

_____

_____

Family Photographs

Next, gather as many photographs of yourself and your family as you can find. Arrange them chronologically, and look at each picture. What does the abuser look like in each photograph? Next, title each photograph. For example, you may name a photo, "the family picnic" or "the only day Dad was nice during the year," or "the day Dad got drunk and beat my brother." After you have ordered and titled the pictures, draw four scenes of family life with the abuser that did not get photographed.

Poetry Writing

Poems are filled with images and feelings, and they do not have to follow the rules of grammar. Even if you have never written a poem, now is a good time to try, because writing poetry can unblock feelings and memories. The following exercise may help you write your poem.

- In your notebook, write words or images that remind you of the abuser. Any words or thoughts are acceptable.
- Next, arrange the words in any way they seem to fit. It does not matter if some words contradict each other: the order in which you think them is more important.
- Now, combine the words into thoughts. Write your thoughts in your notebook. You will have a poem when you are finished. Does your poem reflect your feelings? _____

Masks

In preparing for the next exercise, you will need a small bag of clay. First, find a place where you can be alone for an hour or two. Sit quietly and think of an occasion when you were abused or neglected. Try to remember what the abuser looked like. What color was the abuser's face? What were the abuser's eyes like? The mouth? What expressions did the abuser have?

Now—if you can tolerate the picture—imagine the facial features of the abuser magnified ten times. The eyes are larger; the face and teeth are exaggerated. The face is more intense.

When you are ready, take the clay and, with eyes closed, mold it into the image. When done, open your eyes. You may wish to complete the sculpture with your eyes open.

What are your feelings as you look at this face? Are they similar to what you felt about the abuser when you were growing up? _____

_____

_____

Show the mask to close friends or family members whom you trust. What feelings do they get when they see the mask? _____

_____

_____

_____

Keep the mask for use when you rehearse confronting the abuser.

Expectations

How old were you when the abuse was the worst? When were you least able to escape from it? _____

Who was the abuser? _____

Who were your caretakers? _____

What did you expect from the abuser? _____
_____

What did you expect from the caretakers? _____
_____

What did you get from the abuser? _____
_____

What did you get from the caretakers? _____
_____

If the abuser is still alive, what do you expect from that person now? _____
_____

What do you get from that person now? _____
_____

How do your current fantasies, dreams, or hopes reflect your expectations?
...as a child? _____

...now, as an adult? _____

Do your current relationships mirror your expectations? How? _____
_____

The Outside World and the Abuser

Remember the abuse as clearly as you can. Include:
- the emotional content: what was said, done, implied;
- the sexual parts: inappropriate actions, words, implications;
- the physical acts: what was done, said, threatened;
- the neglect: times alone, times without proper care, times left with others.

Be clear in each area how the abuse hurt you then, and how it continues to block your growth and development as well as your wishes, hopes, and dreams. Think about the abuser: what was happening to him/her (both inside and outside) during the time of the abuse? What was the person feeling? What was the person reacting to?

Imagine next that you are a court psychiatrist, psychologist, or social worker. You have the power to recommend therapy for the abuser, to recommend that a child be placed outside the home, or that the abuser leave the home. You have also been asked for a complete mental health report on the abuser. What is your evaluation and mental health report?

Next, imagine you are young and the abuse has been discovered. It is out in the open. There are no secrets. Visualize yourself as the judge in a courtroom: what would you do with the abuser? What would you say to him/her?

Now, imagine you are the family doctor (a clear advocate of child rights) who has known the family for years. What would the doctor say to the abuser?

What recommendations would you make to the court regarding the abuser and the child?

The Abuser Then

Describe what the abuser looked like when you were a small child. _____

_____

Draw a picture of the abuser in your notebook.

Did the abuser have a different look as you were being abused? _____

_____

How does the abuser look now in your adult life? _____

_____

What are the differences between then and now? _____

_____

_____

_____

The Abuser Now

If the abuser is still alive, have changes occurred? In your notebook, draw the abuser as that person appears to you now.

What has changed? Is the abuser the same age? Does the abuser look smaller to you? Nicer? Kinder? Meaner? The same? _____

_____

How do others perceive the abuser now? _____

_____

Scribble Drawing

Take some construction paper, a dark crayon, and some colored crayons. Sit quietly and get in touch with feelings you had toward the abuser during the abuse. Imagine how you felt and what you were thinking about the abuser. Holding a dark crayon, close your eyes and let the crayon make a scribble—just let the lines flow. When you are ready, open your eyes and see if your scribble has any shapes in it that remind you of the abuser's features. Try to draw the face and body of the abuser, using lines or shapes copied from the scribble. When you have the form, color in your picture.

What do the face and body look like? _____

_____

What feelings do you have as you look at the drawing? _____

_____

Confronting the Abuser

Whether you ultimately choose to confront the abuser, the following exercises will help to make that decision. Practicing a confrontation will help you clarify your feelings toward the abuser and aid you in bringing closure to the early part of your life.

Actual confrontation of the abuser is not something you should be pushed into; rather, it is something you should do only when and if you feel ready. You may choose never to confront the abuser, but recovery is still possible.

A Conversation with the Abuser

Imagine yourself as a child at the time of the abuse. What time of year is it? Is the sun shining or is it cloudy? Warm or cool? What time of day: morning, afternoon or evening? Where are you? What does it look like? Are you inside or outside? Who else is around? What are they doing? How old are you? What do you look like? What are you wearing? How does your body feel?

Now, picture the abuser. What is the abuser wearing? How does the abuser smell? How tall is the abuser? Did the abuser bring anything along? What is the abuser doing? Write down anything you remember the abuser saying (even grunts or single words).

Next, take what you remember the abuser saying and write it down along the first column. When you have finished, fill out the next column.

What you remember	What you would say to the abuser	What you said or did to the abuser	What as an adult you would say
_____	_____	_____	_____
_____	_____	_____	_____
_____	_____	_____	_____
_____	_____	_____	_____

Read through the conversation as you remember it. Visualizing yourself as a strong, healthy adult, write down—in the fourth column—what you would say to the abuser now. Show what you wrote to another adult whom you trust. How did that person respond?

When you feel ready, practice saying your adult responses in front of an empty chair. Speak them in different ways: loud, soft, with lots of feeling, matter of factly, or with no feeling. Once you feel safe, ask a friend, counselor, or other trusted adult to recite the abuser's lines. You can then respond to the "abuser" in any way you feel is effective.

What did you feel during this? What feedback did your friend give you?

_____

_____

Having practiced what you would like to say to the abuser with a friend, and if you decide to do so, take time to become comfortable before confronting the abuser. Do it on your schedule, in your selected way. Be in charge.

Questions to Ask the Abuser

Depending on the abuser's memory, honesty, and ability to respond non-defensively, you may get answers to your questions. Know which questions you most want answered.

Examples of what you might include:

"Why didn't you listen to me when I told you I was in pain?"

"Why didn't you care that I was afraid?"

"Whom were you really angry with?"
"What did you think I felt?"
"Were you abused?"
"Why didn't you get help?"

Now move on to another step in preparing to confront your abuser. You will be better prepared if you can anticipate some of the emotions you may experience. If you plan ahead, emotions are not likely to become crises.

Crisis-planning Sheet

When I am with the abuser, I am afraid of (*examples:* anxiety attack • loss of control • fear • feeling hurt and despondent • being abused again):

_____

_____

If I become afraid of the abuser, I need not worry because I can (*examples:* leave • say how I'm feeling • make a phone call):

_____

Affirmations I will use when I am afraid: _____

_____

I will know when I need to protect myself by: _____

_____

The coping skills I will use are: _____

_____

I need/want the visit to take place at home because: _____

_____

Practice, Practice, Practice

Let people you trust review your likely reactions with you. Rehearse what you plan to say. Decide when and where you are going to make the confrontation. Always be clear with yourself as to what your goals are and what you might feel and do if the outcome differs from your goals.

Practice, Role Play

Practice talking before an empty chair, as if the abuser is sitting right there. Use props such as the mask you made, drawings, or poems. Put them on the chair. Practice in front of a mirror, with videotape, or a tape recorder.

Write up the confrontation as a play with different endings. Examples of endings:
- the abuser admits it
- the abuser throws you out
- the abuser denies it
- the abuser begins to cry.

Practice with friends or a counselor. Make sure you have a plan that will provide for your safety during the confrontation. Write your plan below and then fill out the crisis sheet.

_____

_____

_____

_____

Record your reactions immediately after the practice confrontation in your notebook.

What will you do when you leave the confrontation? Whom will you call? Whom will you visit?

_____

_____

_____

The Abuser as an Adult

How has the abuser used guilt to manipulate others? Give examples:

_____

Give an example of how the abuser has used shame. _____

_____

Give an example of how the abuser has used blame. _____

_____

Give an example of how the abuser has made attempts to grow and develop.

_____

What has the abuser done? (e.g., entered therapy, joined Alcoholics Anonymous or Parents Anonymous?) _____

Has the abuser's behavior improved? Is the abuser different today? Comment. _____

_____

Has aging or illness changed the abuser? Comment. _____

_____

Have these changes affected you? Comment. _____

_____

Do you want to confront the abuser? _____

What are the positives and negatives of a confrontation? _____

_____

What do you hope will happen as the result of a confrontation? _____

_____

How will you know you are ready to confront the abuser? _____

_____

What has this chapter helped you to understand about the abuser? _____

_____

_____

_____

What has this chapter helped you to understand about yourself? _____

_____

_____

_____

_____

12
Spirituality and Beyond: Full Recovery from Abuse

This chapter will help you explore your values, problem solving abilities, and spiritual connection to the world outside yourself. An understanding of these three areas will not only enrich your daily life, but is also essential to achieving full recovery from abuse.

The tasks of childhood and adolescence include finding out who you are and what you believe, then developing methods for solving problems and difficult situations that arise. Children and adolescents need a secure base on which to stand as they make their decisions. Sharing basic values learned at home through discussion and example, they come to know the value system of their family and understand themselves more clearly.

Defining your values can help you to decide what you want to do and what limits you will impose. By setting your limits, you can more easily make decisions, and this will help you grow in self-esteem. Problem-solving methods developed from both trial and error as well as patience and teaching cannot work in an atmosphere where mistakes are never or infrequently tolerated. Problem-solving methods can help people gain perspective on difficulties. Defined thinking processes help a person make decisions and grow in ways that previously were difficult.

The following exercises will help you establish what you value and believe. You may find that your beliefs and values have changed. Change does not indicate the lack of values, only that, as you grew and developed, so did your values and beliefs.

Steps in Problem Solving

1. Describe and define the problem
2. Separate related problems to clarify the issues
3. Identify successful solutions and responses you have used
4. Consider new solutions and options; get input from others
5. Consider the pros and cons of each option

6. Decide on a solution and make a plan

7. Follow the plan, then evaluate your success. Change the plan if it is not working

The best way to practice problem solving is to do it.

1. *Describe and define a problem*. Be clear in describing the problem. You will sometimes need to look for its roots. Addressing a problem in this way can help clarify both the issue and reasonable solutions. Start by writing down your problem, then answer these questions.

- Who? Who is part of the problem? Who was previously involved in the problem and its solution?
- What? What about this situation makes it a problem? What bothers you? What happens? What doesn't happen?
- When? When does this problem occur? When is the situation not a problem? When do you respond? When did you become aware of it as a problem?
- Where? Where does the problem occur? Where does it not happen? Are there places where you have been able to solve this problem?
- Why and How? Why do you think this problem is occurring? Are there recurrent patterns or cause-and-effect relationships that seem to bring it about?

Having thought about the problem, make a clear statement about it.

2. *Keep related problems separate*. Problem solving is easier if the problem is clearly defined. Related problems are best solved with individual solutions.

Define the main problem_____

_____

List related problems_____

_____

3. *Identify solutions and responses you have used*. Identify any past solution or response you have attempted, even if it hasn't worked. Your responses, feelings, and hunches are important since they may have affected the ways you went about solving the problem.

Past solutions_____

_____

Past problems_____

_____

4. *Consider new solutions and options; get input from others*. Brainstorm-

ing can be helpful to problem solving. List all solutions, because even outlandish ideas may help. When brainstorming, do not allow your mind to edit or think of why something cannot work. Be open to all options.

Possible solutions _____

_____

5. *Consider the pros and cons of each option.* List all solutions and alternatives with pros and cons for each.

Solution	Pro	Con
_____	_____	_____
_____	_____	_____
_____	_____	_____
_____	_____	_____

6. *Select a solution and make a plan.* Decide which solution makes most sense. Then, make a plan, outlining each step you will take. Detailing your steps will give you a sense of process. Write down the first step. What happens next? Next?

Solution _____

_____

Plan _____

_____

7. *Change the plan if it is not working, then evaluate.* Set a date on which you will begin the plan. Next, set the criteria by which you will judge the effectiveness of your plan.

Date to begin _____

I will know that this plan is working by _____

How did the plan work? _____

How did you solve problems when you were a child? _____

How is your new method different?_____

What did you learn from this process?_____

_____

To establish a pattern of problem solving, use the problem-solving method on a weekly basis until it becomes automatic.

Value Clarification

Beliefs and values are choices and decisions reflecting how you view and live your life. Beliefs and values are not the same as habits. Patterns of thought and action performed by rote are, at most, "transferred values." For a value to be yours, you must have had a choice and considered the alternatives.

Sid Simon, formulator of "value clarification," says that the process of defining values includes *choosing, cherishing,* and *acting.*

Choosing values means selecting values. *Cherishing values* means liking and appreciating the selection. *Acting* means using your values as guides for living life in harmony with the values. Acting on your values is significant for abused persons. You may have heard much about a family's "values," but not seen values in action.

List your family's three most important stated values. _____

_____

_____

Which family members held to those values? _____

_____

Think about your family's actions. Were the values followed? _____

Action taken: _____

_____

Consistent with stated value? _____

_____

List both your selected and transferred values.

_____

_____

_____

Simon developed a series of questions to define held-values.

1. What are the highpoints of your week? When did you feel most alive, and operate at your kindest, highest level? _____

2. Whom were you in emphatic agreement or disagreement with this week? About what? _____

3. What values did you act on this week? _____

4. What plans did you make for a future event? _____

5. In what ways did you not live up to your values this week? _____

_____

6. How could you have made the week better? _____

_____

Do this exercise for six weeks and then put your answers away. If you have answered all questions, you will find patterns.

In finding these patterns, you will get a sense of what makes you feel good, gives you a sense of accomplishment, and persons whom you value. In noting the persons with whom you agree or disagree, you will find out which people you want in your life at work and at home—and the persons who are making life a bit more trying. You can figure out what is important to you by what you have acted on and by the way you live your life. In looking at the plans you make, you can see what you want enough to plan for.

You can get an idea of where your values are discordant by establishing what actions have not met your values and how you could make your life better.

What have you learned about your values? _____

_____

Are your values different from your abuser's? _____

_____

What do you like about your values? _____

_____

Who shares your values?

My values	Others in my life who share them
_____	_____
_____	_____
_____	_____
_____	_____

Make a plan for telling those whose values you share how much they mean to you. Write your plan in your notebook. What was the result of telling them that you share their values?

Continuing Your Push toward Wholeness

A continuation of the resolution and integration part of recovery from abuse is planning and goal setting. Together, planning and goal setting will help you own yourself and strengthen your power to effect change. The three components of bringing about change are:

- planning
- problem solving, and
- deciding on your values.

The following section on Time Use will help you focus on these three important skills as you continue to develop your own store of inner strength. The exercises that follow will help you understand how you currently live your life, then provide you with some tools to fashion your life as you would like it to be.

Time Use

As the proverb tells us, "For birth and death there is no cure, save to enjoy the interval." Time, and how you choose to use it, is an outline of your life. It is also a model (i.e., a representation of the real thing) because it details what you do, and because it is a model, you can study it to learn how to change your real life. Think about your current life as a segment of one week, 168 hours long. How do you spend your time?

	Now	As I'd like to spend it
Body and self-care		
Sleep and rest	_____	_____
Bathroom, dressing, hair	_____	_____
Exercise	_____	_____
Food shopping	_____	_____
Eating and food preparation	_____	_____
Other _____	_____	_____
Activity—include phone time		
Work	_____	_____
Getting to and from work	_____	_____
Reading—newspapers/books	_____	_____
T.V./radio/videos	_____	_____
Cleaning, chores	_____	_____
Errands	_____	_____
School/education	_____	_____

	Now	As I'd like to spend it
Other _____	_____	_____
Recreation and social—include phone calls		
Friends	_____	_____
Family	_____	_____
Intimate partner	_____	_____
Recreation	_____	_____
Interests and hobbies	_____	_____
Sexuality	_____	_____
Spiritual/giving	_____	_____
Meditation	_____	_____
Lectures or classes	_____	_____
12-Step meetings	_____	_____
Volunteer or charity work	_____	_____
Other _____	_____	_____

Now, draw a pie chart of your current time week so that everything is represented in the circle. Remember that there are 168 hours in a week.

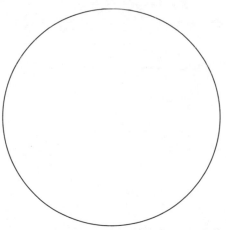

Now, go back to the list and decide how you would like to spend your time. Draw a second pie chart in your notebook.

What is most different about this second chart? _____

What would have to do to make your life the way you want to ?_____
_____

What would be easiest to change?_____

Most difficult?_____

   Changing your time allotment is perhaps the easiest task. But do it slowly. When the change you have made feels natural and it is integrated into your life, make the next easiest change. Proceed in this way until your time allotment is as you want it to be.

How Are You with Others: Are You the Person You Want to Be?*

	As you really are	As you would like to be	Feedback from friends
1. Fun and humor			
2. Warmth			
3. Conversation and intellect			
4. Poise, social comfort, and charm			
5. Adaptability			
6. How I respond to feedback and criticism			
7. Positive outlook			
8. Honesty			
9. Not needing to control others			
10. Caring about others			
11. Other:_____			
_____			
_____			
_____			

_____

*Adapted from Parkview Treatment Centers (1984). *Family program handbook.* St. Louis Park, Minn.: Parkview Treatment Centers.

Change Plan

Behaviors I want to change	How this affected me	Change Plan
Example: Criticizing others at work	I developed a negative attitude	I keep track of when I'm negative
_____	_____	_____
_____	_____	_____
_____	_____	_____
_____	_____	_____

Making a Life Plan

Spirituality and a life plan aid and strengthen every person recovering from abuse. The journey up the path of recovery is a spiritual one. A life plan, or map, can help you chart the way to full personal development. Like many interrelated pairs, spirituality and a life plan produce a synergy when they work together that enhances the value of each, integrates confusing life experiences, and increases one's potential for happiness and accomplishment.

Any kind of abuse is an attack on the human spirit. Abuse damages people's capacity to love and grow. To abuse or neglect a person for whom we are responsible is to trample our own humanity and to deny that which is most valuable in ourselves. Scott Peck, author of *The Road Less Traveled*, defines evil as interference with another person's growth and development. By that definition, abuse and neglect are inherently evil because they destroy life's greatest gifts: growth and development of a life plan.

Many people today yearn for spiritual development and seek guidance from a variety of religious traditions. Alcoholics Anonymous, the foundation of all 12-step recovery programs, has popularized the concept of a "higher power." A.A.'s founders—and the host of self-help leaders who followed them—use this term to describe a "power greater than ourselves." That can be anything that we perceive as more understanding and knowing than ourselves. For some members of A.A., their higher power is the collective conscience of their A.A. group; for others, it is based on the Judean-Christian God, for still others, it is ocean, sun, the earth, or the power of love.

Children learn their notions of God and a higher power from adults, and they frequently see no difference between their God and their parents. Young children, who cannot yet think conceptually, perceive God as a physical being, typically in the form of an adult. They assign to God the same characteristics they use to describe adults: all-knowing, all-powerful, and all-controlling of their universe.

Religion teaches children to honor their parents, but seldom, if ever, encourages children to speak out against abusive parents. Since religion also instructs children that God sees and knows everything, children can understandably feel confused and angry about the teachings of their faith, and may wonder why God did not know they were being abused, or why God did not intervene. An abused child may later have difficulty overcoming this early confusion, or connecting with an all-loving God. A crucial task for an adult recovering from abuse is to overcome childhood ideas of God and spirituality and develop new ones.

Before you try developing your own ideas, answer these questions:

What negative ideas do you still tell yourself about spirituality?

_____

_____

Did you ever pray on your own when someone was not watching you? ____

What did you pray for? _____

You may have had some kind of prayer to help you get through the abuse, something that helped you remain strong and allowed you to go on. These prayers may have been your first contacts with your own spirituality. Think about them. What kept you going as a child? _____

What has helped you survive as an adult? _____

Belief in a Higher Power

Although spirituality includes a belief in God for a large number of people, it need not necessarily do so. Common positive concepts expressed by nontheistic men and women to describe their spirituality are:
- being in touch with and appreciating life's full force
- understanding the God they sense within themselves
- having a relationship with the universe
- expanding one's own consciousness
- believing that everything is connected and interrelated
- maintaining inner peace
- seeking harmony with the universe
- acknowledgment of the creative force of the universe
- celebrating the sacredness of each day

- honoring their uniqueness, but not exclusively identifying with it (Ram Dass)
- being a loving person and following a loving way of life.

Do you know other definitions of spirituality ?

- _____

- _____

- _____

What is your own definition of spirituality?_____

_____

When did you decide on this meaning of spirituality?_____

Has it changed your adult life? _____

Now list several positive ideas or mantras that are counter to your negative concepts of spirituality._____

_____

Say these mantras out loud, then tape them. What do they sound like to you?

_____

Barriers to Belief in a Higher Power/God

Personal spirituality can also include negative aspects. Common negatives include:

- feeling guilt about past actions
- seeing God as judge or scorekeeper
- being angry and resentful at God for what others have done
- holding a rigid sense of rules about religion
- being unable to forgive
- using spirituality only in emergencies
- feeling unworthy
- isolating oneself from others

Barriers I have are:

- _____

- _____

- _____

- _____

Making a Spiritual Connection

To establish a spiritual connection, all you need is a sense of awareness: awareness of the life force in nature, perhaps as it is manifest in trees, flowers, animals, or human physical development. Appreciation of any of these can draw you closer to the essence of life. For some people, the concept of the spiritual, or God, is simply the idea that someone or something is "with me and for me." This concept may be more credible than the notion of a protective guardian—indeed, to one who has been abused, the very thought of a protective guardian may be more than a little alien. To facilitate acceptance of this, think about a person in your life who cared for you and on whom you knew you could depend. Name that person.

_____

Next — if you can — think of the positive energy and beauty of the universe. What healing could it bring? _____

_____

_____

Thinking about these can help you make a spiritual connection to something outside yourself. Making a spiritual connection is done neither easily nor quickly, but you will succeed if you work at it steadily.

Other Ways to Connect

Others have begun to develop a personal spirituality by:
- choosing to hope
- choosing to connect
- choosing to forgive
- developing a life plan and living it
- choosing to seek peace
- choosing to move toward positivity, without negative feelings or angry thoughts.

Talking to Others

Adult spiritual development often starts with a single affirmation, said Dag Hammarskjold. All affirmations need action, followed by practice. Spiritual development requires commitment and perseverance.With commitment and perseverance, spiritual development is possible.

Think of someone you know who has developed a personal spirituality or connectedness to a higher power. Interview that person, asking about spiritual experiences. Did that person have times when spirituality seemed totally absent? What was that like? How was spirituality renewed?

_____

_____

Ask if books or tapes helped. Write a summary of your interview in your notebook.

Did that person mention anything you would like to try? _____

_____

Seeking Your Spirituality

Get a sheet of paper and a paint box, set of colored pencils, or markers. Close your eyes, ask yourself for inner guidance, and draw your spiritual path. As you receive an image, draw it. Later, when you look at the drawing, you may find that your path stops, turns back on itself, or moves ahead. Look closely at your drawing. You may think that you are not on a spiritual path, but you are. Anyone who seeks spirituality has begun the journey. What do you make of your spiritual path? _____

_____

_____

Finding the Path

Finding your own spiritual path lets you claim your own spiritual authority. It is the process that lets you get to know and understand the spirit of the abused child that remains at the core of your being. That small, hurt child needs love and protection to mature. To know, value, and understand the child, like the development of spirituality itself, will take time. When you can, sit in a quiet place, close your eyes, and imagine yourself as a child between seven and nine years old.

What do you look like? _____

_____

What are you wearing and how do you feel? _____

_____

What frightens you? What worries you? _____

_____

Spend a few minutes visualizing the child you were. Now, as the adult you are, imagine putting your arms around that child and making the child feel safe and secure. Ask the child to tell you more about the stored up memories, thoughts, and feelings. What are they? _____

_____

Carry on your dialogue with the child you were. What are you saying? What response does the child give? _____

_____

Continue working with the image of the adult healing the child. No matter how slow your progress, be patient. It may take weeks or months to reach or connect with that child. When you have finally reinvigorated that child, repeat the comforting process again. This time, allow the child to be a year younger. Continue to work with this younger child until you have helped this child to heal and grow. When you are ready, begin to work with an even younger child. Continue in this way until you can visualize, connect, and help the child when he/she was a small baby. This process, though lengthy, will help you claim your own spiritual authority and allow you to help that child grow and personally develop into the spiritual adult you are becoming.

The Rev. Sherre Boothman has suggested that what is not true for the little child is not true for the adult. If the "truth" frightens the child, it is not the truth—certainly not the whole truth. Giving the child the authority to judge truth gives you the authority to reclaim your own adult spiritual authority.

Being Alive and Aware

Being alive and aware is the cornerstone of spirituality—you cannot connect with the life force if you are operating with a deadened body and mind. Being alive and being aware can lead unerringly to personal development and spiritual growth.

Feeling Alive

Howard Clinebell has listed directions for growth in *The People Dynamics*. According to his definitions, you are "alive" to the degree that you feel aware of your feelings; relate to others; own yourself; and love. Being alive also includes being able to enjoy life, be spontaneous, create, take risks, cope, feel connected, and grow. Conversely, you are "dead" to the degree that you are out of touch with yourself, stuck in your own world, manipulating, plodding, and programmed. Other hallmarks of this state include vegetating, playing it safe, being isolated, stagnating, and existing in memories and fantasies of the future.

When do you feel most alive? _____

_____

What areas of your life do you need to work on to help you feel more alive?

_____

What thoughts do you have about how to do this work? _____

_____

Finding a Spiritual Guide or Teacher

Finding someone who you feel is a spiritual person and who can help you develop your own spirituality will make your journey toward spirituality smoother, easier, and more exciting. Your chosen teacher or guide may be a minister, a rabbi, a priest, or a wise and close friend. Your guide or teacher should have values you admire or share.

Is your teacher and guide open and flexible or dogmatic? _____

Does your guide focus on spiritual matters, or do money and material possessions seem to be of greater concern?_____

Be careful not to create a potentially abusive situation. Choose a guide carefully and change your teacher or guide if you feel uncomfortable. Spirituality is not a quick fix or a glib, simplistic answer, nor is it contained in a single, codified, universally correct body of knowledge. Your spiritual pathway is unique.

Increasing Your Spiritual Growth by Giving to Others

Helping others provides you with one of the best ways to deepen your spiritual connection. If it is evil to interfere with another person's growth and goodness, then the opposite is true, as well: it is good to help another achieve personal growth. Think of someone you care about to whom you would like to give a gift, one motivated by sincere, deep feelings. Jot down some ways in which you could help this person grow and develop. How do you help yourself when you give in this manner to someone else? _____

_____

_____

Make a plan to help this person. Be sure, however, that you are giving something—not trying to impose. Think with compassion: put yourself in the other's shoes and ask yourself what might help that person grow. But, before you "help" someone—and this is important—be sure to ask the person whether any help is wanted. Sometimes, being available is the best gift of all.

Reaching out, giving of yourself, and being charitable will further your own spirituality. Getting outside yourself by helping another person will help you gain a new perspective on yourself. If you do not yet know it, you will find that what is given away comes back. Anyone who truly gives of self receives gifts in return. Persons with a background of abuse may find that giving is difficult at first, because others in your family may have drilled into you the idea that you could be "used or used up." That is the "the war and rationing" mentality—that one can only give so much before being used up.

Have you been taught to give to others? _____

Did you see examples of charity in your family? What did you learn about giving and charity from your family, church or synagogue, or others around you?

_____

_____

_____

As personally rewarding as giving is, set limits so that your charity does not lead you to neglect your own needs—or worse, become resentful. Avoid becoming squirrel-like, scurrying and searching for more than enough nuts for the winter and always worrying that your supply will run out. Fear of "never having enough" may have come from your family, if there was not enough food, care, love or kindness to go around. Deprivation engenders a need-to-store mentality. Giving confronts the storage mentality, if you give freely without worrying what you will get back.

Was there a time in your life when you were a giving person? _____

_____

Were there times in your life when you could have given more, but did not?

_____

Why did you not give more? _____

_____

_____

What would have happened had you given at that time? _____

_____

Find some role models for giving. Think about people you perceive as being giving and caring. Who are they? How do they give? Now, write the names of people you know who give of their time as well as their money.

_____

_____

If you can, ask them what they get for themselves by doing this. Write down their answers._____

_____

If you have found the idea of giving difficult, examine your resistance to giving. Why am I afraid? Does giving make me angry? Think about these questions, meditate on them, then see if you are beginning to understand that your giving is really a gift to you.

The Ladder of Charity

Maimonides, a medieval philosopher, wrote about what he called "A Ladder of Charity." Each rung is a way to give that is progressively more virtuous:

1. to give sadly (unwillingly)
2. to give less than is fitting
3. to give only after having been asked
4. to give before being asked
5. to give so that the donor does not know who is the recipient
6. to give so that the recipient does not know who is the donor
7. to give so that neither the donor nor the recipient know the identity of the other
8. to give in a way to help the poor rehabilitate themselves by lending them money, taking them into partnership, employing them, or giving them work, for in this way, the end is achieved with no loss of self-respect.

Many religions teach the value of charity. It is a moral obligation that connects people to their communities and deepens their spiritual connection to the world around them. How do you connect giving with spirituality?

Additional Ways to Deepen Spirituality

Have you ever had what you would call "a spiritual experience?" When? What happened? _____

_____

_____

Was there a time in your life, either as a child or later, when you felt connected to a higher power or to something you felt was greater than yourself?_____

Did you ever feel you had a special understanding of nature and felt a sense of belonging?_____

When? _____

Were you ever able to talk about the experience with anyone? _____

Why or why not? _____

Meditation

Meditation is probably the easiest, most direct route into yourself as well as an excellent way of harmonizing oneself with life. Meditation both clears out superficial thoughts and brings in new, personally important ideas. By increasing the brain's alpha waves through meditation, certain body processes (e.g., pulse rate and muscle relaxation) are beneficially affected. Meditation, as it calms the meditator's internal processes, paradoxically, re-energizes both mind and body. Meditation allows a person to look at complex matters, be open to answers, and find peace in what is learned.

The overall goal of meditation is to still the mind in such a way that it can embrace new insights or ways of understanding. Depending on your personal convictions, you may believe that the understanding and information received through meditation comes from within you, from the universe, or from both. When it is still, the mind has room for thoughts, feelings, and perceptions that are not available to you while you are fully engaged in day-to-day life.

Margo Adair, author of *Working Inside Out,* compares the nonmeditator to a person who never takes out the trash. The mind of the nonmeditator is often cluttered. Thoughts collect, then pile up as they are reviewed over and over. Meditation can help you sort out your thoughts and your feelings, even to leading you to become more perceptive. In a sense, meditation frees you to use your full ability to know and understand.

Understandably, perspective changes with meditation. You may even find that you are able to put distance on your abuse experiences, without denying either the feelings or the experience. Abused persons may find meditation difficult because thoughts "will not stop." It is not unusual for the mind and spirit of an abused person to take months to cleanse themselves. However, after even memories of the most severe abuse situations, daily meditation can bring a person to a point of deep relaxation. Do not give up meditation because you fail to achieve instant results. Everyone can learn to meditate and reap its benefits.

Meditating with experienced meditators may be useful. Persons with more experience can get you started and give you encouragement to continue. Simply knowing that you are with experienced meditators will reduce failure anxiety, and relaxation helps induce a meditative state.

Body Position Is Important

Although some people can meditate lying down, most teachers recommend sitting with your back straight, your feet touching the floor, and your hands in your lap, with the palms slightly cupped upward. This position allows for better energy flow.

Mantras, Counting, and Breathing Methods

Some methods of meditation focus on breathing, counting, or the repetition of a mantra. Though these methods work for many people, focusing on counting or speaking may block access to information or understanding only obtainable during a quieter time. However, you might want to try breathing, counting, or mantras to see if they work for you; meditation tapes may also be of help.

Sensations

Unexpected body sensations may occur as you are learning to meditate. Beginning meditators commonly find they are more tired or jumpy than usual. Remember: meditation is a balancing process that takes time before a balance between daily life and meditation is reached.

Sounds

You may become more aware of external noise. Increased awareness of noise is actually a part of the meditative process as your general sensory tuning increases. If noise is distracting, allow yourself to hear the noise, but turn your attention from it. Do the same for random, distracting thoughts. If you find random thoughts—either unpleasant or pleasant—are distracting you from your meditation, allow those thoughts to float by, but do not struggle to remove your attention from them.

Meditation works best if it occurs in a regular place at a regular time. Be calm, not rushed. If you are feeling anxious, do not force yourself to meditate.

Meditation is usually difficult for those who are sitting quietly with themselves and their own feelings for the first time. If you find a long meditation (20 minutes) difficult, try five-minute meditations. If your mind is blank when you begin to meditate, focus on a pleasant, soft color such as blue or purple, watch a candle flame, or listen to soft, gentle, instrumental music. You will know when you have begun to meditate because your mind, body, and breathing will become more relaxed.

Though you might find yourself becoming drowsy, do not stop. In your meditation, ask questions and ask for insight. Margo Adair suggests that questions be used as a flashlight with its beam of light. Questions can illuminate an idea or situation, and your guide (internal or external) might suggest some possible answer(s).

Create Your Own Ritual

A man I know places a small cloth—which he calls his altar—on the floor of his bedroom to focus on during daily meditation. On the cloth, he places objects of special significance—leaves, flowers, photographs, books— anything important and resonant. He can look at these objects as he goes to sleep and when he awakens. When he travels, he bundles up the items and takes them along. When guests stay with him, he encourages them to place their own special objects on the cloth. In this way he reminds himself of his connections to life, love, and other people. You might find that a similar ritual, or another only you develop that has meaning for you, will help you meditate.

Visualization

Visualization is best accomplished during a meditative state. Unlike meditation, visualization is not listening for an answer. Rather, it is more like programming your mind and body to be who you want and opening yourself to the possibilities of change and goal realization. Visualization is similar to marking a point in the future, and, by focusing on that point, preparing to get there.

Visualization may be difficult at first, because abuse interferes with hope, the sense of future, and possibilities for change. In using visualization, however, you will increase your hope by coming to understand that there can indeed be a future. A sample visualization is included at the back of this book in Appendix II on pages 309–310.

Visualizations work best if they are your own. To begin, write down three things you want to happen._____

_____

_____

Now, write a visualization for each. The more detailed a visualization is, the more likely it will come to be. Write one in your notebook.

Now make a tape of your visualization, filling in with more details, if you can. Listen to your tape. Change the visualization till it sounds just the way you want it to be. Then, close your eyes and begin to fashion the image (or visualization) of what you want to occur. Develop an image for each important step of the process. Let your image speak, act, and show emotion as part of your visualizing process.

Letting Go: Forgiving

Before reading further in this section, sit quietly for a moment. Take a pencil or pen and below the word *forgiveness* write all the associations that come to mind._____

_____

_____

What does forgiveness feel like? Look like? Does it have odor and taste?

_____

What did you learn from your list of associations?_____

_____

Next, ask yourself: What could happen if I let go of my anger and resentment?_____

_____

_____

How would I feel? _____

_____

Would I have an identity? A sense of self? _____

What does the energy I put into resentment cost me? _____

Do I use resentment to keep my life the same? _____

Whom do I resent the most? Why? _____

Does forgiving mean that what happened was right or excusable? _____

Whom is forgiveness for? You? Others? _____

Forgiveness does not mean that the cruelties and brutalities people inflict on one another are right or should be forgotten. We all have a right to be outraged over cruel acts or abusive words against us. To forgive or let go is not the same as excusing past behaviors of the abuser. Letting go and forgiving are steps in reclaiming your power over your own life. Letting go and forgiving establish and assert who you are and what you control.

Letting go and forgiving can draw a person through feelings. Those two steps impart understanding in the deepest sense that you are no longer powerless, that you now can fight back, and that you will never allow yourself to be abused again.

In order for letting go and forgiving to do their work, they must be done by you for yourself. You may come to see that the person who abused you was a "victim of a victim" and acted on unconscious or unrecognized motives and feelings in abusing you. Forgiveness does not mean saying that what happened was right. Forgiveness is a way of saying, "It happened, and now I choose to move on with my life." Forgiveness is the final recognition that you have the power to change your life, but that you have no power to change someone else's life—even the abuser's.

The process of forgiveness starts as you begin to let go of your "abused identity." The process is then pushed along by your deciding that who you are is the total of your life experiences and feelings, not just of the abuse.

Letting Go of Lying

When you repeat the hated behaviors of others—especially telling lies to cover up the fact or effects of abuse—you keep the abuse active. Lying to cover up abuse is, for an adult, like denying one's own life history. And lying about abuse and its effects will continue to disrupt your life.

As an abused person you were lied to in being asked to keep the abuse secret. The abuser's request for secrecy communicated many different lies. You may have been told that:
- you should not to tell anyone
- you are a bad person
- you are responsible for the abuser's behavior
- the abuser cared for you despite the abuse
- you were being "abused" or punished for your own good.

There were probably other lies you were told daily: "We'll eat soon," (then eating two hours later); "We don't have money for this" (while a caretaker was buying extravagant things for personal use); "I'll be back soon," (then the parent stays out all night).

Lying about any matter—even so-called social lies—perpetuates abuse. Letting go and forgiving are positive steps toward ending the lying and also the power of the abuse. Each lie is but a further betrayal of self. Think about the effects of your most frequent lies (example: "I'm fine," when you are not). What lies do you tell?

Why are you afraid?_____

What is the result of your lies?_____

    Recovering from a pattern of lying may also mean revealing your abuse. It is quite possible that you have never told close family members what happened. You may be withholding the information to "protect" or not "upset" the other person—but doing so will only continue (1) your lying and (2) your concealment of the abuse.

List the persons close to you whom you have not told._____

_____

Why have you kept this information from them? _____

_____

What might happen if you tell the truth? _____

_____

List some recent lies you have told:

Lies or important omissions	Told to whom?	What I was fearful of and/or wanted to avoid
1. _____	_____	_____
2. _____	_____	_____
3. _____	_____	_____
4. _____	_____	_____

Now, using the list above, write a brief scenario based on your telling the truth.

Truth	Feelings	What might have happened?
1. _____	_____	_____
2. _____	_____	_____
3. _____	_____	_____
4. _____	_____	_____

There are things you can do to interrupt a pattern of lying. You might keep a "Lie List" to increase your awareness of when you lie. Make a daily or weekly list of lies. Review them, trying to find out what you fear.

If you have friends whom you trust, ask them if they remember lies you have told. Write their observations here:

_____

_____

Ask them to point out when they think you are lying, but make sure you are specific about how you want to receive feedback. Example: "Please make sure we are alone when you tell me that you think I'm lying," or, "Please don't tell me in front of others or when we're having a good time."

Letting Go by Taking Risks

Risk-taking is part of letting go. Many abused people go to great lengths to protect themselves; a few seem to take risks as self-punishment. Review the risks you have taken lately. You may find that you felt you had little choice in your action or that the risks you took actually were self-destructive—a kind of abuse of self.

Taking a risk means being able to handle an unpleasant, frightening, or new feeling. Getting close to someone is a risk; leaving a job is a risk. A good risk is one that has the potential to offer you growth and development. Think about risks you have taken which had a positive outcome.

Risk	Outcome
_____	_____
_____	_____
_____	_____

Now think about risks you would like to take—risks that might help you grow.

Risk	Potential for growth
_____	_____
_____	_____
_____	_____

What keeps you from taking the risks? _____

_____

_____

_____

Make a plan to take some risks. Take one risk at a time (try the least risky first).

Plan	What happened	What I learned from this risk
_____	_____	_____
_____	_____	_____
_____	_____	_____

Forgiveness: Self-love

Abuse robs us of our ability to love and care; forgiveness opens us to letting in love and caring. Self-love and caring, as well as the love of others, are major building blocks for a life of freedom from fear and anger. To help the forgiveness process begin, allow yourself to be open to love.

Think about the things, colors, smells, and tastes that symbolize love and caring to you. An image that comes easily to most people is hearts. Now, take that image further. What color is the heart? What size is the heart? What texture is the heart? Think about changing your environment to reflect positive, caring, loving feelings and thoughts.

Paint your room a new color. Find objects, books, or music that represent love and positivity. Keep them around you. Put a fresh flower in a bud vase near you.

My ideas for changing my environment are: _____

_____

_____

Begin to think about other changes you can make in your life that will reflect love. Below are some suggested areas. You are strongly affected by what you see, think, hear, sense, and do!

Area:	What I can do to reflect self-love
Music	_____
Reading	_____
Interactions with others	_____
My body	_____
My time	_____
My work	_____

How I Have Fun

To renew the process of forgiveness, recite a daily mantra or affirmation that begins with the words, "I am willing to let go of my resentments and hurts. It is time to heal. To replace my feelings of resentment and anger, I ..."

(Complete the sentence with phrases such as):

- will have loving feelings about myself
- I will enjoy today
- I will find inner peace

When you are ready, add the sentence, "I am willing to let go of the abuse and let go of _____ (the abuser)."

When meditating, bring the abuser into the image. At least say you let go or forgive that person (you may still harbor resentment and reservation about forgiving), then bring him or her toward you. Look at that person—walking toward you, standing in front of you, facing you. Now, using your imagination, tell the abuser that you are letting go of him or her—and then watch the abuser walk away.

Ask the child within you if it is time to let go. Listen for the answer. When the child's answer is a clear "Yes," you will be able to let go, forgive, and move on. Practice telling the abuser you are letting go. Now, imagine your life after you have let go.

How is it different? _____

_____

Do you feel more free? _____

_____

You may choose to move from letting go to forgiving the person who abused you, but not the act of abuse. Abusers who fully accept responsibility for what they did and how it hurt you may be willing to hear about your pain and anger. Abusers who perpetrated the abuse while influenced by chemicals, but who have accepted responsibility for their actions (including therapy, and participation in a 12-Step program), can further the mutual healing, forgiveness, and letting go. Without an exchange of feelings, a full relationship based on forgiveness may be impossible. If that is the case, you may want to let go and move on with your life.

Backsliding

You may feel that you had been making progress very quickly in recovery from abuse, but suddenly things either came to a halt or you felt you were backsliding. If this happens, you may become discouraged and think that you will never feel good again. Such a mood swing may be a result of PTSD, or it may be similar to the dynamics of relapse found in recovery from addiction.

A mood change may be a sign that you are moving too quickly, are focused too much on the abuse, or that change and loss are affecting your life.

You will notice signs of backsliding before you come to a crisis. Even then, backsliding can be prevented. Action is the key to continuing recovery. Some of the early signs of backsliding include:

- Increased difficulty carrying out a plan
- Increased indecision and inability to identify feelings
- Increased fatigue or lack of rest
- Return of resentments and anger
- Return of a sense of futility and/or an increased need for control
- Re-emergence of compulsive behaviors—increased spending or eating for example
- Difficulty setting limits, saying "No," or increasing rigidity
- Increased difficulty with impending change
- Decreased self-esteem
- Return of communication difficulties
- Loss of a sense of options
- Return of depression, loneliness, or anxiety
- Increased difficulty with sexual performance

Other signs that I recognize as backsliding are:

_____

_____

If you see these signs—take immediate steps to prevent backsliding. Your actions may include:

- Increasing your meditation time
- Attending a workshop or group on assertiveness/self-esteem
- Talking with your teacher/guide/therapist
- Increasing physical activity
- Connecting more frequently with people
- Revising your stress reduction plan
- Taking a short unstructured vacation
- Reassessing your goals
- Asking friends for feedback and suggestions about behavior change

Other ideas:

_____

_____

Set a time limit on deferring to seek professional help or medical intervention, if either are indicated. If signs of backsliding endure beyond your time limit, seek help. Do not wait.

When Anger Returns

There are times when, no matter how much self-work you have done, you will feel anger returning. The best antidote, once you have reviewed the causes of your anger, is to reacquaint yourself with nature. Meditation may be difficult, since your mind will not be quiet enough to focus. Look for something calming in nature: take a walk outside, drive to the mountains, lake, or beach. Visit a place that gives you inspiration.

Keep your inspiration list handy. Write it down:

_____

_____

_____

A Letter to Yourself

Write a letter to yourself when you are feeling good. Include your list of personal "warning" signs and what you know you need to do about them. Keep the letter taped to something you use regularly (perhaps this book or your journal). If you find yourself backsliding, read the letter and follow your own directions.

Coming to a Positive Resolution

Eliana Gil in her book, *Treatment of Adult Survivors of Childhood Abuse*, has identified what she considered positive resolutions of abuse. They are:
- processing the abuse in a realistic way without feeling you have caused it
- you do not feel compelled to repeat the abuse event(s) consciously or unconsciously
- you do not feel devastated, victimized, or enraged by what happened
- you do not have neurotic thoughts, nightmares
- your emotions are stabilized
- you have a realistic and accurate self-image of your strengths, weaknesses
- you like yourself and feel you are a worthwhile person
- you will not tolerate negative or abusive situations
- you have grieved the losses of childhood

- you can tolerate, express, and resolve pain
- you have tools with which to manage periods of depression and anxiety
- you can tolerate (and even appreciate) being seen, heard, and valued by others
- you are able to assure yourself
- you know the difference between dependence and independence, understanding when each is appropriate
- you can meet your own needs safely and positively
- you can reach out and get your needs met by others
- you have a range of feelings available to you.

In addition, successful resolution of abuse includes:

- disappearance or reduction of psychosomatic illnesses
- an ability to problem solve
- a recognition of your values
- a development of spirituality and inner peace
- the ability to have stable friendships
- an ability to give to others
- learning to trust your intuition.

Like any hard task, resolution of abuse is a step-by-step process. Review the list above every six months and see where you have made progress. Use the chart below to mark your progress.

Chart Your Progress

Stages to chart	Time			
	6 mos.	1 yr.	2 yrs.	3 yrs.
See abuse as past event	❏	❏	❏	❏
Body no longer experiences it as present	❏	❏	❏	❏
No memory of abusive events	❏	❏	❏	❏
Don't feel devastated by the abuse	❏	❏	❏	❏
Don't feel victimized by the abuse	❏	❏	❏	❏
Thoughts and nightmares at a minimum	❏	❏	❏	❏
Emotions feel stabilized	❏	❏	❏	❏
Self-image: honest appraisal of strengths and weaknesses	❏	❏	❏	❏
I like myself	❏	❏	❏	❏
I accept the way I look	❏	❏	❏	❏

Stages to chart	Time			
	6 mos.	1 yr.	2 yrs.	3 yrs.
Negative people/situations are absent from my life	❏	❏	❏	❏
I have grieved my losses of childhood	❏	❏	❏	❏
I can manage my depression	❏	❏	❏	❏
I can manage my anxiety	❏	❏	❏	❏
It is all right to be seen and heard by others	❏	❏	❏	❏
I can assert myself without being aggressive	❏	❏	❏	❏
I am comfortable being independent	❏	❏	❏	❏
I know when and when not to be dependent	❏	❏	❏	❏
I can meet my own needs	❏	❏	❏	❏
I can reach out to others	❏	❏	❏	❏
I feel I can have a full range of feelings	❏	❏	❏	❏
I do not have as many illnesses as I used to	❏	❏	❏	❏
I can problem solve	❏	❏	❏	❏
I can define my values	❏	❏	❏	❏
I am in touch with my spirituality	❏	❏	❏	❏
I have stable friendships	❏	❏	❏	❏
I give to others	❏	❏	❏	❏
I trust in my intuition	❏	❏	❏	❏

Ask your friends to give you feedback on how they see you. Write down what they say.

	Your progress	Suggestions for change
6 mos.	_____	_____
12 mos.	_____	_____
1-1/2 yrs.	_____	_____
2 yrs.	_____	_____
2-1/2 yrs.	_____	_____
3 yrs.	_____	_____

Now, move beyond your limitations. See yourself as being the person you want to be, attaining what you want to have, and keeping in your life people you love and care about.

Work on your own visualizations and rewrite your life story with a happy ending in your notebook.

My Life with a Happy Ending

_____

_____

_____

_____

_____

_____

_____

Appendix I

Definitions of Child Abuse

Many people are unclear about exactly what child abuse is. Although there have been many definitions for child abuse, the definitions from the U.S. Department of Health and Human Services, National Center for Child Abuse and Neglect are useful.

Emotional Abuse

Habitual patterns of belittling, denigrating, scapegoating, or other non-physical forms of overtly hostile or rejecting treatment, as well as threats of other forms of maltreatment (such as beating, sexual assault, and abandonment).

Tortuous restriction of movement, as by tying a child's arms or legs together or binding a child to a chair, bed, or other object, or confining a child to an enclosed area (such as a closet) as a means of punishment.

Overtly punitive, exploitative, or abusive treatment other than those specified under other forms of abuse, or unspecified abusive treatment. This form includes attempted or potential physical or sexual assault, deliberate withholding of food, shelter, sleep, or other necessities as a form of punishment, economic exploitation, and unspecified abusive actions.

Emotional Neglect

Marked inattention to the child's needs for affection, emotional support, attention, or competence.

Chronic/extreme spouse abuse or other domestic violence in the child's presence.

Encouragement or permitting of drug or alcohol use by the child; cases of the child's drug/alcohol use were included here if it appeared that the parent/guardian had been informed of the problem and had not attempted to intervene.

Encouragement or permitting other maladaptive behavior (e.g., severe assaultiveness, chronic delinquency) under circumstances where the parent/guardian had reason to be aware of the existence and seriousness of the problem but did not attempt to intervene.

305

Refusal to allow needed and available treatment for a child's emotional or behavioral impairment or problem which any reasonable layman would have recognized as needing professional psychological attention (e.g., severe depression or suicide attempt).

Other inattention to the child's developmental/emotional needs not classifiable under any of the above forms of emotional neglect (e.g., markedly overprotective restrictions which foster immaturity or emotional overdependence, chronically applying expectations clearly inappropriate in relation to the child's age or level of development).

Physical Abuse

Physical abuse is characterized by inflicting physical injury by punching, beating, kicking, biting, burning, or otherwise harming a child. Although the injury is not an accident, the parent or caretaker may not have intended to hurt the child. The injury may have resulted from over-discipline or physical punishment that is inappropriate to the child's age.

Educational Neglect

Habitual truancy averaging at least five days a month if the parent guardian had been informed of the problem and had not attempted to intervene.

Failure to register or enroll a child of mandatory school age, causing the child to miss at least one month of school; or a pattern of keeping a school-age child home for nonlegitimate reasons (e.g., to work or to care for siblings) an average of at least three days a month.

Refusal to allow or failure to obtain recommended remedial educational services, or neglect in obtaining or following through with treatment for a child's diagnosed learning disorder or other special education need without reasonable cause.

Physical Neglect

Failure to provide or allow needed care in accord with recommendations of a competent health care professional for a physical injury, illness, medical concition, or impairment.

Failure to seek timely and appropriate medical care for a serious health problem which any reasonable layman would have recognized as needing professional medical attention.

Abandonment

Desertion of a child without arranging for reasonable care and supervision.

Other blatant refusals of custody such as permanent or indefinite expulsion of a child from the home without adequate arrangement for care by others or refusal to accept custody of a returned runaway. Custody-related forms of inattention to the child's needs other than those covered by abandonment or expulsion. For example, repeated shuttling of a child from one household to another due to apparent unwillingness to maintain custody or chronically and repeatedly leaving a child with others for days/weeks at a time.

Inadequate Supervision

Child left unsupervised for extended periods of time or allowed to remain away from home overnight without the parent/substitute knowing (or attempting to determine) the child's whereabouts.

Conspicuous inattention to avoidable hazards in the home; inadequate nutrition, clothing, or hygiene; and other forms of reckless disregard for the child's safety and welfare such as driving with the child while intoxicated or leaving a young child unattended in a motor vehicle.

Sexual Abuse

Actual penile penetration—whether oral, anal or genital, homosexual or heterosexual—was required for this form of maltreatment.

This form of maltreatment involved acts where some form of actual genital contact had occurred, but where there was no specific indication of intrusion.

This category is used for unspecified acts not known to have involved actual genital contact (e.g., fondling of breasts or buttocks, exposure) and for allegations concerning inadequate or inappropriate supervision of a childs voluntary sexual activities.

Source: U.S. Department of Health and Human Services, National Center for Child Abuse and Neglect, Study of National Incidence and Prevalence of Child Abuse and Neglect: 1988, and Child Abuse and Neglect: A Shared Community Concern, March, 1989.

Frequency of Child Abuse

The Study Findings of the Study of National Incidence and Prevalence of Child Abuse and Neglect: 1988 (U.S. Department of Health & Service, National Center on Child Abuse and Neglect) found that 16.3 children per 1,000 were abused or neglected each year, with 43 percent of the children involving abuse and 63 percent involving neglect (some children were both neglected and abused). It is important to note that these were children that came to the attention of professionals such as school teachers, mental health professionals, court officers, etc.

However, a different study by M.A. Straus (1,146 parents across the U.S. were interviewed about physical violence) showed that 14 out of every 100

American children were subjected to physical violence annually. The study defined abuse as an attack by a parent involving punching, kicking, biting, hitting with an object, beating up or using a knife or a gun. This study showed that the incidence of abuse was at least 26 times higher than reported by the National Center on Child Abuse and Neglect.

The difference was clearly children that came to the attention of professionals versus study-discovered children that had been abused but never came to the attention of authorities.

A higher prevalence of familial sexual abuse was found by Diana Russell in a random sample of 930 adult women in San Francisco, where 16 percent of the women reported at least one experience of family sexual abuse before the age of 18.

Again, it is clear that reported child abuse is much less than the actual incidence because most child abuse goes unnoticed and unreported.

Appendix II

The following meditation/visualization, written by B. Anne Gehman and Ellen Ratner, is meant to serve as a guide or template for readers who wish to create their own meditations and visualizations.

There are several ways that you can use this model, such as making a tape of your own voice or having someone whom you trust make the tape for you. You many choose to modify the wording to your own preference.

Some of the words, such as self-love, may be difficult for you to use and make part of your own expressions. We urge you to try these words. But, if other words work better for you, those words should be used instead. You may want to add specific images and visualizations regarding the ways you want to see and feel about yourself. We happily encourage your efforts.

Meditation/Visualization

In a quiet place, sit comfortably with your back straight and your hands—with palms open—resting on your legs. Now, slowly relax each part of your body, beginning with your feet and moving slowly upward. Keep relaxing by letting the tension leave each area of your body. Take a deep breath and exhale slowly, feeling your body releasing all tension.

As you relax, let any thought you have pass out of your consciousness. Release them as they flow through your mind. Open yourself, visualizing the person you want to become. See yourself as being open to new experiences and growth.

Continue relaxing, releasing any negative thoughts and see yourself as free from past or present negative experiences. Imagine yourself creating an environment where you feel safe, secure, and where you are in charge.

Now refine your senses as you attune yourself to your feelings, thoughts, and expanded awareness.

While increasing your awareness and sensitivity, extend your understanding and knowledge to include others in your life, and open your intuition to knowing appropriate responses to them.

Recall past experiences of being successfully guided by your intuition, knowledge, and feelings.

As you recall these experiences, release any guilt and shame or sense of worry, replacing these feelings with self-love. Appreciate your ability to overcome and recreate your life. Ask for guidance to continue your pathway and journey toward greater self-realization.

Instruct yourself to feel peaceful and confident. In moments of silence or when you are alone, continue to renew this feeling.

References

Chapter 1 — The First Steps Toward Recovery

American Humane Association. (1988). *Highlights of official child neglect and abuse reporting 1986.* Denver, Colo.: American Humane Association.

American Psychiatric Association. (1987). *Diagnostic and statistical manual of mental disorders.* 3rd ed., rev. Washington, D.C.: American Psychiatric Association Press.

Briere, John. (1988, 12 August). The long-term clinical correlates of childhood sexual victimization. *Annals of the New York Academy of Sciences* 528: 327–334.

Briere, John; Evans, Diane; Runtz, Marsha; and Wall,Timothy. (1988). Symptomatology in men who were molested as children: A comparison study. *American Journal of Orthopsychiatry* 58(3): 457–461.

Bryer, Jeffrey B.; Nelson, Bernadette A.; Miller, Jean Baker; and Krol, Pamela A. (1987, November). Childhood sexual and physical abuse as factors in adult psychiatric illness. *American Journal of Psychiatry* 144(11): 1426–1430.

Burka, J.B., and Yuen, L. M. (1983). *Procrastination: Why you do it, what to do about it.* Reading, Mass.: Addison-Wesley.

Cohen, Frederick S., and Densen-Gerber, Judianne. (1982). A study of the relationship between child abuse and drug addiction in 178 patients: Preliminary results. *Child Abuse & Neglect* 6: 383–387.

Coons, Philip W. (1986). Child abuse and multiple personality: Review of the literature and suggestions for treatment. *Child Abuse & Neglect* 10(4): 455–462.

Courtois, C. A. (1988). *Healing the incest wound: Adult survivors in therapy.* New York: W. W. Norton.

Cunningham, Jean; Pearce, Thomas; and Pearce, Patti. (1988). Childhood sexual abuse and medical complaints in adult women. *Journal of Interpersonal Violence* 3(2): 131–144.

Davies, Robert K. (1979). Incest: Some neuropsychiatric findings. *International Journal of Psychiatry in Medicine* 9(2): 117–121.

Derdeyn, Andre P. (1983). Depression in childhood. *Child Psychiatry and Human Development* 14(1): 16–29.

Finnegan, Dana, and McNally, Emily. (1989). *Dual identities: Counseling chemically dependent gay men and lesbians.* Center City, Minn.: Hazelden.

Finkelhor, David. (1984). *Child sexual abuse: New theory and research.* New York: The Free Press.

Garbarino, J.; Guttmann, E.; and Seeley, J. W. (1986). *The psychologically battered child.* San Francisco: Jossey-Bass Publishers.

Gelinas, Denise J. (1983, November). The persisting negative effects of incest. *Psychiatry* 46: 312–332.

Gelles, Richard J., and Straus, Murry A. (1988). *Intimate violence: The definitive study of the causes and consequences of abuse in the American family.* New York: Simon and Schuster.

Giovannoni, Jeanne M., and Becerra, Rosina M. (1979). *Defining child abuse.* New York: The Free Press.

Haugaard, J., and Reppucci, N. D. (1988). *The sexual abuse of children.* San Francisco: Jossey-Bass Publishers.

Holmes, Sandra J., and Robins, Lee N. (1988, February). The role of parental disciplinary practices in the development of depression and alcoholism. *Psychiatry* 51: 24–35.

Hotaling, G. T., et al. (1988). *Family abuse and its consequences: New directions in research.* Newbury Park, Calif.: Sage Publications.

Kempe, C. Henry, and Helfer, Ray E. (1972). *Helping the battered child and his family.* Philadelphia: J. B. Lippincott.

Kroll, Phillip D.; Stock, Dorothy F.; and James, Mary E. (1985). The behavior of adult alcoholic men abused as children. *Journal of Nervous and Mental Disease* 173(11): 689–693.

Lindberg, Frederick H., and Distad, Lois J. (1985). Post-traumatic stress disorders in women who experienced childhood incest. *Child Abuse & Neglect* 9(3): 329–334.

McGoldrick, Monica, and Gerson, Randy. (1985). *Genograms in family assessment.* New York: W. W. Norton.

Marlin, Emily. (1989). *Genograms: The new tool for exploring the personality, career and love patterns you inherit.* Chicago: Contemporary Books.

National Center for Child Abuse and Neglect Specialized Training. Behavioral indicators of child abuse. Photocopy.

——— Characteristics of abusive families. Photocopy.

——— Indicators of child neglect. Photocopy.

——— Physical indicators of child abuse: For medical professionals. Photocopy.

Ney, Philip G. (1988). Transgenerational child abuse. *Child Psychiatry and Human Development* 18(3): 151–168.

Orme, Terri Combs, and Rimmer, John. (1981). Alcoholism and child abuse. *Journal of Studies on Alcohol* 42(3): 273–287.

Russell, Diana E. H. (1983). The incidence and prevalence of intrafamilial and extrafamilial sexual abuse of female children. *Child Abuse & Neglect* 7: 133–146.

——— (1986). *The secret trauma: Incest in the lives of girls and women.* New York: Basic Books.

Schaefer, Melodie R.; Sobieraj, Karen; and Hollyfield, Rebecca L. (1988). Prevalence of childhood physical abuse in adult male veteran alcoholics. *Child Abuse & Neglect* 12: 141–149.

Van der Kolk, Bessel A. (1984). *Post-traumatic stress disorder: Psychological and biological sequelae.* Washington, D.C.: American Psychiatric Press.

Van der Kolk, Bessel A., and Herman, Judith L. (1987, March 2–6). The psychiatric consequences of psychological trauma. Harvard Medical School Department of Continuing Education and Massachusetts Mental Health Center. Photocopy.

Wisechild, Louise M. (1988). *The obsidian mirror: An adult healing from incest.* Seattle, Wash.: The Seal Press.

Chapter 2 — Support Networks

Alcoholics Anonymous World Services. (1976). *Alcoholics anonymous: The story of how many thousands of men and women have recovered from alcoholism.* New York: Alcoholics Anonymous World Services.

Grant Hospital of Chicago, Inpatient Chemical Dependence Program. (1987). *Early-recovery handbook*. Chicago: Grant Hospital of Chicago.
Luft, Joseph. (1969). *Of human interaction*. Palo Alto, Calif.: California National Press.
——— (1970). *Group process: An introduction to group dynamics*. Palo Alto, Calif.: National Press Books.
Milardo, Robert M. (1988). *Families and social networks*. Newbury Park, Calif.: Sage Publications.
Parkview Treatment Centers. (1984). *Family program handbook*. St. Louis Park, Minn.: Parkview Treatment Centers.
Speck, R. V., and Attneave, C. (1973). *Family networks*. New York: Vintage Books.

Chapter 3 — Boundaries

Duhl, Bunny S. (1983). *From the inside out and other metaphors: Creative and integrative approaches to training in systems thinking*. New York: Brunner/Mazel.
Kantor, David, and Lehr, William. (1976). *Inside the family: Toward a theory of family process*. New York: Harper Colophon Books.
Minuchin, S. (1974). *Families and family therapy*. Cambridge, Mass.: Harvard University Press.
Minuchin, S.; Rosman, B. L.; and Baker, L. (1978). *Psychosomatic families*. Cambridge, Mass.: Harvard University Press.
Olson, David H.; Portner, Joyce; and Lavee, Yoav. (1988). *F.A.C.E.S.: Family adaptability and cohesion evaluation scale*, 3rd ed. St. Paul, Minn.: Department of Family Social Science, University of Minnesota.
Wegscheider, Sharon. (1980). *Another chance: Hope and health for alcoholic families*. Palo Alto, Calif.: Science & Behavior Books.

Chapter 4 — Identity and Self-esteem

Briere, John, and Runtz, Marsha. (1986). Suicidal thoughts and behaviors in former sexual abuse victims. *Canadian Journal of Behavioral Science* 18(4): 413–423.
Bradbard, Marilyn R.; Halperin, Sandra M.; and Endsley, Richard C. (1988). The curiosity of abused preschool children in mother-present, teacher-present, and stranger-present situations. *Early Childhood Research Quarterly* 3: 91–105.
Castaneda, Carlos. (1968). *The teachings of Don Juan: A Yaqui way of knowledge*. New York: Washington Square Press.
Clarke, Jean Illsley. (1978). *Self esteem: A family affair*. New York: Harper & Row.
Fantuzzo, John W.; Stoval, Alex; Schachtel, Daniel; Goins, Cynthia; and Hall, Robert. (1987). The effects of peer social initiations on the social behavior of withdrawn maltreated preschool children. *Journal of Behavior Therapy & Experimental Psychiatry* 18(4): 357–363.
Gawain, Shakti. (1982). *Creative visualization*. New York: Bantam Books.
Harter, Stephanie; Alexander, Pamela C.; and Neimeyer, Robert A. (1988). Long-term effects of incestuous child abuse in college women: Social adjustment, social cognition, and family characteristics. *Journal of Consulting and Clinical Psychology* 56(1): 5–8.
Hay, Louise L. (1987). *You can heal your life*. Santa Monica, Calif.: Hay House.
James, Muriel. (1981). *Breaking free: Self-reparenting for a new life*. Reading, Mass.: Addison-Wesley.
Maslow, Abraham. (1954). *Motivation and personality*. New York: Harper & Row.
Newman, Mildred, and Berkowitz, Bernard. (1971). *How to be your own best friend*. New York: Ballantine Books.
Ney, Philip G. (1987). Does verbal abuse leave deeper scars: A study of children and parents. *Canadian Journal of Psychiatry* 32: 371–377.

O'Brien, John D. (1987). The effects of incest on female adolescent development. *Journal of the American Academy of Psychoanalysis* 15(1): 83–92.

Salman, Akhtar. (1984). The syndrome of identity diffusion. *American Journal of Psychiatry* 141(11): 1381–1385.

Verleur, Donald; Hughes, Ronald E.; and deRios, Marlene Dobkin. (1986). Enhancement of self-esteem among female adolescent incest victims: A controlled comparison. *Adolescence* 21(84): 843–854.

Chapter 5 — Stress Reduction and Body Awareness

Davis, Martha; Eshelman, Elizabeth; and McKay, Matthew. (1982). *The relaxation and stress reduction workbook.* Oakland, Calif.: New Harbinger Publications.

Feldenkrais, Moshe. (1972). *Awareness through movement.* New York: Harper & Row.

Fields, Rick. (1984). *Chop wood, carry water: A guide to finding spiritual fulfillment in everyday life.* Los Angeles, Calif.: Jeremy P. Tarcher.

Kepner, James I. (1987). *Body process: A gestalt approach to working with the body in psychotherapy.* New York: Gardner Press.

Lidell, Lucy. (1987). *The sensual body: The ultimate guide to body awareness and self-fulfillment.* New York: Simon & Schuster/Fireside Books.

Nuernberger, Phil. (1981). *Freedom from stress: A holistic approach.* Honesdale, Calif.: Himalayan International Institute of Yoga.

Roskies, Ethel. (1987). *Stress management for the healthy type A: Theory and practice.* New York: Guilford Press.

Rossi, Ernest L., and Cheek, David B. *Mind body therapy: Methods of ideodynamic healing in hypnosis.* New York: W. W. Norton.

Shaffer, Martin. (1983). *Life after stress.* Chicago: Contemporary Books.

Stevens, John O. (1971). *Awareness: Exploring, experimenting, experiencing.* Lafayette, Calif.: Real People Press.

Chapter 6 — Feelings

Davidson, Glen. (1984). *Understanding mourning: A guide for those who grieve.* Minneapolis, Minn.: Augsburg Publishing House.

deYoung, Mary. (1982). Self-injurious behavior in incest victims: A research note. *Child Welfare* 61(8): 577–584.

Fossum, Merle A., and Mason, Marilyn J. (1986). *Facing shame: Families in recovery.* New York: W. W. Norton.

Green, A. H. (1978, October). Self-destructive behavior in battered children. *American Journal of Psychiatry* 135.

Haldene, Sean. (1988). *Emotional first aid: Coping with grief, anger, fear, joy, parent/child conflicts.* Barrytown, New York: Station Hill Press.

Hibbard, Roberta A.; Brack, Catherine J.; and Orr, Donald P. (1988). Abuse, feelings, and health behaviors in a student population. *American Journal of Diseases of Children* 142: 326–330.

Jeffers, Susan. (1987). *Feel the fear and do it anyway.* Columbine, N.Y.: Fawcett.

Kaufman, Gershen. (1985). *Shame: The power of caring.* Cambridge, Mass.: Schenkman Books.

Kosky, Robert. (1983). Childhood suicidal behavior. *Journal of Child Psychology and Psychiatry* 24(3): 457–468.

Laing, R. D. (1970). *knots.* New York: Vintage Books.

Middleton-Moz, Jane, and Dwinnel, Lorie. (1986). *After the tears: Reclaiming the personal losses of childhood.* Pompano Beach, Florida: Health Communications.

Shapiro, Shanti. (1987). Self-mutilation and self-blame in incest victims. *American Journal of Psychotherapy* 41(1): 46–54.

Sheehan, David V. (1983). *The anxiety disease.* New York: Bantam Books.

Tauris, Carol. (1982). *Anger: The misunderstood emotion.* New York: Touchstone–Simon and Schuster.

Viscott, David. (1976). *The language of feelings.* New York: Pocket Books.

Chapter 7 — Defenses as Coping

Burns, David B. (1980). *Feeling good: The new mood therapy.* New York: New American Library.

Stone, Evelyn M., comp. and ed. (1988). *American psychiatric glossary.* Washington, D.C.: American Psychiatric Press.

Chapter 8 — Communication

Alberti, Robert E., and Emmons, Michael L. (1986). *Your perfect right.* San Luis Obispo, Calif.: Impact Publications.

Camras, Linda A.; Ribordy, Sheila; Hill, Jean; Martino, Steve; Spaccarelli, Steven; and Stefani, Roger. (1988). Recognition and posing of emotional expressions by abused children and their mothers. *Developmental Psychology* 24(6): 776–781.

Ekman, Paul. (1985). *Telling lies: Clues to deceit in the marketplace, politics, and marriage.* New York: W. W. Norton.

Ekman, Paul, and Friesen, Wallace V. (1984). *Unmasking the face: A guide to recognizing emotions from facial expressions.* Palo Alto, Calif.: Consulting Psychologists Press.

Ellenson, Gerald S. (1986). Disturbances of perception in adult female incest survivors. *Social Casework* 67(3): 149–159.

Fast, Julius. (1970). *Body language.* New York: Pocket Books.

Fox, Lynn; Long, Steven H.; and Langlois, Aimée. (1988, August). Patterns of language comprehension deficit in abused and neglected children. *Journal of Speech and Hearing Disorders* 53(3): 239–244.

Goffman, Erving. (1959). *The presentation of self in everyday life.* Garden City, N. Y.: Doubleday Anchor Books.

Hall, Edward T. (1967). *The hidden dimension.* Garden City, N.Y.: Doubleday Anchor Books.

——— (1973). *The silent language.* Garden City, N.Y.: Doubleday Anchor Books.

Helfer, Ray E. (1987). The perinatal period, a window of opportunity for enhancing parent–infant communication: An approach to prevention. *Child Abuse & Neglect* 11(4): 565–579.

Howard, Ann C. (1986). Developmental play ages of physically abused and non-abused children. *American Journal of Occupational Therapy* 40(10): 691–695.

Laborde, Genie Z. (1987). *Influencing with integrity: Management skills for communication & negotiation.* Palo Alto, Calif.: Syntony Publishing.

——— (1988). *Fine tune your brain: When everything's going right and what to do when it isn't....* Palo Alto, Calif.: Syntony Publishing.

McKay, Matthew; Davis, Martha; and Fanning, Patrick. (1983). *Messages: The communication skills book.* Oakland, Calif.: New Harbinger Publications.

Mehrabian, A., and Wiener, M. (1956). Non-immediacy between communication and object of communication in a verbal message. *Journal of Consulting Psychology* 30(5): 5.

Mehrabian, A., and Ksionzky, S. (1974). *A theory of affiliation.* Lexington, Mass.: D. C. Heath Publications.

Morris, Desmond. (1977). *Manwatching: A field guide to human behavior.* New York: Harry N. Abrams.

Scheflen, Albert E. (1972). *Body language and the social order: Communication as behavioral control.* Englewood Cliffs, N. J.: Prentice-Hall.

———— (1974). *How behavior means exploring the contents of speech and meaning.* New York: Jason Aronson.

Smith, Grace. (1982). On listening to the language of children. Photocopy.

Smith, Manuel. (1988). *When I say no, I feel guilty.* New York: Bantam Books.

Chapter 9 — Memories

Evenson, Richard C. (1987). Long-term effects of incest (letter to the editor). *American Journal of Psychiatry* 144(7): 967–968.

Garfield, Patricia. (1976). *Creative dreaming.* New York: Ballantine Books.

Gil, Eliana. (1984). *Outgrowing the pain: A book for and about adults abused as children.* Walnut Creek, Calif.: Launch Press.

Herman, Judith; Russell, Diana; and Trocki, Karen. (1986). Long-term effects of incestuous abuse in childhood. *American Journal of Psychiatry* 143(10): 1293–1296.

Joy, Stephany. (1987). Retrospective presentations of incest: Treatment strategies for use with adult women. *Journal of Counseling and Development* 65(6): 317–319.

Miller, Alice. (1983). *For your own good: Hidden cruelty in child-rearing and the roots of violence.* New York: Farrar, Straus & Giroux.

Morris, Jill. (1985). *The dream workbook.* New York: Fawcett Crest.

Chapter 10 — Relationships and Sexuality

Augsburger, David. (1983). *When caring is not enough.* Ventura, Calif.: Regal Books.

Bach, George, and Deutsh, Ronald. (1979). *Stop! You're driving me crazy.* New York: Berkley Publishing.

Brittain, David E., and Merriam, Karen. (1988). Groups for significant others of survivors of child sexual abuse: A report on methods and findings. *Journal of Interpersonal Violence* 3(1): 90–101.

deYoung, Mary. (1981). Siblings of Oedipus: Brothers and sisters of incest victims. *Child Welfare* 60(8): 561–568.

Fogarty, Thomas. (1978). Triangles. In *The best of the family: 1973–1978.* New Rochelle, N. Y.: Center for Family Learning.

Kinsey, Alfred C.; Pomeroy, Wardell B.; and Martin, C. E. (1948). *Sexual behavior in the human male.* Philadelphia: Saunders.

Weinberg, George. (1989). *Projection principle.* New York: St. Martin's Press.

Wilbur, Cornelia B. (1984). Multiple personality and child abuse. *Psychiatric Clinics of North America* 7(1): 3–7.

Yates, Alayne. (1982). Children eroticized by incest. *American Journal of Psychiatry* 139(4): 482–485.

Chapter 11 — The Abuser

Burgess, Ann Wolbert; Hartman, Carol R.; and McCormack, Arlene. (1987). Abused to abuser: Antecedents of socially deviant behaviors. *American Journal of Psychiatry* 144(11): 1431–1436.

Daro, Deborah. (1988). *Confronting child abuse: Research for effective program design.* New York: The Free Press.

Egeland, Byron; Sroufe, L. Alan; and Erickson, Martha. (1983). The developmental consequence of different patterns of maltreatment. *Child Abuse & Neglect* 7: 459–469.

Erickson, W. D.; Walbek, N. H.; and Seely, R. K. (1987). The life histories and psychological profiles of 59 incestuous stepfathers. *Bulletin of the American Academy of Psychiatry and the Law* 15(4): 349–357.

Erikson, Erik H. (1968). *Identity: Youth and crisis.* New York: W. W. Norton.

Farrell, Lynda T. (1988). Factors that affect a victim's self-disclosure in father–daughter incest. *Child Welfare* 67(5): 462–468.

Geller, Max; Devlin, Mary; Flynn, Terrence; and Kaliski, Judith. (1985). Confrontation of denial in a fathers' incest group. *International Journal of Group Psychotherapy* 35(4): 545–67.

Hirsch, Mathias. (1986). Narcissism and partial lack of reality testing (denial) in incestuous fathers. *Child Abuse & Neglect* 10: 547–549.

Loevinger, Jane. (1976). *Ego development: Conceptions and theories.* San Francisco: Jossey-Bass.

McCarty, Loretta M. (1986). Mother–child incest: Characteristics of the offender. *Child Welfare* 65(5): 447–458.

Newberger, Carolyn Moore, and De Vos, Edward. (1988). Abuse and victimization: A life-span developmental perspective. *American Journal of Orthopsychiatry* 58(4): 505–511.

O'Connell, Michael A. (1986). Reuniting incest offenders with their families. *Journal of Interpersonal Violence* 1(3): 374–386.

Salter, Anna. (1985, July–August). Treating abusive parents. *Child Welfare* 64(4): 327–341.

Wheat, Patte, and Lieber, Leonard. (1979). *A personal history of Parents Anonymous.* Minneapolis, Minn.: Winston Press.

Wild, N. J. (1988). Suicide of perpetrators after disclosure of child sexual abuse. *Child Abuse & Neglect* 12: 119–121.

Chapter 12 — Spirituality and Beyond: Full Recovery from Abuse

Adair, Margo. (1985). *Working inside out: Tools for change.* Berkeley, Calif.: Wingbow Press.

Gil, Eliana. (1988). *Treatment of adult survivors of childhood abuse.* Walnut Creek, Calif.: Launch Press.

Gorski, Terence T., and Miller, Merlene. (1982). *Counseling for relapse prevention.* Independence, Mo.: Herald House.

Peck, M. Scott. (1980). *The road less traveled.* New York: Touchstone Books/Simon and Schuster.

Simon, Sidney B. (1988). *Getting unstuck: Breaking through your barriers to change.* New York: Warner Books.

——— (1985). *Values clarification: A handbook of practical strategies for teachers and students.* New York: Dodd, Mead.

Notes

Notes

Notes

Books from . . .
Health Communications

PERFECT DAUGHTERS: Adult Daughters Of Alcoholics
Robert Ackerman
Through a combined narrative of professional and anecdotal styles Robert
Ackerman helps restore a sense of balance in life for Adult Daughters of
Alcoholics.
ISBN 1-55874-040-6   **$8.95**

I DON'T WANT TO BE ALONE:
For Men And Women Who Want To Heal Addictive Relationships
John Lee
John Lee describes the problems of co-dependent relationships and his
realization that he may be staying in such a relationship because of his
fear of being alone.
ISBN 1-55874-065-1   **$8.95**

SHAME AND GUILT: Masters Of Disguise
Jane Middelton-Moz
The author uses myths and fairy tales to portray different shaming
environments and to show how shame can keep you from being the
person you were born to be.
ISBN 1-55874-072-4   **$8.95**

LIFESKILLS FOR ADULT CHILDREN
Janet G. Woititz and Alan Garner
This book teaches you the interpersonal skills that can make your life easier
while improving your sense of self-worth. Examples are provided to help
clarify the lessons and exercises are given for practicing your new skills.
ISBN 1-55874-070-8   **$8.95**

THE MIRACLE OF RECOVERY:
Healing For Addicts, Adult Children And Co-dependents
Sharon Wegscheider-Cruse
This is about the good news — that recovery from co-dependency is
possible. Sharon offers ways to embrace the positive aspects of one's
experience — to realize the strength that can come from adversity.
Celebrate your own miracle with this inspiring book.
ISBN 1-55874-024-4   **$9.95**

SHIPPING/HANDLING: All orders shipped UPS unless weight exceeds 200 lbs., special routing is requested, or
delivery territory is outside continental U.S. Orders outside United States shipped either Air Parcel Post or Surface
Parcel Post. Shipping and handling charges apply to all orders shipped whether UPS, Book Rate, Library Rate, Air
or Surface Parcel Post or Common Carrier and will be charged as follows. Orders less than $25.00 in value add
$2.00 minimum. Orders from $25.00 to $50.00 in value (after discount) add $2.50 minimum. Orders greater than
$50.00 in value (after discount) add 6% of value. Orders greater than $25.00 outside United States add 15% of
value. We are not responsible for loss or damage unless material is shipped UPS. Allow 3-5 weeks after receipt of
order for delivery. Prices are subject to change without prior notice.

3201 S.W. 15th Street,
Deerfield Beach, FL 33442-8124
1-800-851-9100

Daily Affirmation Books from . . .
Health Communications

GENTLE REMINDERS FOR CO-DEPENDENTS: *Daily Affirmations*
Mitzi Chandler

With insight and humor, Mitzi Chandler takes the co-dependent and the adult child through the year. Gentle Reminders is for those in recovery who seek to enjoy the miracle each day brings.

ISBN 1-55874-020-1 $6.95

TIME FOR JOY: *Daily Affirmations*
Ruth Fishel

With quotations, thoughts and healing energizing affirmations these daily messages address the fears and imperfections of being human, guiding us through self-acceptance to a tangible peace and the place within where there is *time for joy.*

ISBN 0-932194-82-6 $6.95

AFFIRMATIONS FOR THE INNER CHILD
Rokelle Lerner

This book contains powerful messages and helpful suggestions aimed at adults who have unfinished childhood issues. By reading it daily we can end the cycle of suffering and move from pain into recovery.

ISBN 1-55874-045-6 $6.95

DAILY AFFIRMATIONS: *For Adult Children of Alcoholics*
Rokelle Lerner

Affirmations are a way to discover personal awareness, growth and spiritual potential, and self-regard. Reading this book gives us an opportunity to nurture ourselves, learn who we are and what we want to become.

ISBN 0-932194-47-3
(Little Red Book) $6.95
(New Cover Edition) $6.95

SOOTHING MOMENTS: *Daily Meditations For Fast-Track Living*
Bryan E. Robinson, Ph.D.

This is designed for those leading fast-paced and high-pressured lives who need time out each day to bring self-renewal, joy and serenity into their lives.

ISBN 1-55874-075-9 $6.95

3201 S.W. 15th Street,
Deerfield Beach, FL 33442
1-800-851-9100

**Health
Communications, Inc.**

Helpful 12-Step Books from . . .
Health Communications

12 STEPS TO SELF-PARENTING For Adult Children
Philip Oliver-Diaz, M.S.W., and Patricia A. O'Gorman, Ph.D.

This gentle 12-Step guide takes the reader from pain to healing and self-parenting, from anger to forgiveness, and from fear and despair to recovery.

ISBN 0-932194-68-0   **$7.95**

SELF-PARENTING 12-STEP WORKBOOK: Windows To Your Inner Child
Patricia O'Gorman, Ph.D., and Philip Oliver-Diaz, M.S.W.

This workbook invites you to become the complete individual you were born to be by using visualizations, exercises and experiences designed to reconnect you to your inner child.

ISBN 1-55874-052-X   **$9.95**

THE 12-STEP STORY BOOKLETS
Mary M. McKee

Each beautifully illustrated booklet deals with a step, using a story from nature in parable form. The 12 booklets (one for each step) lead us to a better understanding of ourselves and our recovery.

ISBN 1-55874-002-3   **$8.95**

VIOLENT VOICES:
12 Steps To Freedom From Emotional And Verbal Abuse
Kay Porterfield, M.A.

By using the healing model of the 12 Steps emotionally abused women are shown how to deal effectively with verbal and psychological abuse and to begin living as healed and whole people.

ISBN 1-55874-028-7   **$9.95**

GIFTS FOR PERSONAL GROWTH & RECOVERY
Wayne Kritsberg

A goldmine of positive techniques for recovery (affirmations, journal writing, visualizations, guided meditations, etc.), this book is indispensable for those seeking personal growth.

ISBN 0-932194-60-5   **$6.95**

3201 S.W. 15th Street,
Deerfield Beach, FL 33442
1-800-851-9100

Health Communications, Inc.

New Books . . .
from Health Communications

HEALING THE SHAME THAT BINDS YOU
John Bradshaw
Toxic shame is the core problem in our compulsions, co-dependencies and addictions. The author offers healing techniques to help release the shame that binds us.
ISBN 0-932194-86-9 $9.95

THE MIRACLE OF RECOVERY:
Healing For Addicts, Adult Children and Co-dependents
Sharon Wegscheider-Cruse
Beginning with recognizing oneself as a survivor, it is possible to move through risk and change to personal transformation.
ISBN 1-55874-024-4 $9.95

CHILDREN OF TRAUMA: *Rediscovering Your Discarded Self*
Jane Middelton-Moz
This beautiful book shows how to discover the source of past traumas and grieve them to grow into whole and complete adults.
ISBN 1-55874-014-7 $9.95

New Books on Spiritual Recovery . . .

LEARNING TO LIVE IN THE NOW: *6-Week Personal Plan To Recovery*
Ruth Fishel
The author gently introduces you step by step to the valuable healing tools of meditation, positive creative visualization and affirmations.
ISBN 0-932194-62-1 $7.95

CYCLES OF POWER: *A User's Guide To The Seven Seasons of Life*
Pamela Levin
This innovative book unveils the process of life as a cyclic pattern, providing strategies to use the seven seasons to regain power over your life.
ISBN 0-932194-75-3 $9.95

MESSAGES FROM ANNA: *Lessons in Living (Santa Claus, God and Love)*
Zoe Rankin
This is a quest for the meaning of "love." In a small Texas Gulf Coast town a wise 90-year-old woman named Anna shares her life messages.
ISBN 1-55874-013-9 $7.95

THE FLYING BOY: *Healing The Wounded Man*
John Lee
A man's journey to find his "true masculinity" and his way out of co-dependent and addictive relationships, this book is about feelings — losing them, finding them, expressing them.
ISBN 1-55874-006-6 $7.95

3201 S.W. 15th Street,
Deerfield Beach, FL 33442
1-800-851-9100

**Health
Communications, Inc.**

Other Books By . . .
Health Communications